MEDIEVAL IRELAND

The Enduring Tradition

MICHAEL RICHTER

with a foreword by
Próinséas Ní Chatháin

St. Martin's Press   New York

© Michael Richter, 1983, 1988

Originally published as *Irland im Mittelalter—Kultur und Geschichte*
© 1983 Verlag W. Kohlhammer GmbH, Stuttgart, Berlin, Köln, Mainz
Translated in English by Brian Stone and Adrian Keogh

This translation first published 1988

First published in the United States of America in 1988

ISBN 0-312-02338-3

Library of Congress Cataloging-in-Publication Data
Richter, Michael, Professor Dr.
Medieval Ireland: the enduring tradition/Michael Richter;
translated from the German by Brian Stone and Adrian Keogh
p. cm.
Bibliography: p.
Includes index.
ISBN 0-312-02338-3: $35.00 (est.)
1. Ireland—History—To 1603. 2. Ireland—Church history—
Medieval period, 600–1500. I. Title.
DA930.R53 1988
941.5—dc19

Contents

CONTENTS

List of Maps

Foreword

Próinséas Ní Chatháin

This English translation of *Irland im Mittelalter* is a welcome addition to serious literature on the subject. Here we have a book which could not have been written with the same authority by either an Irishman or an Englishman.

A Continental historian who indulges in neither Iromania nor Irophobia, Professor Richter strikes a good balance which may sometimes ruffle insular feathers but which is fresh and free from prejudice and preconceptions.

He is singularly equipped to synthesise the complex tangle of early and medieval Ireland. His sojourn in Wales and experience of Welsh sources (particularly his work on Gerald of Wales), his familiarity with the writings of Bede, his work on Carolingian literacy and learning are all brought to bear on the Irish evidence. The twelve years which he spent in Ireland may not have made him *Hibernicis ipsis Hiberniorem* but he immersed himself in Irish scholarship with more dedication than many an Irishman.

The fruits of his participation in the Medieval Settlement Group, the Medieval Studies Seminar and in Early Irish and Hiberno-Latin studies at University College, Dublin as well as in the International Colloquia on Early Ireland and Medieval Europe are clearly to be seen in the breadth of the material which Professor Richter sets before the reader.

Medieval Ireland: The Enduring Tradition will be read and enjoyed by many.

Acknowledgements

The maps are produced here with kind permission of
W. Kohlhammer GmbH, Stuttgart.

Preface to the English edition

The starting point of this book was a series of lectures which I gave at the university of Vienna in the winter of 1981/82. The keen interest of the students in Irish history and Irish culture prompted me to write a book on the subject. The Continental background may help to explain the title: 'medieval' is understood to mean simply 'post-classical'. On balance, it seems useful to retain this term for English and Irish readers.

The kind reception which the book obtained from Irish, English and Continental reviewers made me agree to a suggestion by F. X. Martin, O.S.A., head of the department in which I then taught medieval history, to have the book translated into English. I decided not to do the translation myself, knowing that I would be tempted to rewrite the book for the new audience. Although I have followed the translation process closely, the book is simply an English version of the German original. Naturally, I have corrected a few errors (a number of which were kindly pointed out to me by reviewers and readers); in two places, I have omitted brief references to things specifically German which would have meant little to English readers, and in one place, in Chapter 9, I have restructured a paragraph. The bibliography has also been updated and revised; it should be stressed that it remains only a basic guide.

It is a pleasure to give thanks to all those involved in the realisation of this book: to F. X. Martin for his initial suggestion and subsequent encouragement; to Maurice Keen for his decision to publish it in the series New Studies in Medieval History; to the late Denis Bethell, founder of that series, both friend and demanding colleague for a number of years; to the publisher, particularly to Ms Vanessa Couchman, Vanessa Graham and to the translators. Unforeseen events in the course of the translation, particularly my move from Ireland to Germany, made it necessary to enlist a second translator. I should like to express my immense gratitude to Adrian Keogh for his help, skill and enthusiasm in translation and revision. I am also much indebted to those who have helped with suggestions and improvements, to Próinséas Ní Chatháin, Jane Inglis and Imelda Gardiner.

In some respects, this book is the result of many discussions I had with my students and colleagues in Ireland. Ultimately, it became an alternative view of Irish history in the Middle Ages. As such, it is intended to enliven the discussion and to call into question what may appear at times to be established truths. History is what we make of it. I am very grateful for the many years I spent in Ireland and taught at University College, Dublin, and for all I learned there. *Habeat sua fata libellum.*

Konstanz, 17 March 1987

To my friends in Ireland

1. The Celts

The history of Europe begins with the Greek civilisation which shaped the Mediterranean world in the last few centuries before Christ. Our information about the Hellenistic world, which was continued in many respects in the Roman Empire, comes just as much from contemporary written sources as it does from archaeological evidence. These sources provide a relatively complete picture which has, up to now, always been used in examining the past.

The culture of the Celts who at that time had a determining influence on Europe north of the Alps is, however, much less accessible. The Celts themselves did not possess any written culture; written accounts which have been handed down from pre-Christian centuries are sketchy and from outside sources. These accounts show particular signs of Greek and Roman moral concepts in their interpretation (*interpretatio Romana*). However, the substantial material culture of the Celts being evaluated by archaeologists does add to an overall picture which is an integral part of the prehistoric and early historic periods of European history.

During the last century before Christ, the remarkable Celtic culture was overshadowed on the mainland by the simultaneous expansion of the Germanic peoples of northern Europe and the Romans from the Mediterranean. The remains of this culture were best preserved in the extreme western areas, particularly in the British Isles. In the Middle Ages, the world of the Celts was regarded as *finis terrae*, a world where many strange phenomena persisted which aroused amazement and often defied understanding.

The Celtic peoples did not, of course, live completely isolated on the outer edges of the world, rather they contributed with their own dynamism to the shaping of Europe in various ways. For this reason alone it is important for anyone wishing to understand the complexity of European history to study the medieval Celtic peoples. This book is concerned with the Irish, the most important and influential of the Celtic peoples in the Middle Ages. We are relatively well informed about the Irish, since they developed a written culture at an earlier stage than most other European peoples. After those of the Greeks and Romans, theirs was the most significant European culture of the early Middle Ages.

Ireland's achievements during this time emerged in conjunction with the mainland. Outside influences which reached Ireland partly via other Celtic peoples were, on the one hand, absorbed and digested, while the Irish culture, on the other hand, influenced its immediate neighbours even more than it did the other peoples of Europe. Any study of medieval Ireland must therefore also include some reference to the neighbouring Celtic peoples, the Picts, Britons and Bretons.

Celtic culture in Europe expressed itself more in the material, artistic and linguistic areas than politically, continuing unbroken up to the present in the linguistic field alone. In the fourth century, Saint Jerome reports quite correctly on the similarity of the (Celtic) language of the Galatians in Asia Minor to that of the *Treveri* (from Trier) in western Europe. At the time he wrote this, Roman rule in western Europe was nearing its end. Gaul, which was previously Celtic, had become a Latin-speaking region, remaining so even after the end of the Roman Empire. In Britain, the development was rather different. Despite 350 years of Roman dominance, the Celtic language had not disappeared, and soon became prevalent again following the withdrawal of the Roman legions, although it had been influenced by Latin in many ways. This Celtic language is still alive in Wales today.

As the neighbouring island of Ireland had never been subjected to Roman rule, the Celtic language was never in danger there. Written documentary evidence of it exists from the fourth century onwards and it is still spoken in Ireland today, particularly in the extreme western regions of the island. The Irish language is quite different from the Celtic language of Britain, in that it is more archaic. Although philologists can recognise certain common features in the morphology, structure and vocabulary of the two languages, it must be assumed that they already differed considerably in early historic times. There are no indications that the various Celtic peoples in the Middle Ages were aware of belonging to one family of languages, just as there was no sense of political or cultural unity.

Exactly when groups of Celts settled in the British Isles is uncertain but it was most probably a complex process lasting several centuries. Groups of Celts came to Ireland both from Britain and directly from the Continent; this process was completed in the first century p.d; after which any disputes were confined to the islands. With the expansion of the Roman Empire in western Europe, Celtic culture became increasingly an insular culture.

Archaeological evidence and accounts from outside indicate that at the beginning of the Celtic period, civilisation throughout Europe was agriculturally-orientated, involved mainly in cattle breeding, just as it was in early medieval Ireland. There were, however, no equivalents of the mainland Celtic *oppida* or of coinage in Ireland. The large stone constructions and tombs still preserved in Ireland are of pre-Celtic origin, dating from the Neolithic period.

In social and religious areas there are, on the other hand, parallels which would indicate some degree of continuity. A learned Celtic class, the druids, documented by Caesar in the case of Gaul, also existed among the Irish and the British. The dynamism of the medieval Celtic peoples, and of the Irish in particular, is based on the fact that they had an intellectual class which was, in many respects, able to match the intellectual demands of the Christian culture.

Finally, there is ample evidence of Celtic art of the La Tène culture in the British Isles. Ornamental work featuring spirals, the plant tendril and the trumpet shape appears frequently on stone and parchment in the early medieval works of art.

Important evidence of the Celtic culture in Europe was preserved in the British Isles into historical times. It has already been made clear that even in Ireland, where the best evidence of continuation of Celtic civilisation survives in language and institutions, the Celtic culture made up only a part and not the whole of the prehistoric legacy. This is even more true for the historical period, which this book is concerned with.

History commences where contemporary written evidence first starts to appear; in the case of Ireland, this was in the fourth century A.D. As everywhere, it begins very gradually with written evidence which, in this case, originates from the Christian-Roman world, dealing initially with the area of Christianity and only gradually including non-Christian areas. Despite the wealth of information available, the earliest Irish sources are not easily accessible and their value and significance are, even today, frequently disputed. Agreement in secondary literature exists, at best, in rough outlines. With regard to the first few centuries, it is often only possible to hint at the contribution of the Celtic insular peoples in general, and that of the Irish in particular, to the development of Europe: any interpretations in this respect must remain largely speculative. It is often difficult to differentiate clearly between what was Celtic and what was simply influenced by the Celts.

The attentive observer of Ireland, nevertheless, cannot help thinking that medieval Europe was much more than the frequently conjured-up synthesis of Graeco-Roman, Christian and Germanic heritage.

PART I

Early Ireland (before c. A.D. 500)

2. Ireland in Prehistoric Times

The Country

Ireland lies on the edge of western Europe, measuring approximately 350 miles from north-east to south-west and 200 miles from north-west to south-east. There is no point on the island which is further than 100 miles from the sea. The island was an ideal size for the political conditions of the early Middle Ages: it was large enough to be able to assert itself as an independent force against Britain, its neighbour across the sea to the east, but was also compact enough to be perceived emotionally as a unit. In this respect, Ireland was quite different from Britain which, because of its size and shape, was divided into various units which were difficult to unite.

There is a considerable amount of evidence that the Irish had the feeling in early times of belonging to a world which embraced the entire island. The sagas repeatedly refer to the 'men of Ireland' and the vernacular name for the country, *Ériu*, is to be found in literature. When one reads 'she was the most beautiful woman of *Ériu*', it does indeed mean 'of Ireland', but it also hints at another meaning, 'the most beautiful woman of the world'. The island was, in some respects, a world of its own; its people retained their own special attitudes and way of life longer than in other less remote European regions.

However, Ireland was remote only in the geographical sense. Both in antiquity and in the Middle Ages, the sea proved more of a link with the outside world than a barrier. Ireland had various contacts with other regions in Europe, yet the sea still represented a certain psychological boundary, which, if anything, did more to deepen the feeling of national unity among the Irish. The sea, which surrounds the island, was almost omnipresent and the inhabitants had a curiously ambivalent attitude towards it. They were prepared to risk going to sea in *curraghs*, lightweight boats which were built for inland navigation and coastal fishing, but their unease in doing so can be seen in the early medieval legendary account of the voyage of the sixth-century Irish saint, Brendan.

There are many references in the hagiography to the trials and tribulations of seafaring. The familiar world ended at the coastline.

Ship burials of kings of the kind known from Sutton Hoo (East Anglia) did not exist in Ireland. There are, however, references in early medieval literature to chariots as a means of transport for high-ranking persons, a legacy of the Continental and land-bound Celts.

The island has a mild, damp climate, and if snow falls it does not remain on the ground long enough for the cattle to have to be brought inside in winter. The southwest of the island has subtropical vegetation. With few exceptions, principally on the northern half of the east coast, low mountain ranges of up to 3,000 feet determine the coastline or the areas near the coast. The inland regions consist largely of badly drained lowland areas, the greatest natural resource of which is still peat.

The island did not have a geopolitical centre. It is quite clear that the coastal regions were settled relatively late, the population choosing instead to live inland. The political centres of early times, Tara and Cashel, offer broad views of the country, which, however, stop short of the sea. This in itself is significant: power in the early Middle Ages meant control of land, particularly grazing land, but it did not mean control of the coastline.

Although the feeling of unity can be seen indirectly in the political sphere, it is more distinct in the social, religious and cultural areas. Politically, the island was polycentrally structured. One reads of a division of the island roughly along a line between Dublin and Galway. The northern half was known as *Leth Cuinn* ('Conn's side'), the southern half as *Leth Moga* ('Mug Nuadat's side', Mug, like Conn, being a mythical figure). There were four large regions which have been preserved up to the present day in the provinces of Ulster and Connacht (*Leth Cuinn*), Leinster and Munster (*Leth Moga*). In historical times, a fifth province was added, Meath ('Midland') which was situated between Ulster and Leinster. The old expression for 'province' was 'a fifth' (*cóiced*). It has been remarked, quite rightly, that 'the fifth' implied a sense of the 'whole'. Nevertheless, there often were more than five *cóicedaig* on the island in historical times, despite the fact that this contradicted basic arithmetic.

The smallest political unit in Ireland was the kingdom, of which there were dozens. The kings were not all equally powerful: various ranks existed, including the kings of the provinces. As early as the end of the seventh century, reference was made to sovereignty over the whole island by Adomnán, Abbot of Iona (+704) who wrote of *totius Everniae regni monarchia* (VC 21b, 'rule of the Kingdom of all Ireland'). However, it is certain that supremacy was not achieved at that time. The closest to a single supremacy that medieval Ireland was ever to know was in the twelfth century.

The absence of effective political unity led to unstable political relations, the complex nature of which is still not clear, especially for the period before 800 A.D. However, despite this, the hierarchy of the kings was sufficient to prevent an all-out internal conflict.

The lack of political unity also had a positive aspect in that battles were not fought solely with weapons, but also with words and writings. As in politically disunited Germany and Italy of the late Middle Ages, there were considerable cultural achievements in Ireland which were sponsored in many different places. Although this encouragement had its origin in self-interest the results are of inestimable value for posterity.

The oldest frequently used learned names for the island date from the late seventh century and are to be found in Adomnán's Life of Columba: these were *Ebernia* or *Evernia*, derived from Greek, the latinised form being *Hibernia* and *Scotia*. From the early Middle Ages onwards the term *Scotia* was gradually applied to the regions in northern Britain with the result that the term *Hibernia* became more usual for Ireland. But certainly those writing on the Continent about *Scot(t)i* almost always meant the Irish. The name 'Ireland' is of Scandinavian origin and first documented during the late Viking era. The official name of the Republic of Ireland today is *Eire*, and the first official language is Irish. English, which is much more widespread, is the 'national language of equal standing'. It is not without a certain irony that the unofficial term for the whole island is the English name 'Ireland'.

The Population

The population of Ireland in the early Middle Ages is estimated at below half a million. It can be assumed that, in the Middle Ages, Ireland was no more thinly populated than the neighbouring island to the east. The large difference in the density of population between Ireland and Britain did not develop until modern times. In England, industrialisation played a decisive role, whereas in

Ireland, the population was dramatically reduced to about half of its original size by the famine in the middle of the nineteenth century from which the country, despite an above-average birth rate, has still not recovered.

It is assumed that Ireland and Britain became separate land masses in the seventh millenium B.C. and it is from this time that the first traces of human settlement in Ireland date: large quantities of stone axes have been found to the east of the River Bann in County Antrim. These early inhabitants supported themselves by hunting and fishing, with no evidence of farming. The first period of advanced civilisation, evidenced by the megalithic tombs throughout the island, is dated to the fourth millennium B.C. and belonged to the so-called Atlantic culture of northern and western Europe.

It has not yet been established when exactly the Celtic-speaking population, which was to become dominant in historical times, came to Ireland. It is assumed that they came in several phases during the last few centuries B.C. The Celtic immigrants would have arrived by various routes, both directly from the Continent, and via pre-Roman Britain. The groups who were later to have a determining influence appear to have left the Continent before the second century B.C.

The Celtic-speaking population became dominant in Ireland, and hardly any traces of pre-Celtic languages have been preserved. Since the early medieval sources deal mainly with the Celtic-speaking ruling class, no conclusion can be drawn from the linguistic evidence as to the numerical relation between Celtic-speaking immigrants and the previous population. All we know is that the Celtic element was not originally indigenous to Ireland. Claims to the contrary go back as far as the earliest written sources; they re-emerge with the romanticism of the nineteenth century in particular, and persist to the present time, but are nothing more than propaganda.

The Celtic Languages

Celtic is an Indo-European group of languages which was widespread on the Continent and was brought by the migration of the Celtic tribes as far east as Asia Minor (Galatians) and as far west as the Atlantic (Gauls). With the exception of Gaulish and a few other fragments, documented linguistic evidence of Celtic is found only in the British Isles. Apart from Gaulish, the Celtic group of languages appears in two large sections which are again subdivided:

1. the Goedelic section (Irish-Gaelic, Scots-Gaelic and Manx, the language of the inhabitants of the Isle of Man);
2. the Brythonic-British section (British/Welsh, Cornish and Breton).

The affiliation of the language of the Picts is still not clear, since only names have survived. While it was presumed for a long time that the Pictish language was not Indo-European, it is today considered as Celtic, although it has not been decided in which section it should be placed.

The earliest evidence of the Irish-Gaelic language dates from the fourth century (Ogam inscriptions), the earliest evidence of Welsh from the sixth century (the poems of Aneirin and Taliesin); Breton dates from the eighth century (cartularies of Landévennec and Redon), whereas the earliest evidence of Manx and Cornish does not appear until the late Middle Ages. Scots-Gaelic was virtually identical with Irish-Gaelic up until the seventeenth century.

The Irish Language (Goedelic, Gaelic)

After Latin, Irish is the language in western Europe with the longest and best-documented development. It is termed a Q-Celtic language in contrast to British which is a P-Celtic language. It must be added that *Q* is written as a *C* (e.g. Irish *cenn*, Welsh *pen*, 'head') in Irish, which is the most archaic of the well-documented Celtic languages and shows a strong affinity to Latin (e.g. deponents ending in -*r*, *sechithir* 'follows'; cf. Latin *sequitur*). From early historical times more abundant and diverse sources have been preserved in Irish than in any other non-Latin language in central or western Europe. A knowledge of Irish is an absolute prerequisite for thorough research into the early, and indeed into the later, medieval history of Ireland.

The development of the Irish language is divided into different stages:

1. Archaic Old Irish, 4th century to c. 750;
2. Old Irish (O.Ir), c. 750–900;
3. Middle Irish, c. 900–1600 ('Classical Irish' 1200–1600);
4. Modern Irish, from 1600.

'Documented' evidence of archaic Old Irish originates in the main from Ireland, the most important being the Ogam inscriptions, the elegy *Amra Coluim Chille* (around 600), the law texts, as well as the Irish names in Adomnán's Life of Columba and in the two versions of the Life of Patrick by Muirchú and Tírechán (all from the seventh century). Evidence of Old Irish is more plentiful; the Christian-ecclesiastical texts of this phase of the language were edited almost in their entirety in the *Thesaurus Palaeohibernicus*. This material is mostly preserved in MSS now in Continental libraries and part of it was also written on the Continent. Most important are the glosses of New Testament texts, the oldest of which are found in a Würzburg manuscript from the second half of the eighth century (Würzburg, Univ. Library, M.th.f.12), in a manuscript originating from the northern Italian monastery of Bobbio, but which was presumably written in Ireland in the early decades of the ninth century and is now kept in Milan (Ambrosianus C 301), as well as in a Priscian manuscript from St Gallen (Sangallensis 904) of about the same period. Apart from these, there are a number of other ecclesiastical texts, the most important of which are the so-called Cambrai homily (with Irish texts, copied on the Continent around A.D. 750, by a scribe who obviously did not have a good command of Irish), a treatise on the mass from the Stowe Missal also containing rubrics in Irish (probably written shortly after A.D. 792) and Irish texts in the Book of Armagh (around 807). A very noticeable feature in Old Irish documents is the astonishing standardisation of the language and spelling. Possible reasons for this could be either the decisive influence of one intellectual centre in Ireland (probably Bangor) or the continuing effect of the pre-Christian intellectual élite. This uniformity was, however, lost in medieval times.

Middle Irish shows significant differences from Old Irish. This is important because a range of texts can, on the basis of their language, be assigned to early times although the preserved manuscripts themselves date from the late Middle Ages; this is the case with the corpus of Irish law, which is as superb as it is difficult. Larger collections of texts with material written in Irish are preserved in manuscripts from the twelfth century onwards.

It is impossible for anyone who is not an expert in the language to classify texts written in Irish according to date and place of origin. Classification has to depend instead upon the judgement of the philologist and research into the substantial corpus of Irish literature in the early and high Middle Ages is still very much in progress. The medievalist familiar with Continental conditions thus finds, unusually, that he can obtain relatively reliable information about early Irish history from texts which, according to palaeographical findings, date from the late Middle Ages. Of course, some of these texts were also changed in the course of being passed on and such alterations cannot always be accurately verified. On the whole, however, early Irish society can be examined on the basis of the extensive information available, though much of it dates from the late Middle Ages; there exists, at most, a lack of precise dates.

Aristocratic Society in pre-Christian Times ('Heroic Age')

The best information on the upper strata of society in pre-Christian Ireland is provided by the epic The Cattle Raid of Cooley (*Táin Bó Cúailnge*), a piece of world literature. The earliest preserved manuscript dates from around 1100, although it is generally assumed that older written versions, which are now lost, went back as far as the seventh century. It is still, admittedly, disputed whether the *Táin* represents the recording of oral 'folk traditions' or the creation of an individual author.

According to the information in the text, which has been handed down in three related recensions, the epic records events that happened during the life of Christ, as one of the principal figures, Conchobhar Mac Nessa, king of the Ulaid, is supposed to have died of grief when he received the news of Christ's crucifixion. This represents a later addition, an attempt, at least superficially, to christianise the epic, thereby making it more respectable. There is no reference given to the dates of the events reported on. The *dramatis personae* are heroic figures with godlike traits rather than actual historical persons. Kenneth Jackson considers it possible that the events described in the *Táin* could be dated to the fourth century A.D.[1]

The *Táin* is an heroic epic in prose dealing with the struggle of the men of Ulster, the Ulaid, under King Conchobhar against the rest of the island, in particular against the people from Connacht led by King Ailill and his wife Medhbh. The main emphasis lies on the description of the heroes' deeds, the most important hero being Cú Chulainn who is staying at Conchobhar's court at Emhain Mhacha and dies in battle. The historical framework is provided by the expulsion of the Ulaid into the northeastern regions of Ireland by the kings of Connacht, a sweeping political process stretching over several centuries and one which will be dealt with again as it extends into historical times. Although an epic of this kind is not, of course, an exact description of historical events, it does convey an impression of the life of the Irish upper class in early times. The *Táin* may be inclined to idealise life but it is by no means completely removed from reality.

The society described in the *Táin* was subdivided into many sections; there were kings, noblemen and officials. It was a society which was constantly confirmed through military conflict, the gaining of fame and glory being the most important task of the warrior. Fame increased the allegiance given to the hero by his followers whom he led to victory and spoils. This does not, however, mean that anyone could become a hero, or that the possibility of social advancement existed. The hero was born as such and his success in battle served only to reveal his status as a warrior to those around him. The hero remaining unrecognised for a time is an old motif which gained additional currency through an important social institution, that of education and upbringing at other courts (fosterage). Sons of noblemen were handed over at an early age to the court of persons of the same or higher rank, or to the king, in order to be brought up and educated, and they were initiated into the craft of war. It was in this way that Cú Chulainn came to Conchobhar's court and was gradually recognised as a hero. This idealised account undoubtedly reflected a factual basis: by handing their sons over to persons of higher rank, the fathers were forced to show a certain degree of political good conduct. The fosterling was, therefore, a sort of hostage. The relationship between the wards themselves became just as close as that of brothers in the same family and, legally, they were treated as equals with the same status as the foster-father's own children. The institution of education and upbringing at other courts was preserved in Ireland throughout the Middle Ages.

A nobleman warrior's equipment consisted principally of a spear and shield, for which there is a collective noun in Irish, *gaisced*, and from which the word warrior, *gaiscedach*, is derived. The warrior fought from a two-wheeled chariot which was drawn by two horses and driven by a charioteer, his close associate. It becomes clear from the sagas that the charioteer had a lower social rank than the warrior who only fought with his equals; the warrior's strict code of honour set him apart from persons of a lower rank.

The battles described in the epic had, in some respects, more of a social and sporting character than a warlike one. The heroes often chose single combat. In chariot battles they could distinguish themselves with masterly performances, leaving the actual seat in the chariot and fighting from the shaft or even from the horses' backs. It may well have been sporting, but it was also to the bitter end, for the battle trophy was the head of the opponent, his equal, which was then kept and displayed. The collection of heads reflected the importance of the hero. The society described in the *Táin* was a pagan one and a commitment was made to the gods of one's own *gens* (*túath*), as in the frequently documented oath, 'I swear by the gods my people swear by'.

There were, however, other activities apart from combat. One reads of purely sporting disciplines, e.g. of a ball-game called *báire* which was played with wooden sticks and is still played in Ireland as 'hurling'. Entertainment at court brought the king's followers together in great feasting-halls, complex timber buildings in which the followers displayed themselves and their beautiful women. The ideal of feminine beauty in Irish society was portrayed in poetry through the distinct sense of colours, typical of the Celts, black hair, black eyebrows, blue eyes, cheeks the colour of foxgloves, white teeth. The importance of the heroes' wives, just as that of the heroes themselves, was measured by the number of people in the retinue. The Irish method of counting was somewhat curious, the retinue of the nobleman frequently being referred to as 'three times fifty'.

The feasting-halls were showplaces for banquets. It was the hero's privilege to carve and he also had the right to the largest piece of meat. The favourite dish of the upper class was roast pork, the preferred drinks being mead, fresh milk and beer.

Apart from culinary delights, entertainment was also provided by the musicians and poets who belonged to each court. The poets had the task of praising in song the deeds of their masters, their heritage and the deeds of their ancestors. In this capacity, the poet was harbinger and at the same time historian and bearer of the genealogical traditions. The excellent qualities of the master were also extolled in various ways. These songs of praise did, of course, have some particular set features in that they had to contain certain basic material. The quality of the poet, and, therefore, the importance of his master were attested to by the variety of the performances. One can recognise here the tendency towards eloquence and verbosity that the Irish displayed in many different ways. They attempted to surpass each other in the variety and accumulation of laudatory adjectives. The power of the spoken word, which could strengthen as well as undermine positions, still showed traces of the magic power which the word possessed in the early period of human history. The *Táin*, however, discloses much more. The elevation of the master had an equivalent in the derogation of the opponent, for eloquence could also be used in a negative way and weaken the opponent considerably. The most powerful weapon of the poet, whose status did not allow him to engage in physical battle, was in the composition of 'defamations' or 'maledictions' (often mistakenly termed 'satires' in English), an area in which Irish literature has produced astonishing material.

Social Stratification

The stratification of early Irish society can best be inferred from the law tracts which were codified in large and small tracts dating back to the seventh and eighth centuries. The language of the legal texts is old, and parts of their contents were already antiquated by the time they were first written down. Quite a few new developments in the political scene of the early Middle Ages did not find their way into the legal texts, and they are therefore neither completely reliable nor exhaustive. The new developments can, however, be gathered from other sources, from the annals for example, and they do not appear to alter substantially the overall picture of early times given in the law texts. With this reservation, an attempt will be made to trace the social structure of that period.

Irish society was hierarchically structured with the king as the political head (Irish *rí*, cognate with Latin *rex*). The king ruled over a people (Irish *túath*; cf. German *theod*) which did not, however, derive its origins from a common ancestor. Early kingship had been of a sacral type and traces of it can still be recognised in historical times. The king was regarded as the embodiment of the people and was responsible for the well-being of the *túath*. He was without physical defects and his beauty was praised by the poets. He led noblemen and freemen in battle and, if he was killed, the *túath* had then lost the battle. The kingship appears originally to have been of a pronounced sacerdotal kind, the office being subject to particular taboos (*gessa*) and privileges (*buada*).

The law tract *Críth Gablach* (early eighth century) says '*rí*, why is he so called? Because he rules (*rigid*) over his *túath*'. This is reminiscent of *rex a regendo dicitur* ('a king is called that because he he rules'), the phrase of Isidore, whose writings were known in Ireland from the seventh century onwards. In what manner then did the king rule? According to the legal texts, he did not have any legislative power as the law was complete, comprehensive and independent. He was not even responsible for the maintenance of law, as this was the responsibility of the people. Offences were settled through the pronouncement of the legal scholars, and were avenged by the victim's clan by way of the blood feud or the imposition of compensation. The king instead defended the *túath* against enemies from outside. Within the kingdom, he presided over the people's assembly (*oenach*), in which 'people' always meant the class involved in the political decision-making process. The king had means of ensuring the good conduct of the people. The noblemen were obliged to provide the king with hostages, as well as paying tribute and affording the king hospitality on his journeys through the kingdom. Originally the king enjoyed, along with the *fili* (poet), the highest honour price (*lóg n-enech*; *enech*, orig. 'honour', comparable with the Germanic 'wergeld'), and was therefore above the law. However, as early as in the eighth century, the possibility is mentioned of fasting against the king, thus forcing him to atone for his wrongs. If he allowed the person on hunger-strike to die, he had to pay compensation to the injured kin. If we disregard the learned class, the only official assigned to the king was, according to the legal texts, the *rechtaire* (Irish *recht* is related to German

'Recht', law or right) whose task it was to exact the payments due to the king. Through the Christianisation of the society from the fourth century onwards, the sacerdotal function of the king weakened without, however, ceasing completely. Irish kings were never anointed in a Christian ceremony. The original sacerdotal power of the kingship is seen by the fact that the bishop in Christian Ireland had the same honour price as the king.

Constitutionally, the *rí túaithe* was the highest political authority. It is assumed that, at the beginning of historical times in the fifth century, Ireland had a great number of kingdoms, somewhere between 100 and 150, which means that a *túath* was fairly small. This meant that the individual king had little political weight, but also that he was in personal contact with his people.

It would be unhistorical to imagine Ireland as a collection of over 100 political units with equal rights. The opposite can be seen in the *Taín*. The concentration of political power was the constant aim, with some kings rising above their immediate neighbours. These more powerful kings are known in the legal texts as *ruiri* 'king of kings'. This type of king was not the ruler of several *túatha* but held the *rí túaithe* in a relationship of personal dependence, who then paid him tribute and provided him with hostages. A further, higher, rank of kingship was king of a province (*rí ruireg*, literally 'king of high noblemen'). His position with regard to the *ruiri* was comparable to that of the *ruiri* to the *rí túaithe*. Here we encounter the predilection of the Irish scholars for clear systematisation which did not match up to the more complex reality. According to the law tracts, the king of a province was the highest political authority in Ireland. Some provincial kings later claimed supremacy over the whole island. The position of such 'high kings' (*ard-rí*) was not, however, legally established. The national kings, who will be discussed later, were, according to their legal position, only provincial kings. Nevertheless, their claim to national kingship shows that the legal texts alone do not provide reliable information about the power structure in Ireland.

The legal texts make only indirect references to the question of royal succession. Eoin MacNeill has established from the annals that there were nevertheless fairly definite rules.[2] The smallest social unit in Ireland was the clan down to the fourth generation (*derbfine*, literally 'the certain family'; the larger family bonds are known as *íarfine* and *indfine*). This group owned the land, it protected the individual's rights and the royal *derbfine* had the right to the royal line of succession. The ninth century witnessed the appearance of an expressive term for those who had a rightful claim to royal succession: *rígdomnae* (Latin *regis materia* which, roughly translated, means 'royal material'). Entitled to succeed were the king's brother, uncle, cousin, son, grandson and great-grandson. However, since the *túath* could not be divided, only one person could succeed at any one time. *Críth Gablach* refers to the successor as *tánaise*. He would appear to have been appointed during the king's lifetime, more than likely soon after his accession, for, as it says in *Críth Gablach*: *tánaise ríg cid ara n-eperr*? '*t.*, why is he so called?'; the answer is 'because the whole people is anticipating his kingship'. The word *tánaise* is derived from *to-ad-ni-sed-* 'the awaited one'. Thus it is assumed that those eligible for succession to the throne reached an agreement with the king on a successor. There was, significantly, land in the *túath* which was tied to the royal office and was not the private possession of the individual king.

Despite the rules regarding royal succession, there was, in practice, frequent discord amongst the *rígdomnae*, stirred up especially by those whose claim to the throne was in danger of lapsing, in other words by those whose family had not provided a king since their grandfather or great-grandfather. The existence of rules governing succession was not, therefore, able to prevent political unrest in early Ireland. Added to this was the fact that the king also had to assert himself against his rivals outside his *túath*.

Only after a candidate had overcome all these difficulties was he confirmed by the people's assembly (*oenach*) and heralded by the poet (*fili*). The ceremonial installing of kings is specifically documented only for the provincial kings of Tara, Emhain Mhacha and Cruacha. The term for this ceremony (*feis* 'festival') alludes to a pagan fertility rite: the king 'slept' (*foaid*) with the *túath*.

The *túath* was subdivided into nobility, freemen, lesser freemen and serfs (see diagram p. 21). Although it is likely that every person originally had had his honour price (*enech*), according to the legal texts, only freemen still possessed it. The subdivision of freemen into seven categories is, like many aspects of the law tracts, an excessive schematisation. In this case the legal scholars probably wanted to present a parallel to the seven orders of the Church. A free person was one who was a legal person in his own right and owned land; one of his most important obligations was military service in wartime. The noblemen were entitled to a retinue (*céle*, pl. *céli*, similar to the Latin *servus* in the sense of 'servant', not 'slave'); the larger the retinue, the more important the nobleman was. The retinue consisted of lower-class free persons. The lesser freemen (*céli giallnai*; there were, however, several other terms, the individual meanings of which have not been completely clarified) had been paid the honour price originally due to them by their master and were no longer full legal persons. Below them was a class of serfs which, in the legal texts, was again divided into seven categories. It is still not known how a person came into bondage. Some scholars suspect that the serfs were the descendants of the pre-Celtic population. One law tract mentions the possibility that a person became a serf if he was unable to pay an honour price and therefore 'sold' himself to a master. Serfs from across the sea, presumably prisoners taken in battle, are also mentioned.

There were certain people among the freemen who, strictly speaking, were not treated at law as persons in their own right. These included women and adult sons who lived on their father's property. The honour price of these people was a fraction (a half, a quarter, etc.) of the honour price of the man on whom they were dependent. *Bretha Crólige*, a law tract, refers to three lawful wives, the principal wife, the concubine and the mistress, justifying polygamy with reference to the example set by the rulers in the Old Testament.

In addition, there was another group in the *túath*, small in number but socially very important, namely the scholars (*áes dána*). It was to this group that the poets (*fili*, pl. *filid*, literally 'seer', cf. Latin *vates*) belonged. Equal to them in importance were the druids (*druí*, pl. *druíd*, referred to in Latin sources as *magi*). The highest position (*ollam*) of the druids was equal to that of the king. Others that should be mentioned are the legal scholars (*brithem*, pl. *brithemin*, anglicised 'brehon') and the experts in genealogy and history (*senchaid*). These scholars had all gone through a long period of training and were the custodians of the oral tradition. The period of training for the druids is said to have lasted between seven and twelve years. The tradition was 'sung' (Old Irish *for-cain*; cf. Latin *canere*). The recitations of genealogies and prescribed stories were learnt in darkened rooms. The learned class was held in high esteem and enjoyed legal protection not only in the *túath*,

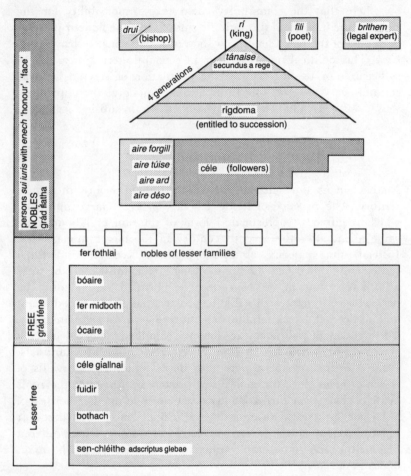

Schematic structure of Irish society according to Críth Gablach

but on the island as a whole. This intellectual élite contributed considerably to the cultural unity of Ireland.

In contrast to the scholars, the other members of the *túath* enjoyed protection and safety only within its boundaries. It was only here that the community could take responsibility for the rights of the individual through the enforcing of the honour price or by means of the blood feud. Few, however, had cause to leave their *túath*. This political unit was also, in economic terms, nearly self-sufficient. For the majority of the population of Ireland life was certainly very meagre. The Lives of the Saints give the impression that it was generally just about possible to attain subsistence level.

Settlement

Neither towns nor villages existed in Ireland before the ninth century. The practice of living together in fairly large numbers, which required a sophisticated form of division of labour, only came about after the seventh century in the larger monasteries. Instead, the majority of the population lived in individual settlements, called *ráth*. The name 'ring fort' is misleading because a *ráth* was not, in its conception, a fortified settlement. The perimeter of an area with a diameter of at least 30 feet was dug out and walled off by simultaneously throwing up an embankment. The remains of palisades can sometimes still be detected in such embankments which had no doubt been erected to fend off animals. Inside the enclosed area were the simple buildings, the walls of which were made of branches and plastered with mud, the roofs being of shingles or turf. Irish law tracts refer to the 'five houses' of a farmer, probably meaning the dwelling house and the four separate animal sheds. If the enclosure was of stone (which differed regionally), the living area was called a *caisel* (English *cashel*, cf. Latin *castellum*).

Around 30,000 *ráths* and *cashels* have so far been recorded in Ireland in the last few decades, principally by means of aerial photography. Only very few of these have been archaeologically examined. Some of them date back to the Bronze Age, but most of them appear to originate from the period between 300 and 1000 A.D. *Ráths* were used right up to the seventeenth century and in some of them subterranean chambers ('souterrains') have been found which, although they may have served the purpose of temporary shelter for weaker members of the community, were normally used as storerooms and were sometimes very elaborately laid out. (Souterrains such as these are also mentioned by Tacitus, *Germania* ch. 16.)

A larger *ráth* (some exist with a diameter of up to 100 metres) was called a *dún*. *Críth Gablach* states in a description of the *dún* of a *rí túaithe* that the king's house was twelve metres long and had sleeping quarters for the twelve-strong retinue of noblemen. The difference between the king and a farmer was, apparently, not particularly great.

A special form of settlement, found particularly in the west of Ireland, were the *crannogs* (from *crann* 'tree'). These were timber residential buildings erected in stagnant waters, usually on artificial islands. There is evidence that this type of settlement existed in the Bronze Age, but it was the importation of iron tools from neighbouring Roman Britain from the third century onwards that really stimulated this rather sophisticated method of construction. About 250 of these *crannogs* have so far been recorded. The building materials were, however, so prone to rot that a *crannog* left behind fewer obvious traces than a *ráth* or a *cashel*. Although it has been established that the *crannog*, *ráth* and *cashel* were not the only forms of settlement in early Ireland, few remains of non-enclosed timber buildings have so far been found, and then usually by accident.

It is difficult to form a picture of life in these settlements. Apart from tools, only a few everyday objects have been found and surprisingly little earthenware. Objects of this kind were probably made principally from wood or leather. In the third century A.D. the plough reached Ireland, but this innovation did not have any decisive influence on the economic system. Frank Mitchell estimates that only five per cent of the cultivated land was used for crops with cattle being the main source of food. Wealth and social position were measured in terms of cattle. The honour price was also expressed in legal texts in terms of cattle or female slaves (*cumal* means three cows). According to Adomnán, a man with five cows was considered very poor (VC 68a, 69b).

A Celtic Society?

Whether there is any justification for referring to the society outlined in this chapter as 'Celtic' depends on how far one wants to take the understanding of that term. Some aspects of early Irish society have their roots among the mainland Celts: one could think here for example of Caesar's account of the druids in Gaul, of his references to head-hunting as well as to the use of two-wheeled chariots (of which no material remains have yet been found in Ireland). However, not every feature of Irish society is necessarily Celtic. The existence in Ireland of a highly-regarded learned class is not attested for all Celts, but it has most impressive parallels in India. Parallels also exist between Ireland and India in the area of language and in the form of epic poetry. The reference to India is not arbitrary, nor are the parallels coincidental; remains of Indo-European civilisation have been preserved on the eastern fringes of the region influenced by Indo-European culture and, on the outer western fringes, in Ireland; they were preserved into historical times. Although nearly the whole of Europe is still Indo-European in linguistic terms, there are considerable distinctions in the social area, created by the powerful and influential Hellenistic civilisation of the Mediterranean region. Ireland had remained outside the Graeco-Roman civilisation and, for this reason, social characteristics were preserved there which, compared with the situation on the Continent in historical times, appear to have been, and indeed were, archaic. There were obvious similarities between the Irish people's assembly and the Scandinavian *Thing*. In Ireland, social systems were preserved right through to historical times which had begun 1,000 years later than in the western Mediterranean. Nevertheless, archaic social systems were preserved there which, in the rest of Europe, were either eclipsed or are not documented in native written sources, as they are, at least to some extent, in Ireland.

To describe Irish society simply as 'Celtic' is to overlook the essential significance of Ireland for an understanding of European development. Its significance lies more in the fact that Indo-European social systems, which had, at one stage, been very common, remained evident in Ireland into the Middle Ages. Apart from the fact that Ireland did not experience any Roman colonisation, the learned class ensured that the Christian–Latin culture which had, in other places, destroyed, eclipsed or silenced a great deal of native culture, did not have the same effect in Ireland.

The particular features of the history of Ireland in the Middle Ages resulting from these conditions are therefore better called Irish than Celtic.

3. Political Developments in Early Times

'Anybody wishing to understand the history of Ireland must be familiar with the history of England'. Although this maxim was coined for modern times, it is, indeed, valid for the entire period since late antiquity. Evidence of the relations between Britain and Ireland in early times may be inadequate, but these relations are certainly perceptible.

We are faced with a contrasting situation at the very beginning of the period we are to examine. Politically speaking, Britain was part of the Roman Empire until A.D. 409, whereas Ireland lay beyond the boundaries of this empire. The withdrawal of the Roman legions from Britain was followed by, what are for historians, two dark centuries when the barbarians threatened the former Roman province, gradually taking possession of it. In keeping with their reputation, barbarians destroyed the ordered development which had existed previously and, with it, the basis for chronologically reliable written records. With the conversion of the Germanic intruders to Christianity from 597, dates and facts begin to emerge again, although this statement must also be qualified. It is not always made clear enough that the political situation in Britain even after 597 is inadequately documented, with the exception of those areas affected by Christianity on a lasting basis. The most important source, the Ecclesiastical History of the English monk Bede, completed in the year 731, conveys an impression of a clear process of development in England in the seventh and eighth centuries. When this is looked at more closely, especially with regard to the political situation, it proves to be misleading in some ways. It was typical of Bede that he held the view that the deeds of those Anglo-Saxon kings who had rejected Christianity and turned once again to paganism should be struck from the annals (HE III, 9). The darkness over barbarian Britain clearly lifted much more gradually than he implies. Hardly anything is known about many of the English kings of the seventh and eighth centuries.

In Ireland, on the other hand, there is, up to the eighth century, a continuous development from the unknown to the better-known. This is because Ireland had never been anything but barbarian before conversion to Christianity; barbarian here in the Roman sense, i.e. not civilised, with no written culture, no reliable chronology. Nevertheless, there was not only a close proximity of peoples on the two neighbouring islands but, from late antiquity onwards, there was also a degree of intercommunication which was to become of great significance for the development of Ireland (and of Britain).

Britain after the Romans

Britain, named after the Celtic *Priteni*, had been a remote outpost for the Romans and in 350 years they had never succeeded in conquering the whole island. The isthmus between the Firth of Clyde and the Firth of Forth formed the northern boundary secured by a *limes*, to the north of which lived the Picts.

Because of its exposed position the island was vulnerable, and from the third century on Britain was exposed to large-scale incursions by the barbarians, of whom the Saxons, Franks and *Scoti* (Irish) are mentioned in particular. These groups threatened the island even before the legions withdrew. When the last legions left Britain in A.D 409, the attacks became more intense since even a former Roman province was still attractive to barbarians. It did, however, take some time for the invading barbarians to assert themselves inland, where the withdrawal of the legions was followed immediately by the British establishing their own realms. The Latin language, which was, until the end of Roman rule, the official language of the country, was relegated to second place nearly everywhere by the upsurge of the Celtic language of the islanders, British. The survival of the Celtic native language in Britain is all the more impressive when one compares the situation with that in neighbouring Gaul. Although Gaul had been a Roman province for not much longer than Britain, the Latin language retained a dominant influence there in post-Roman times. Except in the extreme western areas, Britain did not, however, remain Celtic. This conveys an idea of the intensity of the Germanic conquest and penetration. The Germanisation of Britain was, however, to take several centuries.

The conquest of Britain by Germanic peoples, of whom Bede mentions the Angles, Saxons and Jutes, began before A.D 449, the year in which later traditions are rooted, and thus before the landing of the legendary Germanic commanders Hengist and Horsa. But it is not self-evident that the country under Germanic rule was to be called 'England' after the Angles. Although Bede would appear to have contributed much to the popularisation of this name, the person ultimately responsible for it was Pope Gregory the Great (†604) who up to his death believed that he had dispatched missionaries to the *Angli*, the Angles, in the year 596. His missionaries were, in fact, mainly active among the Jutes of Kent and did not reach the Angles settling further to the north during his pontificate. In any case, the more frequent collective name for the Germanic peoples of Britain, both inside the country and abroad, was 'Saxons', a name which the Celtic peoples have retained up to the present day for their neighbours.

Bede lived in the northeast of England, in the Benedictine monastery of Monkwearmouth in Northumbria. The information for his historical works came mainly from his immediate environment as well as from Canterbury. This is the reason why his somewhat sketchy account of the barbarian incursions into Britain is so biased. He does not mention the threat to Britain's west coast from Ireland, which occurred at the same time as the Germanic incursions were taking place and which will be dealt with later.

Hardly any evidence exists of the individual phases of the Germanic conquest of Britain from the south and east; it has, however, been established that it took several centuries to complete the transition from 'Britain' to 'England'. Small Celtic realms had survived in the west, the most important being in Devon, Cornwall, Wales (the inhabitants of which were referred to up to the twelfth century as 'Britons'), Cumbria and Strathclyde. The British monk Gildas, author of the work *De Excidio Britanniae* 'On the decline of Britain', which was written in the middle of the sixth century, reports that the advance of the Saxons in a westerly direction had come to a halt 50 years previously. We do not know where the decisive battle at *Mons Badonicus* was fought, although it is believed that it took place around the year 500. Gildas warned his Christian fellow Britons that the heathen barbarians would not accept this situation, and would rather continue fighting. His warning proved correct; in the following decades, the Germanic leaders pressed further in a westerly direction. Considerable numbers of Britons fled across the sea to the south and settled in *Aremorica*, the country being named *Britannia minor* 'little Britain' after them, i.e. Britanny.

Gildas reports the survival of a Christian population in the west and north of Britain. Although the Roman Empire certainly did not exist any longer, much of Roman culture still survived, including the Latin language and its written usage. Gildas wrote to his countrymen in this language and his work was aimed not only at the clergy. It must be assumed that a large proportion of Britons were bilingual in the fifth and sixth centuries, having a command of Latin in addition to the native British language. Compared to the Germanic peoples, the Britons considered themselves civilised. Above all, however, they were Christians. They continued to be influenced by Gaulish monasticism right up to the end of the sixth century, as is shown by a church dedicated to St Martin which was encountered by the Roman missionary, Augustine, outside the walls of Canterbury in 597. The British Church was structured territorially according to the Roman model, i.e. subdivided into dioceses. Three bishops from Britain had attended the Council of Arles in the year 314. Two of the diocesan seats are known, London and York, with the third probably situated in the region of Chester. There is evidence that British bishops also attended the councils of Tours (461), Vannes (465), Orleans (511) and Paris (555). Post-Roman Wales was to have particular significance for Ireland in the structuring of the Church, a topic which will be dealt with in the next chapter.

Irish Expansion into Britain

Archaeological finds show that Ireland, although it was not a part of the Roman Empire, had participated in Roman civilisation even before the year 409. The importation of iron tools has already been referred to and there is also evidence of a considerable wine trade. The contacts were, however, not just in one direction.

From the end of the third century, there is evidence of incursions into Roman Britain by the Picts from the north and by the Irish from the west. From the early fifth century, these plundering raids led to settlements and more permanent conquests. The Irish conquest attained greater significance on two fronts, in Wales and Argyll, with Irish dynasties ruling in parts of Wales up to the eighth century. The conquests in the land of the Picts were, however, more lasting and there was such an intensive penetration that the language of the Irish, Gaelic, soon replaced the Pictish language. The more usual name for the country in the Middle Ages also reflects the sustained Irish conquest: the land of the Picts became the land of the Irish, the *Scoti*, 'Scotland'.

Although the attacks on the north and west of Britain took place simultaneously, they were launched from different parts of Ireland and independently of each other. Groups of Irish from the northeast, from the realm of the Dal Riada, encroached on Argyll, where the ruling dynasty then established a collateral line. This bridgehead soon became the starting-point for further conquests in a northeasterly direction. The actual course of the expansion is difficult to determine and it must be assumed that the growth of Irish influence in Argyll was very gradual. The political situation described by Adomnán at the end of the seventh century in the Life of Columba, was such that the Pictish king, Brude, still effectively held supreme authority over Argyll in the year 563, since it was he who handed over the island of Iona to Colum Cille. The long-term influence of the Irish in the land of the Picts was impressive; indeed it led to the Gaelicisation of Scotland. The Irish language was able to assert itself relatively easily, if Pictish was indeed closely related to Irish. The first ruler over the Picts and *Scoti*, Cináed mac Ailpín (843–858), was also the first supreme ruler over a large realm in the British Isles in post-Roman times.

The Irish expansion into Wales is better documented than the expansion into the land of the Picts. Wales was affected on two fronts, north and south. The northwestern part of Wales was temporarily ruled over by Laigin, people from Leinster, whom the British king Cunedda eventually drove out in the fifth century. A reminder of the people of Leinster is preserved in the name of the peninsula, Lleyn, in Gwynedd. South Wales was attacked and settled from Munster, the conquerors coming from the present-day counties of Kerry, Cork and (to a lesser extent) Waterford. The evidence for this expansion, which allows for an unusual degree of precision, are the *Ogam* inscriptions.

Ogam (also *ogham*), in the narrower sense, means writing in the Irish language and, in the wider sense, it means a form of writing in which the earliest records in the Irish language are handed down. It is a script which uses the letters of the Latin alphabet by means of notches (for vowels) and lines or strokes (for consonants) along a vertical axis, usually the edge of a stone hewn for that purpose. *Ogam* was used for inscriptions on the memorial stones of the dead of the Irish ruling class. These inscriptions are generally very simple, consisting of the name of the person commemorated in the genitive case as well as the name of an ancestor, normally the father, e.g. *Maqi Cairatini Avi Ineqaglasi*: '(memorial stone of) Mac Cairthinn, grandson of Enechglass'.

There are numerous memorial stones of this type in the south and southwest of Ireland as well as in the southwest of Wales (Pembrokeshire). Isolated examples are also attested further to the east in Britain. Wherever they are found, they represent the stone remains of Irish domination. Apart from the inscription in the Irish language in *ogam* symbols, the *Ogam* stones in Britain usually carry an identical inscription in Latin letters.

According to the pioneering studies by Kenneth Jackson, the majority of *Ogam* inscriptions date from the sixth century, some from the fifth century and others from the seventh century; it is the significant changes in the British language of the time that allow such precise dating. The *Ogam* stones in Britain are of special significance for the Irish settlement of that country, since they provide evidence of an Irish presence and, what is more, in leading positions. Furthermore, they provide evidence of the retention of the Irish language by the Irish upper class in Britain over a period of more than 200 years. Although one must take into account that the language of inscriptions is generally more conservative than the living language, it is hardly conceivable that the Irish language was retained in inscriptions without having support from the living language of the population, particularly, but not exclusively, in the upper class.

A very intensive domination in the west of Wales, as well as further to the east, during the three centuries after the withdrawal of Roman troops from Britain, must therefore be assumed. This formed the prerequisite for a cultural exchange with the west of Britain, an exchange that was extremely important for Ireland and represents one of the constant features of Irish history in the Middle Ages.

The Political Organisation of Ireland

On the assumption that a king reigned on average for fifteen years there would have been approximately three thousand of them in Ireland between 450 and 750. About a third are known by name and about a tenth of these, in turn, played a role which is still discernible today. However, even for these, the most important kings, only very vague dates and locations are possible. There is certainly no reason to assume that the history of Ireland at this time was any more complex than the history of other peoples at a comparable stage of development; it is only that in the case of most other peoples it is even less well-documented. We must, therefore, content ourselves with broad outlines.

The information concerning the political organisation of Ireland originates from different sources, with varying degrees of reliability, from genealogies, sagas of rulers and their ancestry and lists of kings and annals. These lists are the most easily accessible although they also have their own particular difficulties. It must suffice, at this stage, to state that the annals, which began to be written towards the end of the sixth century, do not cover the Ireland of early times in a uniform manner. The centre for early Irish annals was in the northeast of the island, which means that Leinster and Ulster are better covered than Munster and Connacht. It is quite possible that these records are responsible for the idea that the most important events for the further development of Ireland took place in the northeastern region of the island.

The four 'classical provinces' contained sites dating from neolithic times which, apart from enjoying considerable prestige, were also associated with the provincial kingship, although their significance has admittedly not yet been fully clarified. The principal site (neither capital nor residence) of Connacht was *Cruacha*, those of Ulster being *Emhain Mhacha* and *Ailech*, and in Leinster, *Ailenn*. Munster was an exception in that the principal site, *Cashel* (derived from Latin *castellum*) does not have any traceable prehistoric significance and appears to have been taken over quite late. The case of *Tara* is even less clear. The hill of Tara (Co. Meath), one of the most impressive sites of Irish prehistory, became the principal ceremonial site for the Uí Néill dynasty from the fifth century and is a pre-Celtic site (although there is no reliable evidence of an

association between the provincial kingship and 'law prior to the
fifth century).

It has already been mentioned briefly that the provincial kings
had had an important influence since the fifth century. This does
not, however, mean that the old tribal kingship of the *rí túaithe* had
become meaningless. It is in fact evidence of a change in the
political scene, namely the rise of dynasties which derived their
claims from – mostly mythological – founders and thus began to
supersede the early Irish kingship clearly defined in the legal texts.

It is quite understandable that law tracts schematised the
political order in a manner that did not completely correspond to
reality. However, the strength of the concepts recorded in them can
be seen in how long it was to take for a new, dynastic, form of
kingship to eclipse the old tribal kingship completely, which did
not happen before the eleventh century. This new development is
best documented in the Uí Néill dynasty whose rise extended over
several centuries. At the end of this period the Uí Néill appeared,
paradoxically, once more as provincial kings, only this time in a
different province from that of their origin. The clan, which came
from Connacht, had become the small provincial dynasty of the
O'Neill in Ulster.

The long duration of Irish dynasties has no parallels on the
Continent and was the result of specifically Irish features. It must
be remembered that there was hardly any disruption of development
from ouside. Another factor was the nature of royal succession from
the clan, the *derbfine*, which ensured an almost inexhaustible supply
of *rígdomnae*, eligible heirs to the throne. In addition, monogamy
was not the rule in medieval Ireland, Christianity having changed
nothing in that regard. Contrary to Christian concepts, marriages
were dissolved in agreement with Irish law. The Irish in the
Middle Ages also appear to have been extremely procreative. This
all meant that a dynasty like the Uí Néill was never short of
candidates for the office of king. Typical of medieval Ireland is the
impressive continuity of names in the ruling class.

The Rise of the Uí Néill

The most powerful realm in prehistoric Ireland appears to have
been the province of the Ulaid whose principal site was *Emhain*

Map 1: Ireland c. 800, provinces and principal sites

Mhacha (near Armagh). It extended in a southwesterly direction into the rich agricultural areas of Ireland, to Mide (Meath). There are indications that the Ulaid included a not inconsiderable population of Pictish origin, referred to by the Goidels as *Cruithni*.

A reorganisation of the large-scale political situation on the island was signalled when a dynasty from Connacht threatened and appreciably weakened the dominance of the Ulaid. This dynasty was called the Uí Néill after the king Niall Noígiallach, who claimed descent from Cormac mac Airt, founder of the Connachta, who is thought to have lived in the fourth century. Niall, who died around A.D. 450, is credited with the conquest and destruction of *Emhain Mhacha*. The interpretation of his epithet, Noígiallach ('of the nine hostages'), is that he made the Airgialla ('who provide hostages') dependent upon him. The submission of nine *túatha* of the Airgialla is read into this although in this case history and legend have been interwoven. It was apparently only after Niall's death that the northwest of the province of the Ulaid was conquered, from Sligo, by a branch of his clan, the Cenél nEógain.

One of Niall's first successors, Ailill Molt († around 482) is the first king of the Uí Néill who we can be reasonably certain celebrated the feast of Tara (*feis Temro*) around 467 or 470. Tara (*Temair*) became the principal settlement of the Uí Néill. The legends later associated with St Patrick admittedly give an account of another, somewhat earlier, celebration of this feast by King Loegaire. Tara means 'place with a wide-ranging view' and mountains of all the four provinces of Ireland can indeed be seen from the hill of Tara. The feast of Tara was observed on 1 November (the following dates regulated the seasons in ancient Ireland; *Samain*, 1 November; *Imbolc*, 1 February; *Beltaine*, 1 May; *Lugnasad*, 1 August). It was, for a long time, interpreted as being the inauguration ceremony of the king but is now seen rather as an occasion for the king to assert his overlordship and demonstrate the extent of his power. The feast was celebrated only once by each king, but not at the commencement of his rule. As it had pronounced pagan features, it soon fell into disuse; after Ailill Molt there is only attested evidence for Diarmait (king around 544–65) in the year 558 or 560. Instead, the Uí Néill demonstrated their supremacy from the sixth century onwards through the assembly of Tailtiu (*oenach Tailten*) which was held at the beginning of August every year and lasted a week. The propagandists of the Uí Néill, of whom Adomnán was not the least important, credited the assembly with significance for the whole island. In fact, it only affected those kingdoms which were subordinate to the Uí Néill. It is documented fairly regularly up to the beginning of the tenth century and demonstrated not only the effective power of the Uí Néill (for no other dynasty was able to lay claim to an institution of comparable duration), but also the necessity of seeing the power of the dynasty constantly confirmed.

The almost inexorable rise of the Uí Néill was achieved by means which were not provided for in the law tracts, namely through taking possession of the land of others. However, there is a term in the poems and stories which describes this new reality: *ferann claidib* 'sword land'.

The rise of the Uí Néill was principally at the expense of the Ulaid. It is, however, significant that the Uí Néill set up the centre of their realm a considerable distance south of the former centre of the Ulaid. This was certainly due, in part, to economic factors, but it also shows that the Uí Néill were not able to dislodge the Ulaid easily. In the subsequent period the provincial kings of the Ulaid come on the whole from the Dál nAraidi in County Antrim. Other important groupings were the Dál Fiatach and the Uí Echach Cobo in the east and west of County Down respectively. At the assembly of Druim Cett in the year 575, Aed mac Ainmuired, king of the northern branch of the Uí Néill, laid claim to sovereignty over the Dál Riada. Half a century later Congal Clacn, king of the Dál nAraidi and provincial king of the Ulaid since A.D. 627, was killed in the battle of Mag Roth (637), after which the Uí Néill became the dominant power in the northeast of Ireland, although the Ulaid continued to survive in the outlying regions.

One can see how circumstances in Ireland made the conversion of sovereignty into territorial control very difficult. Although initial steps in that direction are clearly recognisable, they did not progress much further. The difficulty was increased by rivalries within the province between various branches of the ruling clan. From the middle of the eighth century the provincial kingship of the Uí Néill alternated, with astonishing regularity, between the northern branch of the Cenél nEógain and the southern branch of the Clann Cholmain from Mide.

We have seen that the Uí Néill established the focal point of their rule in the southern territory of the Ulaid. They had practically created a new province, but not only at the expense of the Ulaid; the Laigin were also affected in their northern regions.

It has already been mentioned that the Laigin had occupied a part of northern Wales in the fifth century. Their dislodgement from there by Cunedda signals a weakening of which the Uí Néill took advantage in order to drive them out of Mide as well. Although there are allusions in some archaic poems to Tara being the legitimate possession of the Laigin, their northern centre was, from the fifth century onwards, in the Liffey valley.

The most important Laigin dynasty was the Uí Cheinnselaig founded by Fáelán mac Colmáin who died in the middle of the sixth century and who is believed to have been an associate of St Kevin, the founder of Glendalough. His brother, Aed Dub, was abbot and bishop of Kildare, the centre of the Brigit cult. It would appear that a place of worship had already existed in Kildare in prehistoric times, features of which have been partly preserved in the Brigit cult. Like the Uí Néill, the Laigin were subdivided into two fairly large groups. Although the Laigin had been driven out of Mide, it was far from certain that they would bow to the Uí Néill as the stronger neighbour. Not until the end of the eighth century is there evidence that the Uí Cheinnselaig dynasty occasionally gave hostages to the Uí Néill. The development in Munster, the southerly neighbour of the Laigin, is even more difficult to understand. This region was beyond the reach of the Uí Néill and was, therefore, seldom mentioned in the annals before the eighth century. The rulers in Munster were the Eóganachta who looked upon Eógon Már, the grandson of the mythological figure, Mug Nuadat, as their founder. The principal settlement of the dynasty was Cashel, which, in contrast to the other principal settlements, shows no evidence of having once been a prehistoric place of worship. The colonisation of western Britain by invaders from Munster has already been mentioned and it is quite conceivable that Romano-British influences made themselves felt in Cashel (from Latin *castellum*). The connection with late Roman Britain also points to a possible early penetration of Christianity into southern Ireland. It was there that the *Ogam* script, based on the Latin alphabet, was used and perhaps even developed.

Compared to the Uí Néill, the Eóganachta were weak and there is no complete list of provincial kings of Cashel. This weakness was turned into a positive attribute in the propaganda literature of the dynasty, which claimed that the Eóganachta ruled through prosperity and generosity.

The concept of the two halves of Ireland, *Leth Cuinn* and *Leth Moga*, originates from Munster and demonstrates an attempt at delimitation against the rulers of Tara, especially at a time when they were promoting the idea that kingship of Tara meant control over the whole island. To some degree, Munster was indeed a world of its own and we will see later that much work was done there in the field of learning in the seventh century. The political weakness of the kings of Cashel may therefore have had a positive effect in the area.

Connacht, named after Conn Cétchathach ('Conn of the 100 battles'), was, in some respects, also a world of its own. The province had a very distinct eastern boundary in the Shannon and its accompanying lowland plain which abounds with lakes. Its most important dynasty in the fifth century was that of the Uí Fiachrach which, however, encountered significant competition in the form of the Uí Briúin from the seventh century onwards. Their first king, for whom there is reasonably reliably documented evidence, was Ragallach mac Uatach, who died in A.D. 649. The violent methods employed by the Uí Briúin are reminiscent in some ways of the methods of the Uí Néill with whom they also shared rather modest descent. In the eighth century, one branch of the Uí Briúin, the Uí Ruairc, managed to gain a foothold in the outlying western regions of the southern Uí Néill in Bréifne, while another branch distinguished itself in south Connacht against the Uí Mhaine.

Chaos?

The picture we have drawn of the political organisation of Ireland between the fifth and eighth centuries shows no more than the broad outline of a very complex and inadequately documented situation. At any one time, many kings were fighting for their political survival. It must of course be borne in mind that these political disputes really only affected the king and the nobility. In some ways, the struggle was only the realisation of a political pecking order. Many struggles involved nothing more than the rounding up of tribute (rounding up in the true sense of the word as tribute was measured in cattle) and hostages, in other words, rounding up tribute and hostages to which the *ruiri* and the provincial king were legitimately entitled but which were not always given willingly or in full.

Unrest is also a relative term and Bede provides impressive proof of this in an account for the year A.D. 664: 'At that time there were many English noblemen and people of lower rank in Ireland who (. . .) had left their homeland and gone there either for religious study or to lead a more ascetic life there. Some of them soon devoted themselves completely to monastic life while others studied by visiting the cells of their teachers. The Irish received them all in the most friendly manner and gave them, daily, food without charge, as well as books to read and gratuitous tuition'. (HE III, 27) Compared with England, the political situation in Ireland in the seventh century seems to have been quite tolerable.

Bede also attests to the openness of the Irish towards strangers. Although it cannot be determined how large the number of foreigners – significantly not just foreign clerics – in Ireland was, some are known by name and their status makes it extremely unlikely that they came to Ireland unaccompanied. A worthy example is Oswald of Northumbria who had been baptised in exile amongst the Irish before his accession to the throne (634). A generation after the later Austrasian Merovingian king, Dagobert II († 678), also spent some time in Ireland. Oswald plays an important role in Bede's Ecclesiastical History and Eddius, who wrote the biography of the northern English bishop Wilfred, gives an account of Dagobert. It is not clear why Dagobert sought refuge in Ireland of all places; it could, of course, have been due to Irish-Frankish contact as a result of Columban monasticism in Gaul. Another man who should be mentioned is Aldfrith who was king of Northumbria from 685–704 and whose mother, Fín, was the daughter of Colmán Rímid, provincial king of the northern branch of the Uí Néill. Before Aldfrith ascended the throne of Northumbria, he spent some time studying *in insulis Scottorum*.[3]

The accounts of these three foreign rulers in Ireland are each documented in sources which deal with Christianity in England. It must be admitted that the biased nature of these sources prevents any adequate explanation of the political connections between Ireland and the ruling class of western Europe. Nevertheless, these are important insights which show that it was not only the Christian religion which transcended national boundaries. In the field of Christianity, Ireland had meanwhile become particularly dynamic, and it is to this aspect that we now turn our attention.

PART II

Ireland in the first part of the Middle Ages (c. A.D. 500–1100)

4. The Beginnings of Christianity in Ireland

For the year A.D. 431 the chronicler Prosper of Aquitaine writes: *Ad Scottos in Christum credentes ordinatus a papa Caelestino Palladius primus episcopus mittitur* ('Consecrated by Pope Celestine, Palladius is sent as the first bishop to the Irish who believe in Christ'). This is the only reliable date for Irish history in the fifth century. Yet Prosper's statement raises several questions: When had Christianity come to Ireland? How many Christians were there in Ireland in the year 431? Who was Palladius? How long was he active in Ireland? Where did he carry out his work?

Although none of these questions can be answered with certainty, some reasonable assumptions can be made. Let us begin with the last question: Where did Palladius carry out his work? In the Middle Irish Life of Patrick (*Bethu Phátraic*), we are told: 'He (Palladius) founded three churches, Cell Fine, in which he left his books, the casket with the relics of Paul and Peter and the board on which he used to write, *Tech na Rómán* ("House of the Romans") and Domnach Airte containing Sylvester and Solinus' (presumably two of his followers). This information has also come down to us from another source, the origin of which is, unfortunately, unknown. However, the substance of the information does not appear to be without foundation. The three churches mentioned are situated in Leinster, the region lying opposite the northwest coast of Wales. There is good reason to believe that Palladius came to Ireland via Wales, just as it is probable that Christianity had reached Leinster by this route before the time of Palladius.

Palladius was dispatched to the Irish Christians at about the same time as Germanus of Auxerre was sent to the Christians in Britain. Germanus had been dispatched to Britain in A.D. 429 to combat the heretical teachings of Pelagius. Active from around the year 400, Pelagius was a British monk who had developed a doctrine of human free will. Since this conflicted with the Catholic doctrine of grace, Pelagius was declared a heretic in 418. In his Ecclesiastical History Bede tells how Germanus had refuted Pelagianism in Britain through the healing power of relics (HE I, 17ff.). A similar function could be attributed to the relics Palladius brought to Ireland. If this was the case, it would indicate that

43

Rome assumed a rather highly-developed level of Christianity amongst the Irish.

Who was Palladius? Two deacons with this name are known from this period, one from Rome, the other from Auxerre, and it was probably the latter who came to Ireland. However, before, we consider this and other questions regarding Palladius' activities, we must turn our attention to Patrick. Although most of the Irish annals give the year 432 as the date of Patrick's arrival in Ireland as a missionary, this date has proved to be unreliable. The fact that there was a prominent missionary in Ireland by the name of Patrick is well-known, just as there is general agreement that he was active in the fifth century. The exact date when his long period of missionary work began is, however, a completely open question. Opinions range from approximately 400 to around A.D. 460.

Two works by Patrick have survived, his *Confessio* (Conf.) and an *Epistola* (Ep.P) to the soldiers of the tyrant, Coroticus. Despite the many differences of opinion that exist amongst scholars regarding Patrick, these two works were, at least until recently, considered to be authentic. They represent the only, and extremely valuable, testimony, in which the historical figure of Patrick can be seen. However, a few years ago, doubts were raised (which I consider justified) concerning the authenticity of some passages of the *Confessio*, passages which have, up to now, been held to be particularly enigmatic.[4] If these passages do not originate from Patrick, then we have no information concerning where he was born, the position of his father and grandfather, or about his four weeks' march through the desert; the location of this desert in northwest Europe has, for obvious reasons, always created great difficulties. The earliest extant manuscripts of Patrick's works date from the ninth (Conf.) and tenth (Ep.P) centuries. Both works, especially the *Confessio*, are, however, easily recognisable as the sources for the extremely important Life of Patrick by Muirchú, which was written in Ireland in the seventh century. The *Confessio* does not contain any specific dates; the *Epistola* mentions a tyrant named Coroticus. According to the latest research, Coroticus was a leader of British warriors in northeast Ireland who lived from slave-trading,[5] but nothing is known of his dates.

Now, briefly, the most important factual information from Patrick's two works. He wrote the *Confessio* late in life. He was born in Britain, a freeman. His father held the position of a *decurio*, a

Roman civil servant (Ep.P.10). When he was fifteen years of age, and at that time not yet a Christian (it is uncertain whether this means that he had not yet been baptised or that he had not yet emphatically professed his Christianity), he was abducted by pirates and taken to Ireland where he worked in captivity as a herdsman. During his first stay in the country, lasting approximately six years, he devoted himself to Christianity, being moved by visions, and prayed long and often. He eventually managed to escape and return to Britain. Some years later he again had a vision in which he was called upon to convert the Irish. He worked for many years among people who had never had any contact with Christianity, became a bishop, baptised many thousands and travelled, in the course of his missionary work, to the outer limits of the inhabited world. He encouraged those he met to turn towards monastic life. He refers more frequently to monks and nuns than he does to ordinary baptised people and was especially proud of the fact that he was able to win over the children of several pagan kings (*reguli*) to monastic life (Conf. 41, Ep.P.12).

He was apparently envied his position as bishop, for he stressed that he had not acquired it in any improper or unlawful manner. The *Confessio*, in which he defended his work in Ireland, also contains his own very detailed confession of faith. The letter to the soldiers of Coroticus was written with the objective of obtaining the release of Christians who had been sold into slavery to the Picts by Irish pagans. Patrick describes himself as *profuga ob amorem Dei* 'fugitive for the love of God'. He further indicates that he was acquainted with Christians in Britain and Gaul.

Patrick wrote the *Confessio* and the *Epistola* in Latin which, for him, was a foreign language: 'Our words have been translated into a foreign language as can be seen quite easily from the saliva of my writing' (Conf. 9). Traces of British and Irish syntax are noticeable in the rather bizarre Latin of these works. Patrick does not give us any concrete details concerning the region in which he was active, nor does he mention that he had an episcopal see. Indeed, after his writings, nothing more is heard in Ireland about Patrick throughout the sixth century. It was in the seventh century that legends of Patrick's work emerged, based, as previously mentioned, on his writings and supplemented by precise details regarding the very questions which remain unanswered in his writings. The legend grew in the eighth century and became a political issue, a matter which will be dealt with in Chapter 7. For the moment, however, we will confine ourselves to the authentic accounts relating to Palladius and Patrick and consider them jointly.

This gives rise to the following problems: Patrick was a bishop; Palladius is referred to as the first bishop. Palladius came to the Irish who already believed in Christ whereas Patrick was active among those Irish who had never heard of Christianity. Patrick was, according to his own statements, active among the Irish for many years; Palladius apparently spent a long time among the Irish, according to the information in the tribute payed to him by Pope Celestine I and described by Prosper in his work *Contra Collatorem*.

These statements, which may at first appear contradictory, can be reconciled to some extent if one assumes that Patrick was active in a part of Ireland which had not yet been reached by Christianity. Patrick is thought to have worked as a missionary with the Ulaid as well as in northern Connacht and although we have no information regarding a cathedral for Patrick, Armagh became, in the following centuries, the diocesan seat the founding of which was traced back to him. Armagh is situated two miles from Emhain Mhacha, the principal site of the Ulaid, which would tend to indicate that Patrick had placed himself under the protection of the kings of the Ulaid. We have already heard that, in the fifth century, the Uí Néill waged war with the Ulaid, driving them out in a northeasterly direction; Emhain Mhacha was deserted around the middle of the fifth century. The possibility that Patrick was also affected by these political upheavals is supported by the later traditional account that he died in Downpatrick (Co. Down), that is the region where the Ulaid were able to retain control. Nor does the description of Palladius as the first bishop of the Irish pose any real problem: Patrick had no contact with Rome and Prosper apparently knew nothing of Patrick's activities. The later legend tells of Patrick spending many years in Gaul, mainly in the monastery of Lérins. There is, however, no mention of this in the authentic works of Patrick; the Latin in the *Confessio* and the *Epistola* is such that a long stay in Gaul on the part of their author can be ruled out. Gaulish bishops who, according to later sources, worked with Patrick in Ireland (Iserninus, Sacellus), are more likely to have worked with Palladius.

Exactly when the historical figure of Patrick carried out his missionary work in Ireland will probably never be determined. Some scholars are of the opinion that the later legend of Patrick was compiled from accounts relating to the activities of both Patrick *and* Palladius. In this case, the controversy over the description of Patrick as 'the Apostle of the Irish' would become irrelevant. The fact that nothing was heard of Patrick in the century following his missionary work can no doubt be explained by the increasingly important role which the monasteries were to play in the Irish Church from the end of the fifth century. Palladius and Patrick were, however, both bishops. Their work developed from this office and both wanted to establish a diocesan Church in Ireland.

The remaining question concerns the beginnings of Christianity in Ireland, the Christians to whom Palladius was sent. In dealing with this issue, the Latin loan words in the languages of the Irish and Britons (Welsh) provide some very good general points of reference: 'The Greeks, Latin scholars and the barbarians took "Amen", "Halleluja" and "Hosanna" from the Hebrews, the Latin scholars and all those who use the Latin language and books in Latin borrowed "ecclesia", "baptismum", "chrisma" from the Greeks and the Germans took many words, both in colloquial language, such as "scamel" "fenestra", "lectar", as well as almost everything in matters of religious worship from the Latin scholars', writes Walahfrid Strabo, abbot of Reichenau, in the ninth century.[6] This also applies *mutatis mutandis* to the Irish and Welsh.

Among the numerous Latin loan words of mostly Christian content, all of which reached Ireland through the British language, there is one particular group which indicates borrowing into the Irish language, probably during the first half of the fourth century. This not inconsiderable corpus of early Latin loan-words in Irish, which has been maintained along with later borrowings, indicates the strength of the Christian community in Ireland in the fourth century.

The early Latin words can – in simple terms – be recognised from the orthography, especially from the spelling of the Irish 'c' (for /q/) instead of the Latin and British 'p', e.g. Irish *cland*, Welsh *plant* (from the Latin colloquial word *planta*) 'child'; Irish *clúm*, Latin *pluma* 'quill'; Irish *corcur*, Latin *purpura* 'purple'; Irish *cruimther*, Latin *presbyter* 'priest'. Significantly, there is no term for 'bishop' in this early phase of borrowing. The 'p' in Latin loan words in Irish indicates a later phase of borrowing, probably from the middle of the fifth century, although the Latin word *Patricius*, in its two documented Irish versions, *Cothrige* and *Pádraig*, poses problems which remain unresolved.

The second phase of borrowing from British Latin came at a time when the Latin influence on British had considerably weakened. This stage, in contrast to the first, is characterised by ecclesiastical terms. Typical of this phase is the shift of accent, which was on the penultimate syllable in British and on the first syllable in Irish, e.g. Irish *peccath*, Latin *peccātum* 'sin'; Irish *cuthe*, Latin *putēus* 'pit'; Irish *ortha*, Latin *orātio* 'prayer'; Irish *oifrend*, Latin *offerenda* (the term for 'mass' attested from Milan).

Finally, there are a number of Latin loan words both in Irish and Welsh, where the Welsh language has adopted the Irish shift of stress onto the first syllable. This is interpreted as a borrowing-back into Welsh from Irish, e.g. Latin *capitilavium* 'Maundy Thursday', Irish *caplait*, Welsh *cablyd*; Latin *quadragesima* 'Lent', Irish *corgus*, Welsh *carawys*; Latin *beāti* (beginning of Psalm 118), Irish *biait*, Welsh *byweit*.

The linguistic interchange between Latin, Welsh and Irish outlined here must be considered in the context of a much wider-reaching cultural exchange between Wales and Ireland. The directions of this interchange are, in this respect, significant. In the first phase, in the century before the activities of Palladius and Patrick, Ireland was the receiving and Wales the providing part. In the later phase mentioned here, the exertion of influence was reversed. Wales received impulses from Ireland which can be substantiated linguistically, particularly in the area of the Christian religion.

To sum up, it can be established that there are clear signs of the existence of a not inconsiderable Christian community in Ireland since the fourth century which, from Patrick's statements, does not appear to have been located in the northeast of the island but is more likely to have been in the area where later accounts described Palladius's activities, principally in Leinster. Since we know that there were political and military contacts during this time between Wales and *Leth Moga*, a reasonably complete picture can be formed on the basis of the – admittedly very few – sources. Patrick's presumed activities among the Ulaid indicate that he came originally from northern Britain.

Of course, these are not necessarily the only channels through which Christianity reached Ireland. Although direct influences from Gaul cannot be ruled out, especially in Munster, they have not left any lasting mark.

Finally, it should be pointed out that with regard to the organisation of their communities in Ireland, Patrick and Palladius were both committed to the Roman model of the diocesan Church which is attested in Britain from the fourth century onwards. By their activities they also attempted to establish this model in Ireland. It soon became obvious, however, that due to the absence of Roman heritage in Ireland as well as the lack of towns, the Roman ecclesiastical model was quite unsuitable for that country.

5.   The Formation of the Early Irish Church

If the political history of Ireland in the fifth and sixth centuries is regarded as extremely obscure, then the situation relating to the history of Christianity is hardly more favourable. Patrick, Colum Cille and Columbanus appear as credible individuals, be it from their own writings or from those Lives that, as far as can be ascertained, were not excessively stylised. That is, however, about all that is known and it is little enough. An added complication is that Patrick on one side, and Colum Cille and Columbanus on the other, inform us about different aspects of the early Irish Church and in two different centuries. The main problem is that Patrick had planned a diocesan Church while Colum Cille and Columbanus had emphasised the monastic features of Irish Christianity. Although Patrick also refers to monks, and although we will later see the important role played by the bishops even in the sixth century it is not possible to determine the full significance of monastic features in the fifth century and episcopal features in the sixth. There are numerous Lives of the founders of early medieval monasteries, not all of which are, of course, equally reliable; yet – with the single exception of Patrick – there does not exist one single Life of a bishop. According to the sources, the early Irish Church was chiefly monastic in character, an impression which may, however, stem from the fact that traditions were preserved better in the monasteries. Even if the predominantly monastic character of the early, though not the earliest, Irish Church is accepted, the question remains as to how this came about – a question to which there is not as yet a satisfactory answer.

Monastic Founders

The first group of monastic founders can be dated by taking as its conclusion the plague of 548/549 to which some of them fell victim. However, not all of the dates given can be regarded as reliable. Belonging to this first group are Búithe, founder of Mainistir Búithe (Monasterboice, Co. Louth) († 521); Brigit of Kildare († c. 524); Enda of Aran († c. 530); Iarlaithe of Tuam, active around 540; Finnian of Clonard (Co. Meath) († 549); Ciaran of Clonmacnois (Co. Offaly), known as 'the carpenter' († 549); Colum mac Crimthainn of Terryglass (Co. Tipperary) († c. 549).

The geographical distribution of these monasteries shows a wide band in an east–west direction through the middle of the island. The monasteries are all situated, roughly speaking, in the border areas between the provinces. The common Irish placenames with the element *kil-* (from Latin *cella* 'cell') point to monastic origin. Interesting, though still not fully explained, is the single documented occurrence in early Ireland of the term *monasterium* for a monastery, in Monasterboice. The word element *Clon-*, derived from Old Irish *clúain*, appears often with the meaning of 'meadow' (i.e. of non-drained land), land, therefore, which up to that time had not been used agriculturally. Many of the earlier monasteries were situated in river plains (see Map 2).

In the second half of the sixth century, monastic foundations are evident in all regions of Ireland. The most important founders are Brendan of Clonfert (Co. Galway) († c. 580) who, apart from Clonfert (559), also founded monasteries on the islands near Iona; Comgall of Bangor (Co. Down) († 603), founder of Bangor (555/559) and Tiree; Brendan of Birr (Co. Offaly); Ciarán of Saigir (Co. Offaly); Colum Cille († 597), founder of Derry (c. 546), Durrow (Co. Offaly, c. 556) and Iona (563); Finnian of Mag Bile (near Bangor, Co. Down), a contemporary of Colum Cille, who, apart from Mag Bile, also founded Dromin (Co. Louth); Fintan of Clonenagh (Co. Laois) († 603); Molua of Clonfertmulloe (Co. Laois) († 608). Finally, some names from the first half of the seventh century should be mentioned: Kevin (Coemgen) of Glendalough (Co. Wicklow) († 618); Aedán/Maedóg of Ferns (Co. Wexford) († 626); Mochua of Rahan (Co. Offaly) († 637).

According to tradition, Finnian (Latin Vinnianus) of Clonard was the example and inspiration for several founders of monasteries, in particular for Ciarán of Saigir, Ciarán of Clonmacnois (who was also influenced by Enda of Aran), Brendan of Birr and Colum Cille. It should be emphasised that several monastic founders were also active on the islands off the west coast of Scotland: Comgall of Bangor, Brendan of Clonfert as well as Colum Cille. These, then, are the bare facts.

It is only possible to speculate as to how this monasticism reached Ireland. The geographical distribution of the earliest

Map 2: The most important Irish monasteries

known monasteries makes it less probable that Patrick's influence
continued to have an effect; influences from Britain are more likely,
particularly via Wales, at the end of the fifth and the beginning of
the sixth centuries. The political and military contacts between
Wales and Ireland at this time have already been dealt with in
Chapter 3.

It would be unwise, though, to speak of definite influences from
Wales since all that exists are allusions and suggestions. It is true
that Wales provided the best possible conditions for the survival of
Romano-British culture. Important evidence for *one* aspect of
Romano-British continuity in this area was established recently
when it was shown that the deeds of gifts which have been
preserved in the *Liber Landavensis* (twelfth century) date back as far
as the sixth century.[7] It is also a fact that Ireland's longest and
most intensive contact with a former Roman region in Britain was
in Wales.

With regard to monasticism in Britain in the late and sub-
Roman centuries, our knowledge is extremely limited. Reference
has already been made to a church near Canterbury dedicated to
St Martin and thus to traces of Gaulish monasticism. Although
there are records in Wales of a flourishing monasticism towards the
end of the fifth and throughout the sixth century, the Lives of
Saints, which contain the accounts of this, were written quite late
and their reliability has not yet been established. The oldest Life of
a Welsh abbot, Samson, dates from the eighth century; the others
are recorded in versions dating from the eleventh and twelfth
centuries. The most influential personality in the early Welsh
Church according to this tradition was St Illtud who is thought to
have been active around A.D. 520. Samson, Cadoc of Llancarfan
and Gildas are said to have belonged to the same circle. In the Life
of David (late eleventh century) of Menevia (Welsh *Mynyw*), who is
thought to have died around A.D. 601, an account is given of
disputes between David and Maedóg of Ferns, which fits roughly
into the chronology. The presence of British monks among the
followers of Colum Cille and Columbanus is evidence of contact in
the second generation between the Irish founders of monasteries
and the Welsh. Our sources do not, however, allow such precise
detail for the first generation.

The Irish Church comes alive in the second half of the sixth

century and this, mainly, because of what is known about Colum
Cille.

Colum Cille (Columba the Elder, 521/22–597)

After St Patrick, Colum Cille is the first figure in the early Irish
Church to become tangible as an historical figure by means of a
biography. The information concerning his work – not a Life in the
narrow sense, but a collection of vignettes presented thematically
rather than chronologically – was written by a relative, Adomnán,
the ninth abbot of Iona (679–704), approximately 100 years after
Colum Cille's death. Some amount of standard hagiographical
material was used in the Life and the author resorted to older Lives
of Saints even to the extent of borrowing phrases; the conversations
recorded are fictional. Nevertheless, we have in Adomnán's work
the committed writings of an Irishman about his revered compatriot,
predecessor and ancestor which is not only extremely graphic but
also contains important incidental information regarding the
political and social history of Ireland and the land of the Picts.
Adomnán's precise knowledge of the topography of Iona gives a
vivid impression of the scene in which the events took place. Even
if the information does not always include complete details and
does not always appear to be from the period in which the saint
lived, it is nevertheless very valuable.

Colum Cille, originally Crimthann, was born in A.D. 521/22. His
father was descended from the Uí Néill and, on his mother's side,
there is proof of royal ancestry in Leinster. As a monk he received
the name Columba 'dove' (Old Irish *Columb Cille* 'dove of the
Church'), a religious name which was quite frequent in sixth-
century Ireland. For his education he was entrusted to the priest
Cruithnechán whom Adomnán describes as his *nutritor* 'spiritual
provider'. The other teachers of his who are mentioned by name
were bishops Finnio (Finnian of Clonard?) and Finnbarr. Colum
Cille founded monastic communities in Derry, the area under the
control of the northern Uí Néill, and in Durrow, on the boundary
between the southern Uí Néill and the Laigin. Adomnán reports
that he was wrongly condemned by a synod in Tailtiu in A.D. 561;
this was, no doubt, a secular assembly also attended by clerics, and
which he therefore described as a synod. There are strong

indications that this conflict, the intimate details of which are not known, was connected with Colum Cille's decision to leave Ireland. In A.D. 563, at the age of 43, he moved as an *insulanus miles* to the island of Iona (*Iova*, *Hy*) which is situated off the west coast of Scotland. Iona became the centre of Colum Cille's work and he died there in A.D. 597.

The move to Iona was certainly not the kind of life-long exile which was soon to become a characteristic feature of Irish monasticism. Adomnán reports numerous journeys to the still pagan Picts, several longer visits to the islands off the west coast of Scotland, as well as journeys to Ireland where Colum Cille visited 'his' monks in Durrow and other monasteries. Even during his life he enjoyed profound respect. Adomnán tells of hymns in Irish which the laity sang in his praise. A book of hymns from his pen was also used in Leinster.

There are some details concerning the composition of the original community on Iona. Apart from his Irish countrymen – a monk from Connacht is singled out, the other Irish monks appear to have come mainly from the northeast of the island – a British monk is also mentioned, a reference to the continuing links with the Christians from Wales. There is also documented evidence of two monks of Germanic origin, 'Saxons', on Iona.

Life on Iona is described in broad outline. Because of the adverse weather conditions, the island was frequently cut off from the outside world. The available arable land was just enough to feed the monks throughout the year. One of the monks was a baker, and cows were kept in order to provide the community with dairy produce. We are told that the milk was brought from the pasture to the monastery on horseback. The monks did not work on Sundays and holy days but, instead, dressed in particularly festive attire and devoted themselves to prayer and worship.

We do not have any precise details as to how the individual buildings were constructed. We are told only that the church was situated apart from the residential buildings. A bell, no doubt a typically Irish hand bell, was used to call the community together quickly. Somewhat away from the other buildings was the abbot's hut, in which he often sat alone, praying and writing. The manuscripts that Colum Cille wrote were held in high esteem in Ireland. Not even the elements could affect them; some of them which inadvertently fell into the water endured the ordeal without sustaining any damage. The only codex still preserved today which might have been written by Colum Cille is a psalter, the so-called *Cathach* 'Book of the Battles' (Ms now in the Royal Irish Academy). Colum Cille visited the Picts on several occasions, Iona lying within the sphere of influence of the Pictish king. According to later tradition, Colum Cille is said to have received Iona from the Pictish king Brude (around 554–594). Although the Picts were still pagan, the abbot did not go to them as a missionary. We are only told of the conversion of individuals or, occasionally, of a family. Colum Cille also maintained close contact with other monasteries on neighbouring islands.

Readers of Adomnán differ strongly in opinion as to how strict the discipline was which Colum Cille demanded. His personal charisma, on the other hand, was beyond question. The most spectacular example of it appears during a visit to Clonmacnois when Colum Cille was an old man. On hearing of his arrival, the monks left the fields to flock together in the monastery and it was necessary to protect the visitor from too large a throng, and from being annoyed, by means of a wooden trellis carried by four men.

As already mentioned, Colum Cille was more than the model cleric that his biographer depicts. In the year 575, Column Cille attended an assembly at Druim Cett where, according to later tradition, he prevented plans to expel the *filid* from Ireland. Although this may be only a legend, it is a fact that the *fili* Dallán Forgaill composed a long poem in praise of Colum Cille, the *Amra Coluim Chille*, probably soon after his death, a poem not yet completely understood. It is believed to be the oldest preserved poem in Old Irish.

Columbanus (Columba the Younger, 543–615)

Columbanus (also known as 'Columba the Younger' in order to distinguish him from Colum Cille) is much better known outside Ireland than Colum Cille. We are much better informed about him than about the abbot of Iona. We still have writings from his own hand, letters and sermons, monastic rules and poems (the authenticity of the latter has not yet been fully established). Columbanus's work provides us with direct access to his complex personality. About twenty years after his death a *Vita Columbani* was written by Jonas of Bobbio who had not, however, known Columbanus personally. We learn that Columbanus was born in Leinster in A.D. 543, received his monastic training in the monastery of Bangor (Co. Down), left Ireland in the year 587, worked for more than twenty years in Merovingian Gaul (founding Luxeuil in 591), went to northern Italy around 610, via Bregenz, and died in Bobbio in A.D. 615. The spiritual attitudes discernible in the *Vita* can be traced directly back to Ireland; he appears to have received little positive stimulus on the Continent. Columbanus's personal writings, occasionally supplemented by information from Jonas's biography, enable us to draw a reasonably accurate portrait of this cleric, who is often considered to be the typical representative of Irish monasticism on the Continent.

According to Jonas, the most important stages in the life of Columbanus, who was of noble descent, were: firstly, the study of liberal arts and Latin; then, apparently still in Leinster, religious studies under the renowned Sinilis and, finally, his life as a monk in Bangor under Abbot Comgall, who only reluctantly allowed him to go to the Continent with twelve companions (taking Christ as an example). For Columbanus this was a final farewell.

In Frankish Gaul, Columbanus began the life of a hermit, living very ascetically. Some of his companions were Irish, and a British monk had also travelled with him. Two aspects of Columbanus's spiritual attitude are particularly impressive, namely his views on the obligations of a Christian and his assessment of the position of Ireland in the Christian community of the western world. These two themes are closely interwoven and are evident in all his writings.

Central to this is Columbanus's piety which could be described as being strongly emotional. It appears almost programmatically at the beginning of his homilies: 'Nobody should attempt to explore the impenetrable aspects of God (. . .) Believe simply, but strongly, that God is and will be as he has been, for God is immutable' (S. 1). First priority among his spiritual demands is the virtue of humility (*humilitas*). Associated with this is the renunciation of the world, which is particularly difficult because that to which one should turn is unknown. Earthly life is to be abhorred as it is only a shadow, only a preparation for life after death. Man's great challenge is that God created man in His own image. It is necessary to overcome evil, e.g. delight in idle talk and denigration of one's fellow man in his absence (S. 11). Human life must be concentrated solely on Christ: 'Let us love you (Christ), love only you, yearn only for you, think only of you, day and night, so that your love occupies our whole mind and soul' (S. 12). Columbanus occasionally used rather unusual metaphors: 'Even when we consume (literally "eat") Christ through love, even when we devour him through longing, we nevertheless want to long for him as if we were hungry'. *Te rogamus ut sciamus quod amamus* ('We ask you that we may know what we love'), he writes with inimitable and almost untranslatable intensity (S. 13).

Consciousness of human weakness, painful renunciation of the world and its shallow joys, complete devotion to Christ; these extraordinary demands of Columbanus sometimes met with rejection, even among his closest companions, his monks. The force of his language and the power of his argumentation, which shows little display of theological subtlety, are based on a detailed study of the Scriptures with a particular predilection for the psalms. This is in clear contrast to the older form of monasticism which attached greater importance to physical sacrifice than to spiritual devotion. Columbanus wanted both, with no compromise whatsoever. It was with disappointment that he realised that this kind of devotion, which he had learned in Ireland, and which also bore the mark of his own personality, met with considerable lack of understanding in Gaul, although it must be added that Columbanus also enjoyed great success there.

We now turn to the second important aspect of Irish-Columban Christianity of the time, to the conviction that belief in Christ has the effect of a uniting bond which transcends all national boundaries: 'Do not believe that we think of ourselves any different than of you: for we are joint members (*commembra*) of one body, whether Gauls, Britons, Irish or of any other people' (Ep. C. 2). Coupled with this is a trust in the position and power of the papacy as the spiritual leader of the whole of Europe, to an extent that is exceptional for this period. Even more unusual is Columbanus's distinction between ancient Rome and Christian Rome. For him, Rome is great because it is at the head of all the world's churches. 'You have the power to order everything, to declare war, to spur on leaders, to order armies to be destroyed, to set up the line of battle, to have the trumpet blown from all sides, and, finally, to stride into battle' he wrote to Pope Boniface (Ep. C. 5). Did he write this in ignorance of the real situation? Was it rhetoric? Was it meant seriously? To what extent did he give in to the temptation to show that an Irishman could also write good Latin? We cannot say for certain, but some measure of self-portrayal should be taken into consideration which was, however, immediately balanced by self-criticism. It was not without some justification that Columbanus repeatedly referred to his own babbling (*loquacitas*, *garrulus*). On the other hand, he did not display any false modesty and was never sparing with harsh words: 'When I believed everybody (else), I almost became stupid' (Ep. C. 4). Nor was he afraid of being a nuisance to the pope: *Meum fuit provocare, interrogare, rogare* ('I have provoked, asked, begged') (Ep. C. 1); he even says occasionally that he was not at all happy with the way the pope was directing Christendom (Ep. C. 5). And despite all this, his Rule (*regula monachorum*) lists the virtue of silence second only to the duty of obedience; obedience in imitating Christ, silence as a means of combatting the greatest Irish failings, the tendency to gossip and to be self-opinionated. Indeed, the Rule, with its extremely concise wording, stands in a remarkable contrast to the verbosity of the letters. The Rule is impressive simply in terms of its content, but the contrast between its style and that of Columbanus's other writings makes it even more expressive.

Some Aspects of the Early Irish Church

When comparing the accounts of the fifth and sixth centuries, it can be seen that the resistance Patrick encountered during his missionary work had been overcome by the time of Colum Cille. While Patrick had had some difficulty introducing the children of the Irish Kings to the Christian religion, by Colum Cille's time the new religion had found considerable approval in the leading circles of society. This triumph of Christianity is all the more remarkable since there are very few signs that the missionaries received the support of the kings from the very beginning or that they worked under royal protection, strengthened by the prestige of the kings; a rare example of this would be the close proximity of Emhain Mhacha and Armagh. Perhaps it is due to inadequate source coverage from Ireland that there appears such a contrast in Ireland to the support the Roman missionary Augustine received from the king of Kent on his arrival in England in A.D. 597. One sometimes has the impression that the triumph of the early Christian community in the Roman Empire prior to the fourth century was repeated in Ireland, and that Christianity became effective through persuasion and conviction. The Church in Ireland appears to have begun as a popular Church, just as in the Roman Empire. However, because of the different political structures in Ireland, there was no change in the manner that followed Constantine's conversion. An established Church of the kind that had influenced the shaping of Christianity in the Empire since the fourth century did not, therefore, have an equivalent in Ireland.

And yet the success of Christianity in Ireland was determined, just as in the Empire, by the fact that it was possible to integrate the religion into the existing society. A decisive factor in Ireland's case was the existence of an intellectual tradition represented by a class which was highly respected socially. As already mentioned, Irish kingship had originally possessed sacral features, which had, however, weakened by the time Christianity reached Ireland. If one considers religiousness to be an essential part of human nature, it is reasonable to assume that there was also a place for Christian dignitaries in Irish society, both as scholars and as Christian officials. The law tracts of the eighth century, although they only take passing notice of the Christianisation of society, concede to the bishop a position equal to that of the king; the bishop had the same honour price as the king, the *fili* and the *brithem*. It is also accounted that the domain of the bishop was the basic political unit, the *túath*.

We know little about the pre-Christian religious conceptions of the Irish at that time. As in the case of other peoples, Christianity had something essentially new to offer concerning life after death. Columbanus's writings provide impressive evidence that this aspect was important to him. It is, of course, quite another matter whether this central Christian doctrine helped Christianity to a lasting triumph in Ireland. The social aspect appears to have been at least equally important: when members of the nobility became Christians, others followed. The community was also familiar with the existence of a learned class. The Christians, however, as the new learned class, were able to impress through their own visible behaviour, such as through their extreme asceticism, and this contributed greatly to their impact. Furthermore, the tribal structure of Irish society continued unbroken in the monastic community with the individual remaining bound to a group. The Old Irish form *muinter* denotes the community of monks; the term is personalised and contrasts with the original *monos* 'alone' of the monk.

Adomnán's account of the life of Colum Cille shows that there were founders of monasteries in Ireland in the middle of the sixth century who, like Finnian for example, were sometimes abbots and bishops at the same time. Apart from Colum Cille, other founders of monasteries, Brendan of Clonfert, Comgall of Bangor and Finnian of Mag Bile also had several monasteries under their supervision; the same applies to Columbanus in Gaul. These abbots could be regarded as something like the Christian equivalent of the *ruirig*. The organisational bond between several monasteries continued to exist even after the death of the founder. This led, from the seventh century onwards, to the development of quite well-documented confederations of monasteries, known in Ireland as *paruchiae*, which crossed political and territorial boundaries. These *paruchiae* were to become quite important in the following centuries.

The legal procedure involved in founding a monastery is not clear, and although the monasteries of the sixth century were established principally in areas which had not previously been settled, or had hardly been settled, neither were they in no man's land. According to Irish law, however, the land belonged to the family and could not be disposed of by individuals. Although there is some evidence that on occasion the whole family was converted to monastic life, it seems that monasteries were often established without the land passing into the legal possession of the monastery. In this way, monastic communities emerged which were incorporated into the possession of the family. The following centuries provide indications of the existence of distinct proprietory churches. The abbots of the more important monasteries were usually members of the nobility. It can therefore be seen that the Church in Ireland assumed certain features of secular society in the early stages of its history.

It would be a mistake, nevertheless, to describe the Irish Church from the sixth century on as a monastic Church. There were bishops throughout Ireland who carried out functions specific to them alone. The fact that there was no late Roman diocesan structure which could be taken over by the Church was not just the case in Ireland; it was evident in all areas outside the boundaries of the Roman Empire.[8] It is just that Ireland was the first country in western Europe to feel the full impact of these circumstances.

There was never a Celtic Church as such: there were great differences in development between Wales and Ireland but greater still was the awareness among Christians in Celtic-speaking countries that they all belonged to *one* Church. Columbanus has already been quoted in this regard. A dictum attributed to Patrick carries the same message: 'The Church of the Irish, or rather of the Romans; as Christians you should be like the Romans'. Although this dictum probably does not come from Patrick at all, but from the eighth century, this does not diminish its significance. Muirchú described Rome as *caput utique omnium ecclesiarum totius mundi* (Vita 5, 'head of all the churches of the whole world'); Adomnán called Rome *caput omnium civitatum* (VC 135b, 'head of all dioceses'); Maedóg of Ferns is credited with the saying: *Nisi videro Romam cito moriar* ('If I do not see Rome soon, I will die'). The emotional link of the Irish Church with Rome continued throughout the following centuries; occasional differences of opinion never called into question this central issue.

One could even go a step further and suggest that the Irish Church was, in one respect, more Roman than any other regional Church. The abbot or bishop of Armagh thought of himself as *comarba* 'heir' to Patrick. Other monastic founders were also remembered in an unusually intense way in many major monasteries in Ireland as well as in Irish monasteries on the Continent (Ciarán, Colum Cille, Enda, Finnian, Fursa, Kevin, Maedóg, etc.). The similarity with Rome is striking in that the bishop of Rome also saw himself as the successor to St Peter. Was this a case of *imitatio*? The high regard for Christian Rome, widespread in Ireland and documented by Columbanus and others, lends this idea some plausibility.

Regional and social peculiarities did not only occur in the Celtic countries. It was an indication of the vitality of the Christian religion that it could show tolerance in some respects as long as one common faith was upheld. A further special feature of Irish Christianity, already apparent in the sixth century, was an extraordinary dynamism which found its visible expression in the *peregrinatio*.

Peregrinatio – Origins and Significance

An important indication of the success of Christianity in Ireland was the development of the ascetic practice of the peregrinatio. This form of life-long exile from the home country appears for the first time in the case of Columbanus. The concept of 'going to foreign parts' (the original meaning of *peregrinus* is 'foreign') for the sake of Christ, and the renouncing of accustomed shelter and security can ultimately be traced back to Christ's commandment to leave father and mother for His sake (*Mark* 10, 7; cf. also *Matthew* 10, 37). In early medieval society, the individual was firmly integrated into the community, and in it he enjoyed rights and protection according to his position: Christ's commandment therefore meant giving up this protection. In Ireland, it meant initially leaving the *túath*. One then became, in the original meaning of *peregrinus*, alien, without rights (cf. German *Elend* 'misery', *Ausland* 'foreign country'), and one sank to the level of the exile, the outlaw.

Paradoxically, the oldest Irish law tracts contain reference to the exile for the sake of Christ (*deorad dé*) enjoying the same legal status and protection as a king or a bishop, i.e. he belonged to the privileged class throughout Ireland. By the time this state of affairs was reached, the *peregrinatio pro Christo* no longer meant self-denial in Ireland. Columbanus's career shows that this stage had been reached as early as the end of the sixth century (see Jonas I, 3). Only by leaving Ireland could he truly experience the discomforts of a *peregrinus pro Christo*. Columbanus accepted these discomforts and they are the personal expression of his eloquent exhortation to pay little regard to life on earth and concentrate completely on the life to come, even if this proved difficult: *Duret igitur apud nos ista definitio, ut sic vivamus in via ut viatores, ut peregrini, ut hospites mundi* (S. 3, 'We want to persist in living on the road as wanderers, as aliens, as strangers on earth'). On one occasion he was to be sent back to Ireland from Gaul but he resisted successfully (Jonas I, 23; Ep. C. 4). This stance can only be appreciated fully when one realises how much Columbanus was attached to his home country. He wrote, for example, to the pope from Gaul: 'At home (in Ireland), Rome is only great and famous for that chair' (the see of Peter) (Ep. C. 5). In the light of this, it becomes apparent that Patrick had experienced a similar situation in Ireland, for he described himself as *profuga ob amorem Dei* (Ep. P. 1 'fugitive for the love of God'). The fact that Colum Cille frequently returned to Ireland even after moving to Iona shows that this dimension of being alien did not exist in his case even though Adomnán referred to him as a *peregrinus*. His asceticism was less radical than that of Columbanus, in every respect.

The Middle Irish Life of Colum Cille, which is unlikely to have been written before the tenth century, contains a variation on the theme of the *peregrinatio*. It is based upon God's direction to Abraham to leave his land (*Genesis* 12.1). It is emphasised that the spiritual renunciation of the world of one's fathers is more important than physically giving up one's home country. The idea which underlies this concept, particularly the attachment of equal importance to thinking and acting, can be understood as a further development of the ideal of the Columban *peregrinatio*.

The Columban form of *peregrinatio* was principally one of self-denial. It nevertheless had important secondary repercussions, since the *peregrinus* often became, for the community he entered, the positive epitome of radical Christianity which disregarded all that was worldly; it was in this exemplary way that Columbanus had such a lasting influence in Gaul as well as in Italy. But he was not the only one. The conversion of the Anglo-Saxons by Irish missionaries after A.D. 635, which started in Northumbria but continued far into southern England, is another example. Towards the end of the seventh century, English missionaries such as Willibrord and later St Boniface, who were inspired by the Irish, brought, as *peregrini*, Christianity to the Germanic peoples. The vitality of the early Irish Church can therefore be seen to have had wide repercussions.

Ireland – a Christian Country?

A question such as this at the end of this chapter may appear to be a provocation; but developments of later centuries make it imperative to pose it. It cannot be dismissed with the comment that it is not possible to realise Christianity fully on Earth. According to the sources of the sixth and seventh centuries, Ireland was definitely Christianised. The sources were, however, written mostly by Christian authors who had an interest in endorsing their own religion.

Having so far dealt exclusively with Christianity in this chapter, it is now equally important to examine those references, albeit vague, which suggest that Christianity had not penetrated all areas of society. In this regard, the almost complete lack of sources from the century after Patrick is particularly regrettable. When Christianity does return to the focus of attention, it has already become established. By this time, moreover, the monasteries are firmly in the hands of the nobility, who had made their establishment possible. The only known non-aristocratic monastic founder was Ciarán 'the carpenter' of Clonmacnois, although this epithet may easily give a false impression. Since timber was the most frequently used building material, 'carpenters' had a range of activities which brought them into contact with the leading circles of society, especially in the setting up of royal dwellings and banqueting halls; poorer people did not require a carpenter to build their houses.

The most important evidence for the limited influence of Christianity in Ireland is the continued existence of the pre-Christian group of poets or seers (*filid*). It is difficult to say whether the *filid* and their culture should be regarded as being hostile to Christianity and in competition with it; or whether they were simply upholding among Christians a tradition untouched by Christianity: the evidence is ambivalent. It is also debatable whether an attempt was really made in the late sixth century to suppress the *filid*; what is decisive is the fact that they remained. What could be more telling in this respect than the elegy produced by a *fili* for Colum Cille after his death? This means that familiar spiritual values were retained. The continued existence of the *filid* and their further activity in the leading social classes shows that Christianity had a vigorous competitor in the cultural area. It is even quite conceivable that the nobility encouraged this competition and drew entertainment from it. As has already been stressed on several occasions, the atmosphere in Ireland was suitable for an intellectual class. It has been pointed out that this facilitated the adoption of Christianity but it would be inaccurate to think that Christianity replaced the oral traditions. It appears to have been received into the established circles of learning and politics as having equal rights and status without, however, achieving an exclusive position. Apart from the limited impact of the new religion, this also means that Christianity had to be convincing. It was only in this way that it could attain a status even equal to that of the other cultural traditions.

Do the roots of the Irish phenomenon of the *peregrinatio* lie in this very situation? Had Christianity established itself in such a way that, in the eyes of many ascetics, basic values had been abandoned? The stories of the Old Testament must have been very attractive to the Irish upper class with their genealogies and accounts of battles and campaigns – did these stories, in their view, mean more than the doctrine of the New Testament, true Christianity? Did it perhaps disturb them that the Irish legal scholars had justified the polygamy practised in Ireland by referring to the Old Testament? The relevance of questions such as these will become clearer in the following chapters.

It should nevertheless be strongly emphasised that Ireland in the early times produced Christians who were convinced, one could perhaps even say inspired. The extreme ascetic behaviour of particular individuals may have impressed observers and led them to an attitude of respect even where it did not encourage them to imitate it. This is certainly not meant to detract from the daily practice of asceticism by these Christians; it is just that the *peregrini* and ascetics should not be regarded as typical representatives of Irish Christianity. They were outsiders who were, however, tolerated on the fringe of society.

The conceivable objection to the views advanced above, that partial Christianisation was the rule in Europe at the time, is only partly justified. There were bishops in Gaul who in addition to their spiritual office also exercised secular authority i.e. effective control. In his Ten Books of Stories, Gregory of Tours provides evidence of this; he also shows that these bishops were pastorally active as spiritual teachers of their community. There was nothing comparable in Ireland. In England, there were kings in the seventh century who actively supported the spread of Christianity and some even, as in the case of Oswald of Northumbria, suffered a martyr's death for it. It has to be conceded that the wars of these baptised kings against their pagan neighbours did not take place under the banner of the cross to the extent that Bede implies; nevertheless, Christian motivation should not be completely ruled out. It is at least certain that the Christian kings in England attempted to consolidate their position through Christianity. Once again, there was nothing comparable in Ireland. The petulant word of an Irish bishop in 1171 that there had been no martyrs in Ireland before the arrival of the English is appropriate here. If Christianity had 'triumphed' more or less peacefully, it had been at a considerable price. It was regarded as an additional enrichment to life; for many it had the attraction of dramatic entertainment, for some individuals it was their sole purpose in life, but for the population at large, it was by no means an all-embracing way of life.

Extended Roman rule and subsequent invasions had had an extremely destructive effect on earlier cultural traditions in Gaul and Britain. In these lands a relatively weak Christianity had very little competition as a spiritual movement and was therefore able to attain a leading position in society far more easily than in Ireland, particularly since it was actively made use of by royalty. How thoroughly the Germanic, Romance and Slav peoples were 'christianised' would require special study. In the end they would, presumably, fare much the same as the Irish, despite particular regional and cultural differences.

6. Christian Ireland in the Seventh and Eighth Centuries

The two centuries between the death of Colum Cille and the beginning of the Viking raids are regarded as Ireland's Golden Age. It was the time of the first great recording of native and Christian traditions in the Irish and Latin languages, the high point of Irish erudition and art. It was then that the foundations were laid for the high level of learning that Irish scholars were to bring to the Continent from the early ninth century onwards. In these two centuries, more than previously or subsequently, Ireland was the intellectual centre of western Europe. The Irish schools attracted clerics and laymen from England and Gaul. At a time in which the Continent was particularly lacking in culture, Ireland, as the country of learning, exercised an almost magnetic attraction and possessed a wide sphere of influence.

These two centuries witnessed the synthesis of Christianity and pre-Christian Irish society. As in other societies, this meant integration of the Christian religion into the existing society, it meant adjustment, compromise and, often, the abandonment of its earlier rejection of the world.

The emergence of the plague in the middle of the seventh century was to have wide repercussions in Ireland. Although the extent of the epidemic is not as well documented as the great plague of the fourteenth century, the currently accepted view is that it marked an important turning-point. Despite Adomnán's claim that the plague spared the Picts and the Irish of Scotland (VC 103a), the Irish annals leave no doubt as to the extent of the epidemic (AU 663–667).

Scholars now hold the view that there is a connection between the emergence of the plague and the first great period of the recording of old Irish traditions, sagas, genealogies, poetry and law. The community appears to have sensed that this catastrophe marked a caesura in Irish history. There are two other breaks in Irish history which had a similar impact, the one being the period of the first English penetration of the island which commenced in the late twelfth century and continued into the next, the other the beginning of the long-term Anglicisation of Ireland in the seventeenth century. Attempts were also made in these situations to prevent knowledge of past events being forgotten by means of compilation and written records.

Adoption of the Latin Language: Insular Latin

Ireland was the first European country outside the Romance area to be reached by Latin-influenced Christianity and the Irish Church became a Latin Church. In contrast to the Romance countries where Latin was still widely understood, in Ireland the liturgy in Latin was the manifestation of a typical sacral language which was fully mastered only by the clergy.

The prevailing cultural and intellectual situation on the island ensured that the scholars there devoted themselves intensively to the Latin language. The scholarly tradition in Ireland since pre-Christian times had ensured the cultivation of the Irish language. An additional scholarly language was now adopted and likewise carefully cultivated. The scholars educated in the Latin language were known as *fir léighinn* 'men of reading' (from Latin *legendum*); the formation of this term makes it evident that we are dealing here with a second intellectual class since writing in the Irish language was called non-specifically *ogam*.

The evidence for the cultivation of Latin is provided by some treatises on Latin grammar; the result was a Latin which, due to various special features, is recognisable as Latin originating from Ireland. Since it was also spread throughout England through missionary and other contacts, it is known as insular Latin. In its most pronounced form, which is considered to be extravagant and distorted, it is referred to as Hisperic Latin.

The beginnings of systematic study of the Latin language in Ireland can be traced back to the end of the sixth century. As Latin was not dispensed with in the Irish Church, it was considered necessary to learn and teach the language thoroughly and for this the recognised authorities were used, particularly Donatus.

The grammatical works of Donatus (fourth century), *Ars minor* and *Partes maiores*, had been written for people whose mother tongue was Latin. In Ireland, they were revised to serve as textbooks for teaching Latin as a foreign language. The first author of a Latin grammar in Ireland is known by the name Asperius, or

Asporius, and was probably active around A.D. 600. It is evident
from his work that he lived in a monastic environment and felt
himself committed to monastic values. His treatise shows influences
of Cassiodorus's *Institutiones*. Perhaps a generation later, the treatise
known by the title *Anonymus ad Cuimnanum* was written, a
commentary on Donatus's *Partes maiores*. The anonymous author
shows that he was familiar with the early works of Isodore of
Seville which had reached Ireland before his death in A.D. 636. In
contrast to Asporius, one can detect in this work the first signs of
the author breaking away from the exclusively monastic tradition.
The grammarian known as Virgilius Maro, who wrote around A.D.
650, goes even farther in this direction. His work shows the
influence of Isidore even more distinctly. He had completely broken
away from the Christian context of Latin. The Irish scholars had
discovered Latin education for its own sake; in the following
century they were to become famous and very quickly infamous for
it. A Latinity developed which displays particularly eccentric
features.

This can best be seen in the treatise called *Hisperica Famina*
which is written in stilted Latin and is very difficult to understand.
Before Michael Herren established that the *Hisperica Famina*
originated in Ireland, probably around the middle of the seventh
century, considerable uncertainty had existed as to the time and
place of its origin. The treatise is written in long, complex sentences
and is conspicuous through its use of unusual words, loan words
from Greek as well as rambling metaphors. In some respects the
work appears to be an academic exercise in the worst sense of the
word. As regards recognisable influences, the works of Isidore and
Gildas must be mentioned, although Irish literary tradition
contributed to it considerably. In this way the *Hisperica Famina*
epitomises the synthesis of native and Latin literary tradition.

Hisperic Latinity did not remain confined to Ireland. The
profound influence that Irish society had on England in the seventh
century also included the Latin of the Irish schools. Aldhelm of
Malmesbury shows in his works that Hisperic Latin had also been
adopted in southwest England at the end of the seventh century;
one of his teachers was an Irishman, Máel Dub. Remnants of
Hisperic Latin are preserved in the language of English charters
and other documents as late as the eleventh century. Many
distinctive features of insular Latinity point ultimately to Ireland as

the source. The great literary tradition of Bede show particularly impressively that another type of Latin was also written in England. Although living in Northumbria which was strongly influenced by Irish clergy, he was nevertheless able to avoid the vogue for Hisperic Latinity. He took for his inspiration the Latin of the Vulgate and the Church Fathers.

The Hisperic Latin of Ireland shows how a foreign language could be adopted and developed dynamically. Much more important, of course, is what the Latin language was used for.

The following sections deal with the most important genres of literary activity in Ireland. It must be assumed that the making of written records was inspired by the Latin culture of the Irish Church. It is not necessary to discuss whether writing in *ogam* was begun in Ireland or in Britain. From the end of the sixth century and after St Patrick's works, literature in the narrower sense appears in Latin as well as in Irish. This is one of the most important indications of the convergence of pre-Christian and Christian culture in early Ireland. It is assumed that the learned class of pre-Christian origin went over to making written records gradually, which would mean that works in the Irish language were also written down initially by clerics. Due to a lack of precise dates of individual works, we must be content with a general survey of the seventh and eighth centuries.

Biblical Texts and Bible Studies

Although Christianity reached Ireland in the fourth century, the oldest extant Irish biblical texts date from as late as c. A.D. 600. The manuscripts show that two traditions were cultivated in Ireland throughout the early Middle Ages, the Old Latin biblical text (*Vetus Latina*) and Jerome's revised version of the text, the Vulgate. These texts are seldom found in pure form; many codices contain texts which are, to a greater or lesser extent, mixed. There are a great number of biblical texts of Irish provenance preserved on the Continent, either original versions, recognisable as such from the script, or copies. Almost everything that is available of the Old Latin Bible comes from material which had had links with Ireland. The Vulgate reached Ireland directly from Italy during the second half of the sixth century. According to a tradition dating from the ninth century, Finnian of Mag Bile († 579, AU) is thought to have brought the Vulgate with him, and he is perhaps identical with Bishop Finnian, Colum Cille's teacher.

Bibles are essentially books for daily use, written for worship, study or private prayer. Even where they are made of parchment, they have a limited lifespan when used frequently. Most of the early extant manuscripts of biblical texts show signs of considerable wear. The fact that they are still preserved in quite large numbers is due either to coincidence or to the assumption that certain manuscripts enjoyed special reverence and care as the former property of renowned saints. It is written that leather bags with manuscripts hung in Colum Cille's *oratorium*; special rooms, libraries (Latin *bibliotheca* i.e. in the medieval sense 'rooms with bibles'), were not installed until later. Three leather satchels from early medieval Ireland are still preserved and are examples of highly skilled craftsmanship.[9] These satchels were coloured, presumably in order to identify the manuscripts more easily, and the colour of the container was later transferred to the codex kept in it (e.g. 'The Yellow Book of Leccan'). Such leather satchels were also used for carrying manuscripts on journeys; this, as Pope Gregory the Great recounts, was done in Italy (PL 77, 172); Adomnán provides evidence of the same custom in Ireland (VC 59b). Very small Irish Gospel books, presumably pocket books, have been preserved. The smallest of these, the Cadmug Gospels, measures a mere 125 × 112 mm and contains the complete text of the Gospels written in minute script and with numerous abbreviations; evidently the owner was a cleric and very familiar with the text. There are eight 'pocket-sized' Gospel books in existence which originate from Ireland from the period between A.D. 600 and 900.

The early Irish biblical manuscripts generally contain the four Gospels and the Psalms. Monastic rules and penitentials show that the Psalter played a considerable role in monastic life. The Gospels of the earlier manuscripts were frequently written in separate quires which were later bound together. The first and last pages of a quire were often blank and on the inside of the first page was an illustration of the symbol of the evangelist. As the outer pages are often heavily soiled, it is assumed that the quires, each with the text of one Gospel, were used separately for a prolonged period and without covers. This could perhaps explain one particular feature of Gospel books of Irish origin, i.e. that of arranging the Gospels in non-canonical order: Matthew, John, Luke, Mark.

At this stage some of the oldest Irish biblical texts should be mentioned. In 1914, six wooden tablets which were coated with wax and contained the Vulgate text of Psalms 30–32 were found in the Springmount Bog in Co. Antrim.[10] Although the script shows distinctly Italian characteristics, it is without doubt of Irish provenance. This interesting discovery helps to identify the overseas origins of Christian learning in Ireland. The wax tablets were presumably used in school. The Codex Usserianus I, around A.D. 600, contains the complete Old Latin text of the Gospels in the 'Irish sequence'. The almost contemporary text of the Psalter (only Ps. 30: v. 10 – Ps. 105: v. 13), attributed to Colum Cille (the so-called *Cathach*), contains, in contrast, only Vulgate text. A Gospel book from the seventh century, the Book of Durrow, likewise with Vulgate text, is – certainly wrongly – attributed to Colum Cille. In the colophon (the concluding remark of the scribe) Patrick is called upon and it is claimed that Colum Cille had written the text in twelve days. Though it was not written by Colum Cille himself, the provenance of the Book of Durrow does at least suggest the *paruchia* of Colum Cille as the monastery of Durrow had been founded by him. Although the colophon is historically incorrect, it may well have contributed to the preservation of the manuscript.

The so-called Irish mixed type is more frequent than either the Old Latin or the purely Vulgate texts. Of these Irish Gospels the Gospel of Mulling (seventh century) and that of Dimma (eighth/ninth centuries) should be mentioned, both of which are named after the scribe cited in the colophon. A number of manuscripts of the Irish mixed type have been preserved in England and on the Continent, visible proof of the considerable influence of Irish clerics outside Ireland.

The examination of biblical texts used in Ireland in the first part of the Middle Ages is based partly on manuscripts preserved outside the country. Information concerning the study of the Bible in Ireland is contained exclusively in manuscripts which are preserved abroad. Those manuscripts which were written in insular script were conceivably brought to the Continent by Irishmen, fleeing perhaps from the Vikings in the ninth century. However, some manuscripts with Irish biblical exegesis were copied by scribes on the Continent and are only preserved in this form. The basis for the assessment of the Irish contribution to medieval biblical exegesis was laid by Bernhard Bischoff who found 'Irish symptoms' (see Bibliography) in Continental exegetical manuscripts. Since the directions indicated by Bischoff have not yet been systematically followed, the Irish contribution to the understanding of the Bible cannot yet be fully appreciated.

Many of the exegetical works of Irish origin have been handed down under the names of the great Fathers of the Church, (pseudo-) Augustine, Jerome, Hilary, etc. with this reputed authorship contributing to their preservation. The authors' names are a case of consciously selected pen-names. Ancient pseudonyms were not just used in an ecclesiastical context (cf. Virgilius Maro the grammarian, adopting the name of the classical poet) nor were they confined to Ireland; look, for example, at the use of pseudonyms at the 'academy' of Charlemagne (where Charlemagne was 'David', Angilbert 'Homer', Alcuin 'Horace', etc.).

In seventh-century Ireland there was an extremely active exegetical tradition which was strongly influenced by the School of Antioch with its preference for historical interpretation, whereas the Continental patristic tradition followed rather the moralising School of Alexandria. The works of Theodore of Mopsuestia in their Latin translation played an important role for Irish exegetics. The intense preoccupation with the Bible in Ireland at that time contrasts very favourably with the situation on the Continent where, in the seventh century, almost no exegesis was written or preserved.

The Irish commentaries strongly emphasised the examination of the historical content of the Christian message and therefore remain mostly quite superficial. It is typical of the schoolroom tradition to set a question and begin the answer to it with the phrase 'That is not difficult' (Latin *non difficile*, Irish *ní anse*). The answers themselves tend to bear this out. This leads to the conclusion that this kind of material derives from the study of the Bible in schools.

'Irish symptoms' in exegetical writings, in addition to the *ní anse*, are a preference for excessive numerical symbols, details of how certain names and things are written in the three 'sacred' languages (Hebrew, Greek, Latin) as well as the question concerning the first mention of a thing or a deed. Bischoff speaks of the tendency 'to examine material problems thoroughly and to give hair-splitting answers' to questions which are basically unimportant. There remains, however, the impression that an attempt was made to understand the Bible in its entirety.

These observations should not be misunderstood because, even though the commentaries often appear trivial, they are nevertheless evidence of an intensive preoccupation with the biblical text on a broad basis which was unique in Europe at that time and which prepared the way for many aspects of the Bible studies of the Carolingian Age. Characteristic of the Irish inclination towards curiosities is the work *De mirabilibus sacrae scripturae* ('of the wondrous things of Holy Scripture') which originated in Munster in the middle of the seventh century and has been handed down under the name of Augustine. Adomnán's *De locis sanctis* was the product of a similar curiosity.

Having seen how 'Irish symptoms' demonstrate the origin of an exegetical work, the manuscripts give occasional insights into Irish society in the form of marginal glosses (often in Irish) and additional observations. A commentary on *Luke* 4:5 on the words 'the kingdoms' and 'their glory' reads: 'the kingdom, that means gold and silver, fine materials and crimson, towns and lands, chariots and riders'; 'their glory, that is the king and the army, bejewelled women and glorious singers'; similarly on *Luke* 7:25 'Behold, they which are gorgeously apparelled and live delicately, are in the king's court': 'It is they who sing flattering words to the kings and change their song as they see fit, they who utter praise or defamation'.

The Irish exegetes were industrious and inquisitive. They often neglected the depth of the exegesis in favour of the breadth. Evidently, however, they enjoyed the study of the Bible and others were infected by their enthusiasm. In their endearing way they often succeeded in relating the alien world of the Bible to their own familiar environment, something which is also an important Christian principle.

The Penitentials

The oldest penitentials typical of the Irish Church date from the sixth century. They were produced for clerics, monks and nuns, and contain detailed lists of transgressions with the appropriate penance. In this respect they are not unlike the secular Irish law tracts. It is constantly stressed that a sin in thought is just as grave as an actual sinful deed; both kinds of transgression have to be atoned for. It is significant that, in a society which was extensively bound by the oath, perjury was regarded as a sin greater than murder. Upon carrying out the penance imposed, the sin was atoned for. An extreme example of this can be found in Finnian's penitential (Ch. 21): 'But if, as we have said, a woman (evidently a nun) bears a child and her sin is manifest, she shall do penance for six years, as is the judgement in the case of a cleric, and in the seventh year she shall be joined to the altar, and then we say her crown can be restored and she may don a white robe and be pronounced a virgin'.

The penitential of Finnian is generally attributed to St Finnian of Clonard, Columbanus's teacher. Columbanus also wrote a penitential, the first part of which was directed at the clergy and the second at the laity. Apart from the penitentials already mentioned, Cummean's (perhaps Cummaíne Fota, † 662) also became particularly influential. The Irish penitentials are, by and large, very similar to each other. Their common feature is that they were directed at the entire Christian community; however, the penance for the laity was only ever a fraction of that prescribed for the clergy. There were also differences in the extent of punishment. Finnian, for example, prescribes fasting on bread and water as well as temporary exile; Columbanus places greater emphasis on physical chastisement. In the provisions for the clergy, sexual offences are dealt with at particular length. The Irish penitentials reached the Continent in the eighth and ninth centuries where they exerted considerable influence. It was the Irish penitential practice that was responsible for personal, private confession becoming generally widespread in the Church, whereas the old Church had prescribed open, public confession.

The penitentials mentioned so far were written in Latin. In their attempt to make provisions which are as comprehensive as possible, they came close to the secular Irish law tracts. An even stronger influence in this regard can be seen in a penitential written in Irish. Judging from the language, this penitential dates from the late eighth century and is, in content, similar to the Latin penitentials even if the penances are generally less stringent. However, what it does provide, more so than the Latin penitentials, is an insight into Irish society of that time. Thus it becomes clear that fines were

payable to the Church. Pre-Christian practices such as keening the
dead were forbidden, which shows that they were still carried on.
Druidic art and the use of maledictions are considered to be sins
which cannot be forgiven; evidently, these had not disappeared
either. The penitential in the Irish language also contains a detailed
list of how imposed penances, which were often applicable for
many years in the case of serious offences, could be curtailed. It
says, for example, that former lay people could atone for their sins
by spending one night in water, on nettles or on nutshells. What is
also interesting is how scholars and uneducated people were dealt
with in different ways:

> Commutation of a three-day fast for one who can read: reciting
> the Three Fifties [i.e. the 150 psalms] standing and celebrating
> each canonical hour, twelve genuflections with arms outstretched
> towards God at each canonical hour, and diligent meditation
> upon heaven. Commutation of a black fast due for grievous sin
> for one who cannot read: three hundred genuflections and three
> hundred properly administered blows with a scourge, at the end
> of each hundred a cross-vigil until the arms are weary. 'I beseech
> pardon of God', 'May I receive mercy', 'I believe in the Trinity' –
> that is what one sings without ceasing until the commutation is
> completed; further, frequent striking of the breast and perfect
> contrition to God. To do this thrice is a commutation of a three-
> day fast.

The following provision reflects the extent to which people felt
bound to the tradition of the early Irish Church, also with regard
to this calculation of punishments:

> If there be danger of death, the following is a commutation of a
> year of penance when accompanied by intense contrition: to
> chant 365 Paters standing with both arms extended towards
> heaven and without the elbows ever touching the sides, together
> with fervent concentration on God. And the words are not
> spoken aloud. And to recite the *Beati* (Psalm 118) in a stooping
> position with the two arms laid flat by the sides. Or the whole
> body is stretched out along the ground face downwards and both
> arms laid flat by the sides. Patrick has recommended this type of
> vigil and so have Colum Cille and Maedóg of Ferns and Molacca

Menn and Brénainn moccu Altae and Colum mac Crimthain and Mocholmóc of Inis Celtra. And this tradition was deposited with Enda in Aran. The four chief sages of Ireland, viz. Ua Minadan, Cummaíne Fota, Murdebur and Mocholmóc mac Cumain from Aran, have recommended its continual practice to every son of life who desires to obtain heaven.

The Beginnings of Latin Literature

The oldest Lives of Saints still preserved were written in Ireland in the second half of the seventh century. Their value as source material varies considerably. The order of their appearance has been definitely established even though no precise dates are known. They begin with the Life of Brigit of Kildare, written by Cogitosus probably around the middle of the seventh century; the next is the Life of Patrick by Muirchú, inspired, according to the author, by Cogitosus, with the third work being Adomnán's Life of Columba. A collection of accounts about Patrick by Tírechán from the late seventh century, although not as important as Muirchú's work, must also be mentioned. All these works are written in Latin and they all show, to a greater or lesser extent, the influence of Irish in the syntax, orthography and use of prepositions. The language of these works is Hiberno-Latin.

Cogitosus maintains that Brigit's *paruchia* stretched throughout Ireland. However, in contrast to Patrick and Colum Cille, Brigit remains so colourless as an historical person that one doubts whether she had lived as a saint at all. There is more to be said for the existence of an important pagan site of worship in Kildare which was later 'christianized'. The feast of St Brigit on 1 February is *Imbolc*, one of the four great feasts in the Celtic year. The fire cult in Kildare associated with Brigit certainly also has pagan roots. The significance of Cogitosus's Life lies in areas which have little to do with Brigit herself; firstly in that it is the oldest preserved Life from Ireland and the one which also inspired Muirchú to write the Life of Patrick and, secondly, in the information Cogitosus gives regarding the Kildare of his time. This information is considered to be reliable and the following three excerpts from the Life[11] serve to illustrate this.

No church buildings have been preserved from the seventh

century because at that time construction in Ireland was carried out almost exclusively with timber. The oldest stone churches in Ireland with their characteristic steep stone roofs (e.g. St Kevin's, Glendalough; 'Colum Cille's house', Kells) were modelled on these timber constructions. As there is no material evidence for the churches at that time, the description of the church of Kildare by Cogitosus is all the more significant:

On account of the growing number of the faithful of both sexes, a new reality is born in an age-old setting, that is a church with its spacious site and its awesome height towering upwards. It is adorned with painted pictures and inside there are three chapels which are spacious and divided by board walls under the single roof of the cathedral church. The first of these walls, which is painted with pictures and covered with wall hangings, stretches widthwise in the east part of the church from one wall to the other. In it, there are two doors, one at either end, and through the door situated on the right, one enters the sanctuary to the altar where the bishop offers the Lord's sacrifice together with his monastic chapter and those appointed to the sacred mysteries. Through the other door, situated on the left side of the afore-said cross-wall, only the abbess and her nuns and faithful widows enter to partake of the banquet of the body and blood of Jesus Christ. The second of these walls divides the floor of the building into two equal parts and stretches from the west wall to the wall running across the church. This church contains many windows and one finely wrought portal on the right side through which the priests and the faithful of the male sex enter the church, and a second portal on the left side through which the nuns and congregation of women faithful are wont to enter. And so, in the one vast basilica, a large congregation of people of varying status, rank, sex and loyalty, with partitions placed between them, prays to the omnipotent Master, differing in status, but one in spirit.

A settlement had emerged around the church. Although there were neither towns nor villages in ancient Ireland, in the seventh and eighth centuries some of the largest monasteries became town-like settlements. Cogitosus writes of Kildare:

Who can describe in words the exceeding beauty of this church and the countless wonders of that monastic city we are speaking of, if one may call it a city (*civitas*) since it is not encircled by any surrounding wall. However, as numberless people assemble within it and since a city gets its name from the fact that many people congregate there (*cives – coeuntes*, following Isidore), it is a vast and metropolitan city. In its suburbs, which Saint Brigit had marked out by a definite boundary, no human foe nor enemy attack is feared; on the contrary, together with all its suburbs it is the safest city of refuge in the whole land of the Irish for all fugitives and the treasures of kings are kept there; moreover, it is looked upon as the most eminent for its splendid temple. And who can count the different crowds and numberless people flocking from all the provinces – some for the abundant feasting, others for the healing of their afflictions, others to watch the pageant of the crowds, others with great gifts and offering – to join in the solemn celebration of Saint Brigit's feast day on the first day of the month of February.

Finally, Cogitosus also gives an account of how a road was built. The subject has nothing to do with Brigit, but it can be inferred from the Lives of the Saints and from the *Collectio Canonum Hibernensis* that chariots drawn by two horses were still used in the seventh century; roads would be needed for them. Note in the following description the influence of the New Testament on the language of the author:

There went out a decree from the king of the country where she (Brigit) was living to the peoples and provinces which were under his jurisdiction that all the noblemen and commoners (*populi et plebes*) should come together from all regions and provinces and build a solid wide road. They were to lay a foundation of felled trees and rocks and some very solid earth work in the deep and virtually impassable bog and in the sodden and marshy places through which a large river ran so that, when it was built, it could bear the weight of charioteers and horsemen and chariots and wagon-wheels and the rushing of peoples and the clash of enemies from all sides. When many people had gathered, they divided into their own sections by kinship groups and families the road which they had to build so that each him and family built the segment allotted to them.

It should be mentioned that the word for a road in Irish, *slige*, is derived from the verb *sligid* 'fells, cuts down'. The excerpt from Cogitosus illustrates this phenomenon very well.

Muirchú ('the Sea-hound'), inspired by Cogitosus, wrote a Life of Patrick on the instruction of Bishop Aed of Slébte (Sletty, Co. Laois, † c. 700) towards the end of the seventh century. This Life forms the basis of all later Lives of Patrick and, for that reason alone, is of the greatest importance. Muirchú used Patrick's *Confessio* and *Epistola* and because we know these sources we can determine what slant he gave in his presentation of Patrick. In addition to these primary sources, Muirchú also apparently used popular tales of his own time about Patrick. His account is characterised by repetitions, digressions and very bizarre Latin. The intention of his work is expressed towards the end when Patrick is referred to as *totius Hiberniae episcopus* ('bishop of all Ireland'), a title which is in no way borne out by the preceding account. Muirchú's writings claim for Patrick national significance just as Cogitosus does for Brigit.

The account of Patrick's youth and imprisonment in Ireland is taken from the *Confessio*, after which, however, the story differs. Patrick set off for Rome without ever arriving there; he spent 30 to 40 years with Germanus at Auxerre. He was made a bishop in Gaul along with Auxilius and Iserninus after it had become known that the Roman archdeacon Palladius had had little success in Ireland as a missionary and had died in Britain. Patrick then made his way to Ireland, but there is no further mention of Auxilius and Iserninus. There are no details of Patrick's country-wide missionary work. Instead Muirchú places great emphasis on Patrick's disputes with certain people, especially with King Loegaire of Tara, 'the capital of the Irish'. There was nothing Christian about Patrick's methods of combatting the druids. Rather, he showed that he was superior to them in their own art. Despite this, he was unable to convert the king and those around him; he cursed the Loegaire line and withdrew from Tara. He received land in Armagh from King Dáire, but only after the king had vainly tried to deceive Patrick.

Muirchú's Patrick is the supreme druid. He performs fantastic miracles, raises the dead, commands the elements; he causes a druid to spin into the air and then be crushed to the ground. Patrick is self-assured, punitive and strict. There is no more mention of the humility which makes Patrick's *Confessio* so credible; his Christian faith is not even mentioned. Muirchú's Patrick presumably bears some of the traits of Patrick's successors in Armagh in the seventh century.

In comparison with Muirchú's work, Adomnán's Life of Columba is remarkably sober. It has already been mentioned that it often appears to idealise the hero and re-interpret some historical events so there is no further need to go into the content of this work by Adomnán; instead, something should be said about the superior literary quality of Adomnán's work. In contrast to Cogitosus and Muirchú, Adomnán of Iona was active in a place which had been a centre of learning for a hundred years, and this is reflected in his work. In addition, Adomnán had a written source which he used extensively, namely a Life of Colum Cille by Cuimíne Ailbe, abbot of Iona (657–68) which is now lost. Finally, Adomnán had already been active as an author before he wrote the Life of Columba. In *De Locis Sanctis* he had described the important places of worship of the Holy Land. He received the information for this from the Frankish bishop Arculf who had himself been in the Holy Land and who was for some time a guest of Adomnán on Iona. It can be seen from the imaginative descriptions of the Christian places of worship that Adomnán had found in Arculf an attentive observer and excellent reporter. *De Locis Sanctis* is, in several respects, the more important work by Adomnán; through Aldfrith of Northumbria, the former scholar from Iona, it reached Bede who was in turn patronised by Aldfrith. Bede used Adomnán's *De Locis Sanctis* extensively in the fifth book of his Ecclesiastical History and wrote an entire book with the same title; the work then reached the Continent from Northumbria where it became very influential. Adomnán's sober style is also evident in his Life of Columba.

The Annals

The annals are the most important sources for the political history of Ireland in the Middle Ages. They are of ecclesiastical origin and remained by and large in the hands of clerical authors throughout the Middle Ages. They began as short notes concerning ecclesiastical and secular events such as the term of office of abbots and bishops, dates of kings, battles, natural disasters and similar matters.

The oldest Irish annals are not preserved in the original; they can only be inferred as a basis for later compilations. Very few of the Irish annals still preserved are available in critical editions and, for this reason, uncertainty still prevails concerning the development of annalistic writing in Ireland. An absolute chronology consisting of the enumeration from the birth of Christ was developed in Italy by Dionysius Exiguus in the sixth century. The first time it was used in England to any great extent was by Bede in his Ecclesiastical History and it did not reach Ireland until the latter part of the eighth century. Previously and for a long time afterwards, a different form of dating was used in the annals. The commencement of the year was denoted by the number of the day of the week on which the first of January fell: *Kl.*: this is the abbreviation for Latin *Kalendae*, originally the beginning of each month, in this case the beginning of the month of January. Thus, *Kl.* ii denotes the year which began with a Monday. Whether the earliest annalistic records of Ireland were entries on Easter Tables is not certain. In later transcripts of the annals, the Roman numeral after *Kl.* was sometimes omitted. In the case of there being no entry after *Kl.* for several years, incorrect dates tended to find their way into later transcripts.

It is now generally agreed that the earliest Irish annals were written on the island of Iona, presumably from the time of Colum Cille onwards. This 'Chronicle of Iona' contained the dates of abbots of the island monastery, recorded events in the land of the Picts, in Dál Riada and Northumbria as well as the dates of the deaths of the first three abbots of Lindisfarne, Aidan, Finan and Colman (who all came from Iona). From the end of the seventh century, more and more events from Bangor were recorded, presumably under Adomnán's influence. The best impression of what this 'Chronicle of Iona' might have looked like is given by the Welsh *Annales Cambriae*, the oldest version of which (known as version A) contains largely Irish material and was completed in the late tenth century.

In Ireland, the rather laconic accounts of the 'Chronicle of Iona' were adopted and expanded through accounts of local and regional events. From about 740 onwards, it was continued separately in two different locations, probably Armagh and Clonard. Taken together these chronicles form the basis of the Annals of Ulster (AU) which are preserved in late medieval manuscripts.

Almost identical in their essential features down to the middle of the tenth century, are the Annals of Tigernach (Tig.), the *Chronicon Scotorum*, the Annals of Clonmacnois, the so-called Cottonian Annals (the Annals of Boyle), the Annals of Inisfallen (AI) and the Annals of Roscrea. From the tenth century onwards these annals became largely local chronicles. Finally, it is worth mentioning the so-called Annals of the Four Masters (AFM), a scholarly compilation from the seventeenth century which contain material from some local chronicles now no longer extant.

The 'Chronicle of Iona' was written in Latin, and Latin remained the language of the annals, with the exception of Irish names and short phrases, down to the early ninth century. After this time the Annals of Ulster have long entries in Irish, especially for secular events. The same occurred sooner or later in the other annals in Ireland which were written in the high and late Middle Ages in a mixture of Latin and Irish. The Annals of Clonmacnois have come down to us only in the form of an English translation from the seventeenth century.

As already mentioned, the 'Chronicle of Iona' was begun towards the end of the sixth century. The Annals of Ulster, however, begin in the version preserved today in the year 431 with the mission of Palladius to the Irish, while AI and Tig. actually begin with Adam. All the accounts before the late sixth century are later additions and are also immediately recognisable as such in AU, since they are written in Irish. It was not until later that the chroniclers came to think that Irish history commenced in the year 431. The question is when were the earlier entries written, when was the prehistory of Ireland placed into the framework of world history? From where did the information concerning events of antiquity come into the hands of the medieval Irish historiographers?

In or around the year 609, the annals state: *Finis Cronici Iusebii* (AU); *Finis Croníce Euséui* (Tig., 'the end of the chronicle of Eusebius'); *Finis Cronici Issiodori* (AI, 'the end of the chronicle of Isidore'). These entries show that the great world chronicle of Eusebius of Caesarea had been used. Written in Greek in the early fourth century, this work had presented the story of the Old

Testament alongside that of the great oriental empires as well as
that of Greece and Rome. It was widely distributed in the form of
the Latin translation by Jerome and was also used by Isidore of
Seville who continued it down to the year 615. Bede's chronicle
also draws on it.

How this world chronicle reached Ireland has not yet been fully
explained. There are indications that not only Jerome's translation
and revised version and Isidore's continuation were used there, but
also a Greek version which differs from Jerome's (shortened)
revised work.[12] Furthermore, it would appear that a copy of this
version also found its way into Bede's hands; this must have
occurred before A.D. 721 when he wrote his own chronicle. There is
an Irish story which can be associated with this problem. Cenn
Fáelad was badly wounded in the battle of Mag Roth (Moira) in
A.D. 637. A doctor from the school of the druids operated on him,
saving his life. He removed 'forgetting' from his brain and implanted
instead great knowledge. Cenn Fáelad became a famous scholar
who is said to have written in Latin old accounts on wax tablets
and, later, on parchment. That is the essence of the story, as it is
told; what we really are seeing is how a writer to whom history that
is not part of folk memory is an unfamiliar idea tries to account for
its acquisition, and mythologises the process, turning what has
been learned from a chronicle into ingrafted memory.

A nephew of Cenn Fáelad was Fland Fína who, for his part,
studied for many years in Iona before he became king of
Northumbria in 685 (where he is known by the name of Aldfrith).
Aldfrith was Bede's patron. It is not unlikely that the 'Eusebius'
was brought to Northumbria by him, although it is impossible to
say how the version of the chronicle of Eusebius, for which there is
otherwise no evidence in western Europe, reached Ireland. On the
other hand, it can be seen from the sources that as early as the
seventh century the Irish chroniclers had the possibility of placing
developments in their country in the framework of world history.

Writings on the Subject of Kingship

Perhaps the oldest medieval European Mirror for Princes comes
from the south of Ireland. It is 'The Bequest of Morann' (*Audacht
Morainn*), written in archaic Old Irish. Although the language of

the extant version probably dates from around A.D. 700, the text appears to be based on older exemplars. It deals with the ruler's ethos in the form of advice from an older man to a young ruler and shows hardly any perceptible Christian influences. The work is characterised by short maxims which are easily memorised, the underlying oral tradition being particularly evident. It is conceivable that such maxims were recited when inaugurating a king: 'Tell him before every (other) word, bring him with every word this lasting advice: let him preserve justice, it will preserve him; let him raise justice, it will raise him; let him exalt mercy, it will exalt him.' etc. In this treatise, the king appears as the embodiment of the *túath*, the people. His correct manner of action brings peace, joy and prosperity, tall corn, good pannage and pasture land which can be used indefinitely. 'The true ruler is moved towards every good thing, he smiles on the truth when he hears it, he exalts it when he sees it. For he whom the living do not glorify with blessing is not a true ruler.'

A further treatise on this theme exists which was also written in the seventh century, possibly also in the south of Ireland, but this time in Latin: *De duodecim abusivis saeculi* ('On the twelve abuses of the world'). Although it was printed among the works of St Cyprian, its Irish origin has been established. The section concerning the good ruler was incorporated into the *Collectio Canonum Hibernensis* (XXV, 4). The following example shows that there are similarities with *Audacht Morainn*: 'The justness of the king is the peace of the peoples, protection of the land, the invulnerability of the people, protection of the people, care for the weak, the joy of the people, mildness of the air, calmness of the sea, fertility of the soil, consolation for the poor, the heritage of the sons, hope for future salvation, abundance of corn, fruitfulness of the trees'.

This catalogue of the effects of the *iustitia regis*, scattered with only a few truly Christian elements, would also be conceivable in a secular Irish text. The succinctness of expression, the delight in variations (which, in translation, seem repetitive), the form and content are all reminiscent of *Audacht Morainn* although it is not necessary to think in terms of a direct dependence. The same environment led to writings in which the similarities outweigh the differences. In contrast to the vernacular treatise, the section in Latin on the ruler contains the following Old Testament warning: 'Woe betide the land whose king is a child'. The classical and

Christian idea of the wisdom of old age combined with the youthful vigour of the ideal Irish ruler. The Latin treatise puts kingship into a Christian framework, a framework which, according to preference, could be a decorative accessory, a concession to the environment as it then existed (as was apparently the case in Ireland), or a matter of central importance, as on the Continent. *De duodecim abusivis saeculi*, especially in its section on the right of resistance, was to have quite considerable reverberations in the Carolingian Mirrors for Princes.

This raises a question as to what extent the office of king in Ireland was subject to Christian influences. In view of the fact that the community was nominally Christian, this influence was surprisingly small. Adomnán tells of how Colum Cille ordained Aedan, King of the Uí Néill, in Iona by the laying on of hands at the command of an angel who appeared to him three times: *imponens manum super caput eius ordinans benedixit* (VC 108a). Whether this 'ordination' was to have any influence on the office of the ruler is not evident. Adomnán's account makes it impossible to postulate the anointing of kings in Ireland at that time although it is possible, if not certain, that some Irish kings were anointed towards the end of the eighth century. Aed mac Néill of Tara (797) was given the epithet *Oirdnide* (from Latin *ordinatus*) and, by that time, the anointing of rulers had already reached England from the kingdom of the Franks. If Aed was anointed, which is by no means certain, it would have been due to outside influences. In Ireland, the anointing of rulers was at best passing fashion.

The Secular Law Tracts

The secular law tracts of Ireland were first written down in the seventh and eighth centuries. They are not laws but rather textbooks for the instruction of legal scholars (*brithem*) whose training took place in special schools. The law was held to be ancient and comprehensive, it was sacred. Its keepers were also regarded as 'sacred' (*nemed*; cf. Latin *nemus*, a sacred grove). The *brithem* was the arbitrator in legal quarrels and worked in a house specially provided for this purpose.

The collection of the early Irish law tracts was partly and inadequately edited and translated from Irish in the nineteenth century ('Ancient Laws of Ireland'). The complete *Corpus Iuris Hibernici* has been available since 1978 in D. A. Binchy's edition. All the known law tracts are printed as they are preserved in the late medieval manuscripts. This is the first step towards a comprehensive assessment of Irish law and a deeper understanding of early Irish society. However, it will take decades for this task to be completed.

The material is particularly difficult to use because the texts were originally written in archaic Irish and the later transcripts are full of errors. But that is not all. Even at the time when they were first written down, many passages were no longer fully understood. They were therefore provided with shorter or longer glosses, 'explanations' many of which have proved to be inaccurate. In addition, extensive commentaries were added in later centuries.

The oral tradition of Irish law is known as *fénechas* 'the lore regarding the *féni*'. Settlements were made *la féniu* 'amongst the freemen', and, in a secondary sense, 'according to Irish law'.

The largest extant compilation of law tracts is *Senchas Már* 'the great old knowledge', which was compiled in the northern half of Ireland, in *Leth Cuinn*, presumably in the first third of the eighth century. It was apparently prompted by the compilation of the *Collectio Canonum Hibernensis* which originated between A.D. 700 and 725. (The Annals of Ulster, however, give the year 438 for the compilation of *Senchas Már*, placing it on a par with the *Codex Theodosianus*.) A similar compilation was made in the southern half of Ireland, in *Leth Moga*, probably half a century earlier, *Bretha Nemed* 'the sacred law' of which only fragments are preserved. Its very existence at that time is an indication of significant intellectual activity in Munster in the seventh century which is less apparent than the political struggles of that period in *Leth Cuinn*.

For the time being the layman must rely on the translated and annotated individual editions of Irish law tracts some of which have come down to us independently of the large compilations. The most accessible is the text *Críth Gablach* ('the branched purchase'), edited and copiously annotated by D. A. Binchy which has as its theme the social structure of the *túath*. Since this treatise has already been referred to several times, it would be beneficial to mention other treatises at this stage: *Uraicecht Becc* ('the small instruction'), *Bretha Crólige* ('judgements on sick maintenance') and *Coibnes Uisci Thairidne* ('affinities of conducting of water'). A few examples from these texts will show what a valuable contribution they make to the social history of early Ireland.

The excessive systematisation which is peculiar to Irish law is demonstrated in *Uraicecht Becc:* 'How many categories of *nemed* (here, persons according to the law) are there? Answer: two, free *nemed* and lesser free *nemed*. How many categories of free *nemed* are there? Four: the scholar, the cleric, the nobleman, the poet. People who follow other occupations are lesser free *nemed*, the craftsman, the smith, the coppersmith, the metalworker'. It should be noted that the cleric was included in the (otherwise pre-Christian) Irish hierarchy.

Bretha Crólige deals with the claims for the nursing of unlawfully injured persons having suffered great loss of blood. The arrangements extend to the most minute detail, e.g. how often the person concerned may receive a visitor with a specified number of retinue who are entitled to food and board. The details regarding what food the wronged party was or was not to receive give an impression of what foodstuffs were normal. He cannot receive: seafood, whale meat, horse meat, honey; he is to receive fresh meat (in winter), butter, bread and herbs, 'for gardens are laid out for this purpose, namely to care for the sick'. It goes on: 'Where somebody is injured in summer, he is entitled to salted meat only on Sundays and Thursdays; the amount should not be smaller than a piece of ham two fingers thick'.

Coibnes Uisci Thairidne is particularly interesting as it deals with something new in Ireland. It concerns the rights and obligations of landowners through whose land a millstream runs as well as of those owning a mill. Watermills were introduced into Ireland in the seventh century, in particular by monasteries, but also by secular landowners. Previously corn had been crushed with stone hand mills. The text deals with the problem of the millstream in a noticeably archaic manner; it is not clear whether it was actually able to solve any problems and one can certainly question the practical application of the treatise. The land on which the spring, watercourse and pool of the millstream are situated is classified according to the Irish kinship groups (*derbfine, iarfine, indfine*) and the rights to the use of the mill are determined accordingly. It leads to the somewhat surprising conclusion that the person with the source of the millstream on his land enjoys greater profit from the mill than its owner!

Although such absurdities are not typical of the law tracts, they are by no means exceptional. They allow insights into the Irish mentality which can be confirmed through other observations.

The Irish Canon Law Collection

The *Collectio Canonum Hibernensis* (abbr. *Hib.*) was compiled in the early eighth century by Cú Chuimne of Iona and Ruben of Dairinis. Although it does have something in common with the Continental European canon law collections of the early Middle Ages, it has also many unique features. The early canon law collections on the Continent mainly contain decisions by popes and Church synods or councils on questions of canon law. The *Hib.*, on the other hand, goes much further, dealing also with moral and social aspects of the Irish Christian community. Quotations from the Old Testament, especially from the five books of Moses, which are also generally known as *lex*, take up considerable space in the collection whereas the New Testament appears less frequently. There are quotations from the writings of the important Church Fathers as well as from other works, such as the Ecclesiastical History by Rufinus, various writings of Isidore of Seville, accounts concerning Egyptian monasticism, etc. In these sections the *Hib.* gives a good impression of the extent to which works of the universal Church had been received in Ireland by the eighth century.

Yet more important is the appearance of specific insular ecclesiastic works, of which Gildas and Vinnianus are mentioned by name. However, by far the most important sources are those quoted frequently, namely *Synodus Romanorum* and *Synodus Hibernensis*, both of which refer to Ireland. The decrees cited under the heading *Synodus Romanorum* have come down to us in different forms as *Synodus I. S. Patricii* and *Synodus II. S. Patricii*. Although they bear Patrick's name, the content of these canon collections would seem to suggest that they originated in the seventh century since the Church appears in them to be well integrated into Irish society. What, however, does the title *Synodus Romanorum* mean?

One of the great controversies of the Irish Church in the seventh century concerned the calculation of Easter. Around A.D. 630, the Roman method of calculating the date for Easter was adopted at the Synod of Mag Léna in *Leth Mugu* (the southern half of Ireland) whereas in *Leth Cuinn* the older tradition was preserved up to the late seventh century; Iona did not change to the Roman calculation until 716. From the time of their decision to adopt the Roman date for Easter, the clerics in the south of Ireland referred to themselves as *Romani*; *Synodus Romanorum* in the *Hib*. therefore gives information on the ecclesiastical affairs of southern Ireland; the decrees which have come down to us under the title *Synodus Hibernensis* provide an insight into the affairs of the Church in the north of Ireland where, according to the information given in the *Hib.*, it had a clearly monastic character. The bishop was the crucial figure among the *Romani*, but this role was filled among the *Hibernenses* by the abbot who is often referred to as *princeps*.

It is therefore clear that there were considerable differences in the Irish Church of the seventh and eighth centuries but, despite these factions, there was also, in fact even more, basic common ground. Both the *Romani* and *Hibernenses* provide evidence of the almost complete integration of the Church into Irish society. Nevertheless, the secular lawyers still had an important function in this Christian Ireland, and the structure of society was preserved in almost every respect. However, neither the *Romani* nor the *Hibernenses* were prepared to tolerate the secular law governing marriage which was practised in Ireland.

The *Hib*. gives insights into the situation in Ireland at that time which are often better than those gained from other sources. Most important perhaps is the impression that the episcopal Church was still (or once again) a powerful force in the seventh century. The monastic Church did not gain (or regain) the upper hand until somewhat later. The unusually high esteem accorded to the Old Testament by the authors of the *Hib*. can be explained by the apparent similarities of the social structures in ancient Israel and early medieval Ireland. Both the *Hib*. and the secular Irish law tracts show how traditional society was modified under the influence of Christianity.

One further phenomenon in the Irish Church of the eighth century should be mentioned here, namely the attempt to limit acts of violence in society. Several factors made the Church suitable for the role of peacemaker. In addition to the Christian commandment of peace, the land belonging to certain churches in Ireland enjoyed special legal protection. In this they benefited from the respect for taboos which had a long tradition in Irish society. The three circles around the sacred site, referred to in the *Hib*. as *sanctus, sanctior, sanctissimus*, guaranteed special protection for the laity, priests, bishops or abbots. It also states: 'The boundary of the sacred site is marked by crosses. Wherever you find the sign of the cross of Christ, do not violate it' (XLVI, 3).

However, the Church also reached out beyond consecrated ground. In the year 697, 'Adomnán's Law' (*Cáin Adomnáin*) was enacted in Birr which placed women, children and the clergy under protection in times of war and it is therefore also known as *Lex Innocentium* 'the Law of the Innocent'. It was to apply throughout Ireland. Other such 'laws' ('Patrick's'. 'Dáire's', etc.) are known to have existed although the actual texts are not preserved. These forbid the killing of clerics and the theft of cattle or horses. A 'law' then followed in the ninth century regarding the observance of Sunday as a day of rest (*Cáin Domnaig*). One can see here the beginnings of a type of *treuga Dei* ('truce of God') which, however, was made impossible by the Viking raids. It is, indeed, uncertain how successful these 'laws' were even in the eighth century as they were enacted quite frequently which would appear to indicate that they did not have any great effect. The churches also gained materially from their peace initiatives since the proclamation of the 'laws' had to be paid for by means of a tribute. This demonstrates that the Church opened itself increasingly to the outside world, but it also implies a certain secularisation.

Art

Ireland's artistic achievements in the seventh and eighth centuries are of the same high standard as those in other areas. Since it is impossible to convey even a general impression of them without illustrations, a few references will have to suffice. Fortunately, early Irish art is quite well-known.

The most important artistic activities were in three areas, manuscript illumination, sculpture and metalwork; those that have been preserved are almost exclusively objects associated with the Church. It is still possible today to inspect the sculptures on their original sites. Manuscripts with Irish illumination are scattered throughout the libraries of Europe and they illustrate the widespread influence of Irish culture in Europe. Although artefacts made of gold and silver are to be found in Ireland, a large number were brought to Scandinavia by plundering Vikings, especially to Norway. In this respect the history of art is a reflection of the political history of the time. Although the number of sculptures and manuscripts available can be considered as final, new metal artefacts occasionally come to light. A particularly impressive example is the Derrynavlan hoard which was discovered in 1980 and consists of a chalice similar in quality to the Ardagh Chalice, a paten and long-handled metal spoon; it has rightly been hailed as the find of the century.[13] There are close links between the artistic shapes and forms used in sculpture, manuscript illumination and metalwork. On the one hand, indigenous pre-Christian motifs such as trumpet, spirals and leaf ornamentation continued to be used, on the other hand, foreign influences also found expression.

Manuscript illumination from the seventh century displays influences from Italy as well as from Egypt and Syria, influences not evident for that period anywhere else in Europe. The initials surrounded with red dots in 'Colum Cille's Psalter' (*Cathach*) have parallels only in Coptic art. The inspiration for the full-page abstract illustrations, the carpet pages and the interlaced borders, also appear to have come from the East and were combined in Ireland with the spiral form. The carpet pages show an astonishing degree of detail and ornamentation reached a climax in this period. Interlacing designs can also be seen on the grave slabs of the time.

Metalwork had been cultivated in Ireland since pre-Christian times and its craftsmen were highly respected. The technique of enamelling was known from around the time of the birth of Christ. The techniques of filigree and millefiori were introduced in post-Roman times. There are brooches, bronze hand-bells and hanging lamps from the early medieval centuries, all featuring very simple decorations.

It was in the middle of the seventh century that foreign influence made itself felt in this and other areas. Grave slabs took on more distinctly the form of the cross and from this time circular shapes appeared on the crosses. The crosses of Carndonagh and Fahan Mura (Co. Donegal) were the first to have one complete side decorated; their motifs show great similarity to the decorations in the Book of Durrow. It is here that animal motifs appear for the first time. The design of the symbols of the Evangelists remains decorative rather than striving for naturalism. Despite interlace and the first appearance of intertwined animal motifs, the overall impression is one of tranquillity and harmony; this effect is heightened by the use of only three colours. Anglo-Saxon influence is evident in the animal motifs; however, Irish influences have been detected in objects from the royal grave of Sutton Hoo in East Anglia which dates from the early to mid-seventh century, indicating that the influence was two-way.

The Lindisfarne Gospels, written around 700, display both Irish and Continental traces in their decoration. The Book of Kells combines in a masterly way both Irish and European traditions; it was completed 100 years after the Lindisfarne Gospels and is quite rightly the best known Irish manuscript. It represents not only the climax but also the virtual conclusion of Irish illumination. In it, the complex though still tranquil illustrations of earlier times have become an excessive end in itself and the detail hardly serves the whole.

The chalices of Ardagh and Derrynavlan, which can be compared in quality to the Tassilo Chalice from Bavaria, and the brooches with an ornamental ring, the best-known of which is the so-called Tara Brooch, are recognised as unsurpassed examples of metal work. The bronze relief of the book cover of Athlone is in some respects similar to the impressive stone crosses of Clonmacnois and Monasterboice.

Artistic development in Ireland can be summarised as follows: it displays astonishing vitality and virtuosity, is open to outside influences and successfully adapts them; a style is formed which lives and develops without ever quite cutting itself off from its roots. The great expert on Irish art of the Middle Ages, Françoise Henry, refers appropriately to this achievement as a successful tightrope walk between realism and purely geometric art.

Ireland and her Neighbours

We have now highlighted the most important aspects of Ireland's Golden Age. In the artistic and spiritual spheres, Ireland displays a standard which, in terms of breadth and diversity, was unparalleled in Europe at that time. It has been shown that many influences coming from outside found an extremely favourable climate in

Ireland. The fact that Irish society, although somewhat archaic, was open to outside influences, was one of the essential conditions for this. The other was the contact with Europe which made these influences possible. Directly or indirectly they made themselves felt in just about every area although the stimuli from abroad can only sometimes be linked with particular individuals. Ireland had contacts with the Mediterranean world, with Egypt, Italy and especially Spain although the links were even closer with her immediate neighbours across the sea, Gaul and Britain.

Ireland exerted its strongest influence on Britain; Northumbria and Ireland were part of one and the same cultural area. In the seventh and eighth centuries, links between the Saxons and the Irish were particularly close. In his Ecclesiastical History, Bede places considerable emphasis on the Irish missionary work in Northumbria from 635 on. He also writes that countless Englishmen were being educated in Irish schools in the seventh century. Nevertheless, he conveys the impression to many of his readers that Irish influence decreased perceptibly in the wake of the Easter controversy at Whitby in 664. Five years later a Greek scholar arrived, Theodore of Tarsus, dispatched from Rome to Canterbury as the new archbishop along with Abbot Hadrian from Naples. It is generally held that this was the second factor in the growth of Roman influence on the English Church at Ireland's expense.

This view does not, however, correspond to the facts. Bede himself, albeit rather discretely, writes that the positions in the English Church which had become vacant in the year 664 were filled by other Irishmen. The Roman date for Easter had, after all, already been accepted in many areas of Ireland and the Irish and English Christians had much in common even though opinions differed regarding the calculation of Easter. The career of Aldfrith of Northumbria, mentioned earlier, is evidence of the continuous contacts between England and Ireland in the latter part of the seventh century. In addition, there is much to be said for the view that the study of the Greek language promoted by Theodore of Tarsus in England was also taken up in Ireland. In this case England was the giving and Ireland the receiving party.

The following example serves to show the palpable effects of the continued contact between the two islands. Bishop Colman of Lindisfarne, who suffered defeat at the synod of Whitby in 664, returned subsequently to Ireland. He took with him all the Irish from Lindisfarne; in addition, he was also followed by 30 Englishmen. They travelled with Colman via Iona to Ireland where he established a monastery for them off the west coast on the island of Inisboffin. Within a short time, arguments broke out between the Irish and English monks which led Colman to found a separate monastery for the English, Mag-eo (HE IV, 4). The monastery continued to be visited by English monks and Bede testifies that it was still drawing large numbers from England two generations after its foundation. A letter from Alcuin to his countrymen at Mag-eo provides evidence that there were still English monks there at the end of the eighth century.[14] In the light of this, Einhart's reference to Irish kings corresponding with Charlemagne is plausible.[15] Ireland was a part of Europe and not an insignificant one.

7. Secularisation and Reform in the Eighth Century

A Church which embraces the whole community will always show, at any particular time, various trends more or less 'typical' of the period. The process of adjusting to society almost inevitably involves reform within the Church. This feature can be seen particularly clearly in eighth-century Ireland. There were increasing trends towards secularisation and at the same time a reform movement developed with the aim of strengthening the weaknesses which had appeared in the Christian community.

The Rise of Armagh

At the beginning of the ninth century, Armagh, the residence of the successors of Patrick, claimed the leading position in the Church in Ireland. This claim is most clearly formulated in the Book of Armagh, a pocket-sized Gospel Book which, according to the colophon, had been written in the year 807 by the scholar Ferdomnach at the command of Torbach, Patrick's successor (*comarba*, lit. 'heir') in Armagh. In addition to a nearly complete text of the New Testament, the Book of Armagh contains the Life of St Martin of Tours, the Lives of Patrick by Muirchú and Tírchán, an abridged text of Patrick's *Confessio* as well as a treatise with the title *Liber Angeli* 'The Book of the Angel'. The *Liber Angeli* claims that Patrick had been invested with the supremacy of the Irish Church and that his successors were to retain this position. This book was known in Armagh as *Canóin Phátraic* 'Patrick's testament' and venerated as one of the most valuable relics of the Apostle of the Irish.

The texts which were added to the New Testament in this manuscript indicate a particular aim when considered together; they are propaganda writings designed to elevate the position of Armagh. The Life of Martin of Tours is immediately conspicuous in this regard. What connection did Martin have with Patrick? As already mentioned, the biographers of Patrick wrote that he had spent many years in Gaul where Martin was the most important saint. By including the Life of Martin in the Book of Armagh, Patrick was visibly linked with this saint. It has already been pointed out that Muirchú and Tírechán presented a picture of Patrick which considerably distorted the character that appeared in the *Confessio*: according to his biographers, Patrick was the glorious victor of heroic struggles. This view tallies with the incomplete text of the *Confessio* contained in the Book of Armagh, a text which suppresses those passages in which Patrick told of his fears, adversities and difficulties. These passages did not suit the propaganda purposes of his successors in Armagh. It is also significant that Patrick's letter to the soldiers of Coroticus, which likewise tells of his difficulties and which had been used by Muirchú, is not even included in the Book of Armagh.

In the *Liber Angeli* the supremacy of Armagh is clearly stated: all churches which had been founded by bishops and did not belong to a specific *paruchia* were to be placed under the authority of Armagh; the bishop of Armagh was the head of the Church in Ireland. In case of disputes which he was unable to resolve an appeal was to be made to the See of St Peter 'who holds the authority in the city of Rome'. The *Liber Angeli* closes with the statement that Brigit should hold the leading position in her *paruchia*. Brigit and Patrick are referred to as the two pillars of the Irish Church. This retreat is at first sight surprising because it contradicts other claims made in the Book of Armagh. Inconsistencies such as these are, however, not uncommon in medieval documents. In this case, what was meant was that Armagh claimed to hold the leading position at least in the northern half of Ireland. Although it was still only a claim, it was accredited with divine origin to which it was difficult to object, even in Rome.

The veneration of Patrick reached its highest point so far in the Book of Armagh. The beginnings of this cult can be seen in the seventh century. Around A.D. 630, Cummian refers to Patrick as *papa noster* (PL 87, 975). By about 670, Patrick was known in Gaul; in the Life of St Gertrude of Nivelles, Patrick's death is given as 17 March.[16] The veneration of Patrick must therefore have begun some time earlier. The fact that Patrick was venerated in Gaul in the later seventh century is a further indication that the Irish Church was in close contact with Continental Christendom. It is, however, remarkable that Patrick is not mentioned by Bede. The circumstances of the development of the cult of Patrick in Ireland cannot easily be determined. There is a gap of more than 100 years between Patrick's work in Ireland and the first evidence of his recognition as the Apostle of the Irish.

The promotion of the cult of Patrick by the officials in Armagh had a political dimension. Armagh grew in influence through its connections with the Uí Néill dynasty. The secular aim of the Uí Néill, to be kings of the whole of Ireland, corresponded with the aims of Patrick's *comarba* in the spiritual sphere. Just as the Uí Néill ruler was the mightiest individual king in Ireland but not yet king of Ireland, the bishop of Armagh asserted similar claims in the Church.

It also becomes clear from the *Liber Angeli* that there were a considerable number of churches in early ninth-century Ireland which did not belong to any monastic *paruchia* but in which bishops held the leading position. There is, of course, more extensive historical information about *paruchiae* directed by abbots; the institution of the monastery had always guaranteed continuity in tradition for as long as it existed.

It has already been mentioned that the monasteries were usually proprietory churches where the secular ruler had a decisive say in the appointment of the abbot. This can be seen most clearly in Iona where, for over a century after its foundation and with only one exception, the abbots were members of Colum Cille's family. A high degree of continuity was thus guaranteed and although it was not necessarily an indication of corruption, this became a distinct possibility. There are also numerous references in the eighth century to hereditary succession amongst the abbots of other important monasteries. This has been shown particularly clearly in the case of the monasteries of Lusk and Slane. It was a sign of the increasing secularisation of the Church although opinions differ as to its significance. The abbots usually came from noble families that had been unsuccessful in attaining kingship.

Another indication of secularisation is the fact that no Church synod was held between the Synod of Birr (697) and the Assembly of Tara (780) under the leadership of Dublittir. The accounts of wars between monastic communities provide even stronger evidence of secularisation. Clonmacnois fought against Birr in 760 and against Durrow in 764 when Durrow was reputed to have mourned 200 dead.

There was, therefore, a considerable degree of secularisation in the Irish Church but, as will be seen, this should not be regarded as the all important feature.

The Reform of the Church (*Céli Dé*)

Céli Dé 'followers' or 'servants of God' has become the established term describing the reformers of the Irish Church in the eighth century. In the contemporary sources, the supporters of this reform are also referred to by other names, 'true clerics' (*fírcléirigh*), 'son of life' (*mac bethad*) or 'clerics in the South' (*cléirich ind deiscirt*), the last expression indicating the roots of the *Céli Dé* movement in Munster.

Documents written in Irish around the year 800 by unnamed *Céli Dé* are the best sources for the study of the reform movement. They outline the ideas of recognised leaders of the reform in short texts and occasionally in aphorisms. Máelrúain of Tallaght (†792) and Dublittir of Finglas (†796) are particularly prominent among the leaders of the reform movement towards the end of the eighth century. Tallaght and Finglas are situated in Co. Dublin, but it should be remembered that the town of Dublin was not founded until the ninth century although there is evidence of earlier settlements there.

The roots of the *Céli Dé* reform are to be found in Munster. Máelrúain describes Ferdáchrích (†747) of Dairinis (Co. Cork) as his teacher. Other centres of the reform were Lismore (Co. Waterford) under Mac Óige (†753), Terryglass and Derrynavlan (Co. Tipperary). *Leth Moga*, the southern half of Ireland, had distinguished itself in the seventh century in the intellectual field, something from which the *Céli Dé* also benefited. As already mentioned, one of the compilers of the *Collectio Canonum Hibernensis* came from Dairinis. The reform spread from Munster to other parts of Ireland and as far as Iona while the centre of the movement lay, according to the sources, in Leinster. Finglas is first mentioned in the year 763; in 774 King Cellach mac Dúnchada of Leinster granted to God, St Michael and Máelrúain the land on which the monastery of Tallaght was established.

It would be too narrow to see the *Céli Dé* reform as merely a rejection of the world; although this was one part of their programme, there was also an active participation in the affairs of the world. In the year 737, 'Patrick's Law' was proclaimed in Terryglass; in 780, Dublittir presided over the clergy at an assembly in Tara, and in 811, Abbot Echaid of Tallaght succeeded in preventing the Assembly of Tailtiu. These activities show that the leaders of the reform had achieved considerable social standing. The last great representatives of the reform were Maeldíthruib of Terryglass (†840) and his contemporary, Heláir of Loch Cré († c. 807).

The monasteries of Tallaght and Finglas are particularly prominent and were called, even at that time, the 'two eyes of Ireland'. The idea that this was the centre of the reform at the end of the eighth century is strengthened by the fact that the most important documents of the *Céli Dé* movement whose place of origin is known come from the Dublin area. Although the reform spread throughout the island, its impact can only be surmised.

The *Céli Dé* movement placed the greatest emphasis on individual piety. Ferdáchrích inspired Máelrúain who in turn had a decisive influence on Maeldíthruib. Dublittir also had considerable charisma; his way of life was more flexible than that of the austere Máelrúain, his closest neighbour and critical but well-intentioned partner. Normative documents of the *Céli Dé* movement, such as sets of vows or rules, have not survived from Tallaght or Finglas. The ideals of the *Céli Dé* can, however, be inferred from the accounts of everyday life in Tallaght, Finglas and other communities; the most surprising feature of them all is the flexibility of the reformers.

As in all ecclesiastical reforms, prayer played a central role for the *Céli Dé*. Dublittir recited the entire Psalter ('the three fifties') while standing, prostrating himself after each psalm; others said a *paternoster* at the end of each psalm. Particularly popular was Psalm 118 which is mentioned frequently in the documents by reference to its opening word, *Beati*. Maeldíthruib spoke the following words after each psalm: 'St Michael, pray for us, blessed Mary, pray for us, . . .', also adding the saint of that particular day. During communal meals the Gospel was read, one Gospel for each of the seasons. It is mentioned that the monks were questioned about the content of the reading; great emphasis was placed on the understanding of Holy Scripture rather than on mechanical repetition. Apart from this, the monks also devoted themselves to physical work.

The accounts from Tallaght contain detailed information on eating and drinking habits. It is quite clear that these sources were not official documents although the question of diet was important in spiritual life. The *Céli Dé* were supposed to feed themselves in a way that was conducive to prayer. General rules were varied according to the needs of the individual. Extreme fasting was not advocated; even so, one was only to eat as much as was necessary to remain healthy. Physical enjoyment of food was regarded as sinful, which is perhaps why it occupied the monks' thoughts all the more. Drinking water and whey was generally permitted, albeit in small quantities, whereas milk was seldom allowed and, if so, was not to be fresh. Máelrúain resolutely opposed Dublittir's demand that beer sometimes be allowed, whereupon the latter calmly remarked that his monks would also enter into Paradise. The most essential foods were bread and porridge to which the abbot sometimes secretly added, for the well-being of the monks, a little extra butter. It was unusual for food to be stored. Anything remaining from the daily meals was distributed among the poor. Fasting on Sundays was very much frowned upon; in some communities, as a concession to the Old Testament, it was also forbidden on Saturdays. The generally recognised virtues were those of poverty and chastity. Máelrúain also demanded strict obedience while other teachers relied on the individual's voluntary submission. Extreme forms of asceticism were frowned upon because of the dangers of gossip or the sin of pride. Mac Óige is credited with the dry remark: 'Never was it said: this man is too steady'. The *Céli Dé* were generally admonished to face up to their own personal weaknesses. As Máelrúain put it: 'The fire thou most dreadest to burn thee, to it shalt thou go'. Another more moderate saying points in the same direction: 'Every man should regulate his pittance for himself. It should be limited to men's natures, for the course of nature differs in each man'.

The *Céli Dé* reform was essentially orientated towards the exemplary personality which accounts for its strength and its weakness. The *Céli Dé* lacked firm structures and thus it is not surprising that the movement lost much of its impetus from the middle of the ninth century onwards, once the leading figures had died. It did, however, leave behind an unmistakable legacy and furthered the use of the Irish language in the recording of spiritual texts. It is thought that the Irish glosses of New Testament texts preserved today in Milan and Turin originate from the circle around Máelrúain. They underline the efforts of the *Céli Dé* to understand the Christian message although they were always careful not to deal too directly with the 'mystery of the faith'.

An important document of the *Céli Dé* reform is the Stowe Missal which probably originates from Terryglass and was written soon after Máelrúain's death. It contains the Gelasian Mass canon as well as rubrics in Old Irish. The term *oífrend* (Latin *offerenda*) for Mass points to an influence from Milan. This manuscript contains a treatise on the Mass in Old Irish in which the following sentence is included: 'It is not proper for it (the host) to go under the back teeth, (this) symbolising that it is improper to dispute overmuch on God's mysteries, lest heresy should be increased thereby'. At that time, communion was offered in both forms, in bread and wine. This is illustrated clearly and vividly by the size of the Derrynavlan Chalice; coming from a *Céli Dé* monastery, it is large enough to hold wine for a sizeable congregation. Derrynavlan provides the only complete early medieval Irish altar service.

Other evidence of the piety of the *Céli Dé* is provided by literary works. These include, above all, the 'Alphabet of Piety' (*Apgitir Crábaid*), written in Lismore in the early eighth century, and *Saltair na Rann*, a collection of 150 Irish poems on subjects from the Old Testament and from the life of Jesus. The rich treasure of Irish lyrical poetry on themes of faith, nature and man cannot be ascribed entirely to the *Céli Dé*; much of it is attributed to hermits who were in close contact with nature but who seem to have been encouraged by the *Céli Dé*. A typical example of the religious poetry is a poem about 'little Jesus' (*Ísucán*); at that time the use of such a familiar expression for the Saviour was highly unusual.

The veneration of the saints by the *Céli Dé* should also be mentioned. It has already been shown that Mary and Michael were venerated in Tallaght; that monastery also provided a martyrology (a list of saints' days). This is based on the *Martyrologium Hieronymianum*, but it also includes Irish saints. It is thought to have been started by Máelrúain and it was continued for another 100 years after his death. The following remarkable entry appears for 20 April: 'The feast of all the saints and virgins of Ireland, Britain and all of Europe, and especially in honour of the saint, bishop Martin'. This is typical of the way in which the *Céli Dé*, like Columbanus before them, considered themselves quite naturally a part of the European Christian community. The Martyrology of Oengus (*Félire Oengusso*), which contains a large number of Irish religious poems, originates from the same area and the same period.

The *Céli Dé* reforms appear to have arisen in Ireland itself without any obvious influences from outside. They began at roughly the time when Bede was deploring the decline of the Church in Northumbria and before the Continental reform of Chrodegang of Metz. Although it is generally assumed that the reform remained confined to the Celtic regions, possible influences on the Frankish area cannot be ruled out. Virgil, abbot and bishop of Salzburg (746/47–784), was an Irishman, and the names of two men of his entourage are reminiscent of supporters of the *Céli Dé*, namely Dobdagrecus and Dupliterus.[17] The Irish forms of these names, Dub dá Chrích and Dublittir, are attested in Ireland in the eighth century. It is, therefore, worth considering whether Virgil and his companions on their way to Gaul had passed through Munster. It should be noted that the reform of Chrodegang of Metz began almost ten years after Virgil's arrival in Gaul. It remains to be examined whether there are any links between the two reforms.

8.   The Age of the Vikings

The significance of the Viking raids in western Europe from the end of the eighth century on is less clear today than it once appeared. The Norsemen were seen for a long time as plunderers and destroyers of political order, both in Frankish Gaul and in England; recently there has been a tendency towards more varied assessments. Firstly, it can be seen today that the Viking raids appear in hindsight more severe and more intense than they actually were. Secondly, it is now accepted that the Vikings were able to have such a destabilising effect on western Europe because the societies they threatened were themselves unstable. Thirdly, it is becoming increasingly clear that the Vikings made positive contributions, be it directly through the founding of states or indirectly where various regions strengthened their defences against them.

These points also apply to Ireland and are gradually being reflected in scholarly work. The Irish public at large is also beginning to realise that the destructive role attributed until recently to the Vikings does not correspond to the facts. The archaeological excavations in the centre of Dublin in the 1970s in particular have contributed to this change in public awareness. The attempts by the city authorities to end the Wood Quay excavations prematurely brought tens of thousands of people onto the streets, not only to protest, but also to visit the excavation sites. The public could see for themselves the contribution of the Vikings to the shaping of Dublin. Excavation sites admittedly show the more peaceful sides of life and are therefore just as one-sided as the written sources which tend to concentrate on conflict. The truth presumably lies somewhere between these two extremes.

Opinions differ as to the significance of the Viking Age in Ireland but it is agreed that it was of prime importance. For the first time since prehistory the island experienced sizeable military attacks, raids and subsequent settlement from outside. Although there had been isolated attacks from England, the Irish themselves had been active in military expansion in the previous four centuries. While the country was by no means peaceful, many basic social rules were adhered to. The Vikings, however, did not abide by these rules and in the long term this was to influence the Irish.

The monastery of Lindisfarne on the northeast coast of Northumbria was first plundered by the Vikings in A.D. 793. A few years later, Iona suffered a similar fate, followed by the entire north and east coasts of Ireland. The next generation experienced almost annual raids by the Vikings which are recorded with horror in the monastic annals. Monasteries and churches were favourite targets for the Scandinavians as they contained gold, silver and other valuables in large quantities. Adomnán reports that the doors of the churches in Ireland were bolted (VC 83a), but they could not resist the intruders who did not share the Christians' respect for their places of worship. The people in the monasteries were badly prepared for attacks of this kind.

The Church prescribes the use of precious metals for its liturgical vessels; thus the individual churches presented the gold-hungry Vikings with a continuous supply of treasure. Nowhere else on the island were such spoils to be found in similar quantities or so conveniently accessible as in the churches and monasteries. Those reporting and recording the Scandinavian raids were also their victims and it must therefore be assumed that the picture given by the chroniclers was more gloomy than the reality.

A considerable amount of Christian Irish art from the early Middle Ages is preserved today in the museums of Norway. They were the spoils taken by the Vikings and provide the clearest indication of the origins of the Scandinavians who plundered Ireland. Few Irish art objects are found in Denmark and it has been shown that some of these had come there from Norway rather than directly from Ireland. The majority of the Vikings who raided and later settled in England came from Denmark. The Irish annals generally call the Vikings foreigners or strangers (*gaill*, Latin *gentes* 'pagans'). The groups from Norway were referred to as *Finn-gaill* whilst the Danes, who began their incursions in the middle of the ninth century, were called *Dub-gaill*. This differentiation shows that the Norsemen in Ireland did not act together but as separate groups. Since the northern part of Ireland was initially more seriously affected by the Viking raids than the south, the kings of Munster could expand their power considerably.

The first phase of the Viking Age in Ireland began in 795 with a raid on the island of Lambay and by 830 25 further raids had been recorded in the annals. For obvious reasons the northern and eastern areas were initially much more strongly affected than the other parts of Ireland. The attacks on Ireland had been preceded by the occupation of the Orkney Islands and the Hebrides by the Vikings. After several attacks, the monks of Iona fled to Ireland in 807 and founded a new monastery in Kells which was completed in 814. It was not until 823 that the entire coastline of Ireland was affected by the Vikings. Remarkably, they spared the *Céli Dé* communities of Tallaght and Finglas, probably because these were so poor.

Because of their great mobility, the Vikings were difficult to confront during the first three decades of their attacks. Their ships could navigate rivers just as well as the open sea; the Vikings were much more mobile than the Irish. In addition, the monasteries were badly equipped for battle.

The remarkable career of Feidlimid mac Crimthainn, king of Munster (820–46), belongs to this period. He was the first Irish king who was a cleric and was also the first Irish king to wage war against monasteries on a large scale. Feidlimid associated himself with the *Céli Dé* community of Tallaght; his family held the kingship of Munster for 100 years after his death and several of his successors also held clerical office. Feidlimid cleverly used the ambitions of Armagh by proclaiming 'Patrick's Law' in Munster together with the bishop of Armagh in 823. In the following decade he extended his influence to Leinster and waged war against the monasteries of Durrow and Kildare, also launching several attacks on Clonmacnois. In 836 he became abbot of Cork and in 838 abbot of Clonfert; he was even to interfere in the affairs of Armagh. Feidlimid's main targets were the old-style monasteries which he considered to be too worldly. He also attempted to gain influence by appointing his own people, especially in Clonmacnois; in this he showed not only his religious but also his political intentions. His swift rise to national importance was made possible by the fact that Niall mac Áeda of the Uí Néill was a weak opponent. Feidlimid's propaganda claims that Niall submitted to the king of Munster in the year 838. Although this is improbable, Feidlimid did manage to advance as far as Tara and in 840 captured Niall's wife, Gormlaith. His last major undertaking was directed once more against Clonmacnois where he is reported to have tied up a high-ranking cleric together with his wife, servant and dog and then to have recited a malediction against him. He died on 28 August 846 and was widely praised as a hero, even as a saint. His career shows that the struggle for supremacy in Ireland continued almost unabated despite the Viking raids.

Meanwhile, the Vikings were intensifying their attacks and in 840 they spent their first winter in Ireland. This was the first step towards settlement, towards the establishment of fortifications which were later expanded into towns. Nearly all important Irish towns originated as Scandinavian settlements and are situated on or near the coast: Dublin, Wicklow, Arklow, Wexford, Waterford, Cork, Limerick. In the long term, the Vikings were only able to settle along the coast of the southern half of Ireland. A strong king of Munster like Feidlimid was as exceptional for that time as was the temporary weakness of the Uí Néill. Although it is known that the Vikings periodically spent the winter along the coast of the northern half of Ireland, the locations where they wintered did not develop into towns. The first Viking settlement, which was also to become the most important one, was Dublin; 841 is taken as the year of its foundation. The Scandinavian cemetery of Islandbridge was used from around 850 on. The Vikings settled on a hillside ridge south of the River Liffey where the River Poddle joined the Liffey. This was preceded by *Dubh-linn* 'black pool', another settlement presumably on the north bank of the Liffey, at a ford which Adomnán referred to as *vadum Clied* (VC 55b; Áth Cliath).

In spending the winter in Ireland and settling on the coast the Vikings became a greater threat. At the same time, however, they became more predictable through having settled down, and it gradually became possible to fight them by traditional methods. Máel Sechnaill (846–62), king of the southern Uí Néill, made a name for himself in this regard; in the year 846 he drowned a Viking leader by the name of Turgesius. In 851, a Danish fleet came to Ireland from the north of England. The Danes were not made welcome by the Norwegians of Dublin and there were indications of an internal struggle among the Scandinavians. The threat to Ireland, as it had existed in the first half of the ninth century, had subsided.

In 851, the Danes asserted themselves in Dublin under the leadership of Ivar, two years after which another fleet arrived under the Norwegian, Olav. The two appear to have come to a temporary agreement with each other. Olav took the daughter of Áed Finnliath as his wife which shows that the Vikings had, in some areas, become socially acceptable. Máel Sechnaill on the other hand, appears to have united many of the Irish against the Vikings. Even their former ally Áed Finnliath abandoned them upon succeeding Máel Sechnaill as king of Tara in 862. A year later, the Vikings plundered the legendary prehistoric graves of the Boyne Valley, a deed Máel Sechnaill regarded as sacrilege and which he avenged in a bloody manner. In 866, Áed Finnliath drove the Vikings from the north coast from Donegal to Antrim. Ivar then appears to have returned to the Scandinavian kingdom of York while Olav remained in Dublin. It was not until 871 that Ivar came back to Dublin, having destroyed Dumbarton in 870. Following Olav's enforced departure to Norway, Ivar remained for the last two years of his life the supreme power in Dublin and further afield. On the occasion of his death he is described in the Irish annals as 'King of the Norsemen of all of Ireland and Britain' (AU: *Imhar rex Nordmannorum totius Hiberniae et Britanniae vitam finivit.*). This entry illustrates the wide-ranging influence of the Viking settlements.

Towards the end of the ninth century the native rulers in England and Ireland intensified their struggle against the foreigners. At much the same time as Alfred the Great († 899) succeeded in checking the Danes in England, an important breakthrough was achieved in Ireland with the destruction of Dublin in 902. In the early tenth century the influence of the Vikings in Ireland was very weak; at the same time the kingdom of York was under strong pressure from Aethelstan. This lull provides the opportunity to review the situation.

What had changed in Irish society and which of these changes can be attributed to the Vikings? The most obvious area is the field of learning where some developments can be seen to be directly connected with the Viking raids. Those Irishmen who made their way to the Carolingian Empire in the first half of the ninth century (the grammar teacher Muiredag, Sedulius Scottus around 848, John Scottus Eriugena and others) had probably fled from the Vikings. For the time being, the conditions for study on the Continent were better than in Ireland. The Annals of St Bertin mention in the year 848 that the king of the Irish claimed in a message to the Franks that the Vikings had been driven out of Ireland. Contacts, therefore, existed in both directions. Numerous manuscripts must have reached the Continent through the fugitive scholars and many other unknown Irishmen, as is shown by the earliest library catalogues which list bibles, bible texts with glosses, exegetical works, *De duodecim abusivis saeculi* and others. At about this time, too, some monks also left Ireland for Iceland, to be plagued by the Vikings at the beginning of the tenth century.

In Ireland itself, the arrival of the Vikings signalled the end of the great period of manuscript illumination; the last great example of this is the Book of Kells. The monasteries changed in appearance; they were increasingly constructed from stone and the first Round Towers (*cloictech*, 'bell-house') were built. The finest High Crosses date from the ninth and tenth centuries. The monastic communities were now interested in objects of greater durability.

The beginning of the Viking Age coincides with another major change in the Irish Church. Laymen had, until then, occasionally become the abbots of a monastery: this now became the rule rather than the exception. The monasteries needed the leadership of men who could protect the Church in battle. Many of the monasteries had already been proprietory churches but now they came even more strongly under the control of the local nobility. The position of abbot was treated as hereditary: for example, the Uí Sinaich, provided the abbots of Armagh for 200 years.

Changes can be seen in secular society, changes which often reach back to before the Viking Age. The lowest rank of king, the *rí túaithe*, had diminished in significance since the eighth century, such kings frequently being referred to in the annals as *dux* or *tigerna* (Latin *dominus*). As already mentioned, certain provincial kings rose to a position where they could lay claim to the high-kingship, supremacy over the whole of Ireland. From the eighth century onwards, these claims seemed less unrealistic than they would have been in the fifth or sixth centuries. Collateral lines of the leading dynasties which had been unable to gain control of a province or part of a province instead set up local lordships which approximated the position of a *rí túaithe*. The extended family (*derbfine*) appears to have diminished in importance in favour of the nuclear family.

Just as elsewhere in Europe, there were signs in Ireland of internal colonisation, indicated by placenames with the element *dísert* 'barren land'. The search for new agricultural land points to a rise in the population. The need for an increase in the food supply affected the social and economic position of the lower classes.

Through the Vikings, slavery had also become widespread in Ireland. Slaves, often prisoners taken in battle, were traded, imported and exported, but this was only one aspect of the growth in trade brought by the Vikings. The Irish were also introduced to more advanced techniques of seamanship, a precondition for the settlement of Iceland. Long ocean voyages created the demand for the popular tales of travel, the most famous of which was the Voyage of St Brendan (tenth century). From the ninth century on, the Uí Néill maintained close contact with the Irish in the west of Scotland; this again was facilitated by improvements in shipbuilding techniques.

It is not clear to what extent the Vikings contributed to the increased brutality, which is discernible especially in war. Signs of growing brutality accompanied the secularisation of the large and influential monasteries from the late eighth century onwards. Some Irish kings would appear to have been ritually murdered by the Vikings who were, however, converted to Christianity as early as the second half of the ninth century. Meanwhile, the Irish learned quickly from the foreigners how to enrich themselves by capturing prominent men in battle and releasing them on payment of an appropriate ransom; this, in turn, led to changes in the means of payment. Whereas cattle had been used as the unit of payment in the early medieval centuries, the ounce of silver (*uinge*) began to take over from the ninth century. Coins were introduced by the Vikings in the tenth century.

The expulsion of the Vikings from Dublin in the year 902 did not mark the end of the Viking Age; by 925 at the latest, Dublin was once again in Scandinavian hands. The other Viking foundations along the coast also survived, and it would be wrong to underestimate their size. Towns were dependent upon their hinterland and here the Scandinavian layout of fields has sometimes remained visible up to the present day, indicating agricultural settlements.

The Scandinavian settlements in Ireland were small kingdoms, presumably larger than one *túath*, the essential difference being that a town formed the centre of the kingdom. The economic definition of a town involves the idea that its residents produce less of their own food than those living in the country; instead, they support themselves rather through barter and trade. The early Scandinavian towns of Ireland were, naturally enough, in contact with the Scandinavian kingdoms in Britain.

The saying *pecunia non olet* ('there is nothing wrong with money', lit. 'money does not stink') is particularly apt in this case, and the trade links of the Viking towns indeed extended beyond the Scandinavian settlements in England. Finds of coins are evidence of trading connections with the south of England along the coast from Bristol via Cornwall as far as London from the end of the tenth century onwards. The Irish Vikings adopted English coinage in the mid-tenth century. The earliest known coin struck in Ireland in the English style, from the period shortly before A.D. 1000, was discovered in 1980 during the Wood Quay excavations in Dublin.

The contacts of the Vikings in Ireland also extended beyond the coastal towns. There are several indications that the Scandinavian kingdoms became integrated into the Irish political scene from the end of the tenth century onwards. The conversion of the Vikings to Christianity removed the last ideological barrier.

Although the annals do contain accounts of 'national' resentment towards the foreigners, this is more likely to have been propaganda on the part of the ruling classes than the feeling of the country as a whole.

The significance of the Viking Age in Ireland can be put into perspective by comparison with the situation in England. Here there was a major wave of new Danish attacks at the end of the tenth century, and some further settlement, particularly in the Midlands. In the eleventh century, the Danes took over the national kingship, their most prominent king being Canute the Great (1016–38). Ireland did not experience the second wave of Viking invasions on such a large scale; the peak of Viking power had already been reached around the year 900.

The usual practice of allowing the Viking Age in Ireland to continue into the eleventh century or even extending it up to the 'Norman Age' (from 1169 onwards) is partly the result of popular simplification and the convenient division of historical periods. In any case, that Ireland's experience of the Vikings was different from that of England must be taken into account. There was never any indication that the Vikings established in Ireland kingdoms on the scale of those in England. This was impossible due to the political diversity in Ireland, the fragmentation of the country into numerous small units which were the best protection against

conquests from outside. Nevertheless, the existence and survival of
the small Scandinavian kingdoms was important as the Irish could
also benefit from the trading connections. It has been plausibly
suggested that the decline of the Uí Néill from the tenth century
onwards was perhaps connected with the fact that they had not
tolerated any Scandinavian settlements on their coasts and therefore
benefited less from the trade links.

The adoption of Scandinavian terms into the Irish language is
also worth mentioning. Irish has Scandinavian loan words for
seafaring, trade, market and coin; the names for the provinces of
Leinster, Munster and Ulster go back to Scandinavian word
formations as does the term 'Ireland' for the whole island.

The Scandinavian kingdoms in Ireland did not play any
significant political role from the tenth century onwards. They
often appear almost insignificant alongside the power struggles
among the Irish dynasties, which continued undiminished. However,
it is not certain whether such an impression may not be misleading
in the light of long-term changes of a political nature that occurred
in Ireland from the tenth century onwards. Most important is the
fact that the Uí Néill were no longer the undisputed leading
dynasty. Powerful kings of Munster, Leinster and Connacht now
attempted to gain supremacy over the whole island, the so-called
high-kingship, and some of them succeeded in this. Although their
success was generally short-lived, it signals a considerable change
on the Irish political scene.

During the two centuries before the arrival of the English in
Ireland (1169), the political scene was dominated by the struggle
for the kingship of Tara. The confusing sequence of alliances,
battles and rulers and the rise and fall of individual dynasties
cannot be discussed in detail here. However, the struggle is
certainly important and is closely linked to the existence of the
Viking kingdoms: all the leading dynasties in Ireland aspired
towards national kingship. Just as elsewhere in Europe, the
Scandinavians appear to have acted as catalysts in the formation of
larger states from the tenth century onwards.

The radical political changes which ensued in the tenth and
eleventh centuries cannot always be attributed directly to the
Vikings but seem instead to be connected with the new political
order in Ireland. Generally speaking, there are two principal lines
of development, on the one hand the rise of new dynasties and, on

the other, the intense struggle for supremacy in Ireland symbolised by the kingship of Tara. The latter had been the focus of attention in the early ninth century with Feidlimid mac Crimthainn; over a century later, Munster would once again achieve prominence.

The leading Munster dynasty were the Eóganachta with their headquarters in Cashel. The Eóganachta Chaisil had virtually monopolised the provincial kingship in the period from 820 to 964 without, however, extending their influence beyond Munster for any length of time. They were weaker than the Uí Néill in that they were unable to prevent the Vikings from gaining a foothold on the coast of Munster. In the course of the ninth century a new group came to prominence in the western part of the province which was known from 934 on as Dál Cais.

The Dál Cais were part of the Déisi with the name Déisi Tuaiscirt. Although they were overshadowed nationally by the Eóganachta, they managed to expand in the direction of Clare. An attack on Limerick in the year 967 shows that their king, Mathgamain mac Cennétic, was a man of great ambitions. The actual founder of the new dynasty, however, was his brother, Brian Boru, who succeeded him as king in 976.

Brian Boru is one of the great legendary figures of Ireland. He was long regarded as a 'national' hero whose supposed objective was to drive the Vikings out of Ireland, an objective he came close to realising in the Battle of Clontarf. The legends tend to play down the fact the he lost his life in this battle. Nowadays Brian Boru is seen more as a talented, ambitious and ruthless politician who battled against the Vikings among others but whose real aim was to become high-king.

Brian Boru's career is characterised by an almost inexorable rise. In the first two decades of his rule he forced both Munster and Leinster to recognise his authority. In order to achieve this he was prepared to form an alliance with the Vikings of Waterford. He then forced Máel Sechnaill II to relinquish his influence in the south of Ireland, thereby considerably undermining the claim of the Uí Néill to supremacy over the whole of the country. But Brian Boru went still further. In 1001 he attacked the territory of the Uí Néill and five years later was able to carry out a royal tour of the north completely unchallenged; only the Ulaid remained outside his reach. He did not concern himself with Connacht any further and made Armagh bend to his will through gifts. His brother,

Marcán mac Cennétig (†1010) was abbot of Killaloe, Terryglass and Inis Cealtra and could thus ensure that the Church did not afford any protection to his opponents in the south.

Although Brian Boru's rise was greeted with suspicion everywhere, the only signs of resistance against it came from those most affected, namely Leinster and Dublin. King Sitric of Dublin called for assistance from Jarl Sigurd of Orkney as well as from the Vikings of the Isle of Man and also had the Leinster king, Máel Mórda, on his side. This opposition was so strong that Máel Sechnaill refused to fight on Brian's side. On Good Friday, 23 April 1014, the battle of Clontarf (now a district of Dublin on the north side of the Liffey) was fought. The battle claimed the lives of Máel Mórda and Sigurd as well as those of Brian Boru and his son, Murchadh. His other son, Donnchadh, became an inglorious successor of his father and survived until 1064. Brian Boru was laid to rest in Armagh; the Book of Armagh has an entry (f. 32rb) where he is called *imperator Scotorum*.

This title may appear exaggerated at first sight, but it does have a certain justification. If it is meant to denote a supremacy founded on the might of the sword, there is not much difference between Brian Boru and the emperor Otto I even though the title hardly implies an 'Empire'. Yet the mere fact that Brian Boru, as a Dál Cais, was buried in Armagh shows that his achievements were respected even after his death. What were these achievements? The claim of the Uí Néill to the monopoly of the kingship of Tara had been broken effectively for the first time and, from then on, it was clear that the contest for the high-kingship was open. Without wishing to glorify the politics of the sword, it must be seen as one of Brian Boru's achievements that the high-kingship of Ireland now attracted a range of candidates. His successors, often termed 'king with opposition' (*rí co fresabra*), went further in the direction of a central monarchy which, by the twelfth century, began to show more European features. The English intervention from 1169 on was to end these developments.

It is not surprising that Brian's descendants called themselves O'Brien after him. Similar developments could also be found in other parts of Ireland. The O'Neills called themselves after King Niall Glúndub mac Áeda (916-19), the O'Tooles after Tuathal Ua Muiredaig (†917), the O'Connors after Conchobhar mac Taidg (967-73), etc. Family names became common from the eleventh century on. It was then that families developed that were to determine the political and cultural landscape of Ireland right into the late Middle Ages.

An almost unbroken succession of high-kings can be recognised from the eleventh century onwards. Brian Boru's son, Donnchadh (†1064 on a pilgrimage to Rome) was unable to retain his father's pre-eminent position. Leinster in particular won back its independence under Diarmait mac Máel na mBó (1032–72) who himself attempted to gain supremacy. Diarmait is called in the annals 'king of Ireland with opposition'; in Leinster his rise meant virtually the beginning of a new dynasty. Diarmait belonged to the Uí Cheinnselaig who had not provided a king of Leinster since 738. The kingship had been occupied in regular succession from 738 to 1042 by three other groups, the Uí Dúnlainge from the Liffey Valley, the Uí Faeláin and Uí Muiredaig. This alternating succession of power is regarded as the classic example of the Irish political order but is unparalleled in its consistency. According to Irish law, the Uí Cheinnselaig had lost all further claim to kingship; yet their success shows that great differences had emerged between political theory and practice. Diarmait's great-grandson, Diarmait mac Murchada, was later to achieve historical significance by sending for the English. Donnchadh's nephew, Tairrdelbach Ua Briain, rose to the leading position in Munster from 1063 onwards; from 1072 to 1086 he was regarded as king of Ireland (*rí Erenn*, AU) in succession to Diarmait. His position involved supremacy over Leinster, Meath and Connacht. His son Muirchertach became king of Dublin in 1075, and he was 'King of Ireland' from 1088 to 1119. It was here, however, that the supremacy of the O'Briens ended. From then on, the O'Briens were confined to the northern half of Munster, to Thomond (*Tuadmumu*), while in the southern half, in Desmond (*Desmuma*), the Mac Carthys became prominent. The high-kingship then was taken by Tairrdelbach Ua Conchobhair of Connacht (1119–56).

If one regards the intellectual history of a people as an integral part of their political history, then the effects of the Viking Age can also be identified in this area, in two definite respects. Through the Vikings, Ireland's contacts with the neighbouring island, England, had once again been strengthened. This is clearly shown in an Irish work, *Saltair na Rann*, a biblical story in Middle Irish written in verse. The material is based partly on the Apocrypha but also on

Anglo Saxon poetry. The writing of magnificent manuscripts had been brought to an end by the Viking invasions.

Another development had an even greater impact. Judging by those manuscripts which can be localised, the centre of Irish intellectual life moved gradually from the east coast westwards between the ninth and eleventh centuries. The monastery of Clonmacnois on the River Shannon became the new intellectual centre and many important manuscripts of the period are attributed to its scriptoria. Better conditions appear to have prevailed there although it is not necessary to credit this to any particular individual such as Brian Boru. However, one can see here the beginning of a long term development: in the following centuries, the West was to become the guardian of the old traditions. Literary production had temporarily weakened during the Viking Age only to increase again from the twelfth century onwards.

Ireland in the second part of the Middle Ages (c. 1100–1500)

9. Ireland under Foreign Influence: the Twelfth Century

The author of this book divides the Middle Ages into two sections, a concept widespread especially in France and Italy but which also seems to suit the Irish situation particularly well. The transition between the two sections, however, cannot be neatly confined to one century as suggested by the chapter heading, although some very important developments took place in the twelfth century. Justice is rarely done to the actual course of events by using years or even decades as turning points. Events that are of long-term importance tend to have a prehistory which also has to be considered, and thus one has to go beyond mere description.

Here this means that we depart from the usual division of Irish history, knowing, however, that the usefulness of this division has been questioned for some years now. We will deal later with the reform of the Irish Church usually called the 'twelfth-century reform', the roots of which, however, stretch back well into the eleventh century; this reform was not completed, as often suggested, by the synod of Kells-Mellifont in 1152. We will also deal with the English intervention in Ireland particularly from the 1160s onwards, an event that also has a recognisable prehistory. We also want to look at subjects beyond these two major events. Naturally, all these subjects overlap to some extent. Whether or not these events in the course of the transition from the first to the second part of the Middle Ages are indicative of 'progress', of the emergence of something new, will be discussed in the last chapter.

Ireland as seen by a Foreigner

As already mentioned, Ireland had always had contact with neighbouring countries, but until the twelfth century the Irish had succeeded in maintaining their independence. From the twelfth century onwards the English became a new, threatening and lasting influence on Irish life, in that they involved themselves in Irish affairs with varying degrees of intensity, down to the present century. The first description of Ireland dates from the early years of this new phase of Irish history, from the late twelfth century. Its author was a foreigner, a cleric of Anglo-Welsh aristocratic descent, Giraldus Cambrensis (Gerald of Wales, 1146–1223). His considerable range of writings includes a description of Ireland (*Topographia Hibernica*) and an account of the first few decades of the English conquest of Ireland (*Expugnatio Hibernica*). The two books were dedicated to the English rulers of the time, Henry II and Richard I.

Modern readers, including historians, especially in Ireland, have often seriously misunderstood these two books because they failed to assess them in their proper historical context. To accuse the author of a lack of objectivity is to demand the impossible. Since the author was both British and a cleric, he approached his subject with certain preconceptions and expectations. His books about Ireland certainly are subjective, often decidedly biased. They had been written for entertainment and for the glorification of the English rulers. The well-travelled and highly educated author obviously enjoyed comparing Irish society with other societies; it is hardly surprising that he judged the Irish way of life according to what he was familiar with and that he described the differences in a negative way. This applies even more strongly to the peculiarities of the Irish Church.

The most important feature of the *Topographia* is that it is the first major description of Ireland by a foreigner who had visited the country personally. Giraldus collected the material for this book during a full year spent in Ireland. The *Topographia* remained the only description of Ireland of its kind for centuries to come and was very widely read. The *Expugnatio* is one of two surviving near-contemporary accounts of the invasion of Ireland by the English. The other account is by another (anonymous) foreigner, a verse epic in French ('The Song of Dermot and the Earl'). No history of the conquest can be written from Irish sources alone because the Irish annals deal chiefly with the infighting among the Irish. Despite their obvious weaknesses, the great importance of the works on Ireland by Giraldus derives from the information they contain relating to the conquest of Ireland.

The *Topographia* is divided into three sections, a description of the country, an account of the marvels of Ireland and an outline of Irish history. Part I deals in detail with the topography, the climate and the fauna, and Giraldus comments on a number of natural phenomena from a theological and allegorical point of view. Towards the end he compares the Eastern and Western fringes of the world and concludes that the West is preferable to the East. Part II is concerned with the miracles of Ireland; the entertainment value of this section can be appreciated particularly well. The author was of the opinion that nature tolerated on the fringes of the world many marvels that were unthinkable in 'normal' countries. In Ireland there were fabulous beings, part animal, part human, there were islands on which no female creature would survive, others on which corpses did not decompose, there were fish with gold teeth and much else. The legends of the saints offered more scope for fabulation; some of these saints had particularly close contacts with the animal world. Even the English in their few years in Ireland had experienced miraculous things that had to be reported.

In many respects the most interesting section of the *Topographia* is the third part, the account of the history of Ireland from the earliest times to the twelfth century. In this section Giraldus depended almost completely on information provided by the Irish. He may well have been taken in by some unlikely yarns, without his noticing, but this section nonetheless shows how the Irish viewed their history. The tradition persisted that immigration to the island had happened in various stages as in the 'Book of Invasions' (*Lebor Gabála*). Giraldus was also informed that St Patrick converted the people of the whole island; the date of his death was given as 468. Besides Patrick, Brigit and Colum Cille were held to be the most important saints. Giraldus then gives an assessment of the Christianity of the Irish and his views here are particularly narrow although he admits that Irish Christianity still corresponded to Continental expectations in some respects. He mentions the reorganisation of the Irish Church by the papal legate Paparo but does not mention the reforms before the synod of Kells (1152). Giraldus regarded the Viking Age as an important landmark in Irish history. He notes establishment of towns and development of trade links by the Vikings. He draws a straight line from Scandinavian rule (the extent of which he exaggerates) to the arrival of the English in Ireland. It is particularly significant that Giraldus had apparently been told by the Irish that there had been a national kingship from the very beginning. Giraldus merely adds the comment that kingship in Ireland was conferred neither by anointing nor by crowning. Power alone, not heredity, determined who would be king.

Obviously, this outline of Giraldus's view of Ireland is simplified even in its details and is thus somewhat distorted. However, it should be emphasised that essential elements of the view of Irish history that were conveyed to Giraldus have remained common property right into this century, even to the present. This applies both to the views on St Patrick and the Vikings; likewise, the arrival of the English in Ireland in the 1160s is held by most people to be another turning point in Irish history.

A thorough reassessment of Irish history is beginning to emerge from the archaeological excavations at Wood Quay in Dublin the full publication of which is eagerly expected. Admittedly only a small segment of Irish history was excavated at Wood Quay, but the results are highly significant. The excavations show that Dublin had been exposed to new influences from the beginning of the twelfth century. On the basis of the finds it has become clear that the town had been closely involved in the North Sea trade with Scandinavia until the late eleventh century. From the early twelfth century onwards the links with the south of England and the north of France became more important. The archaeological material thus provides the evidence of Ireland's political and ecclesiastical links with the Anglo-Norman world, links that are otherwise poorly attested.

In the mid-eleventh century Dublin was surrounded by a stone wall; the part of that wall that crossed the Wood Quay site was destroyed in 1978 while the excavations were still in progress. In the course of the twelfth century the town was extended in the direction of the river by means of land reclamations and earthen walls; these were strengthened by using the hulls of disused boats. The remains of these boats show that by the twelfth century the ships were larger than ever before. On the other hand these ships do not show any Norman influence in their construction. This could indicate that the initiative for the reorganisation and expansion of the Dublin trade came from within Ireland.

The politics of twelfth-century Dublin are far from clear. To what extent was the town still Scandinavian? A dynasty of Scandinavian descent was still in power, but this dynasty had intermarried with Irish families. The town of Dublin, originally set up on the southern bank of the Liffey, had been extended to the northern bank. The name of that extension, Óxmantown (town of the Ostmen), emphasises the foreign origins of its inhabitants, yet those finds from Wood Quay dating from the twelfth century show few Scandinavian features, in contrast to the tenth-century stratification where gold, silver, amber and glass were quite common. The twelfth-century finds are predominantly made up of earthenware, pewter and bronze with northern French features. The excavated remains of houses from the eleventh and twelfth centuries are quite similar to houses from other parts of Ireland of that time. Ash timber was the main building material. The average house at Wood Quay measured 12 × 18 ft and consisted of a single room with a living area and fireplace in the centre and sleeping spaces along the walls. Walls and roofs were made of wattle and daub; houses of this kind had a lifespan of about one generation. They were then taken down and another house of the same type was built on the remains of the previous structure.

Dublin in general and Wood Quay in particular illustrate the complex nature of Ireland. There are many indications that the Irish element in Dublin was quite prominent and that the town had become part of the Anglo-Norman trading world. The Irish world was not as backward as Giraldus described it in his *Topographia*.

Naturally, there were regional differences. An exceptionally detailed report from the northwest of Ireland shows the continued existence of traditional social obligations and at the same time allows an insight into the structure of society. The Annals of the Four Masters report for the year 1150: 'The visitation of the Cenél nEógain was made by the successor of Colum Cille, Flaithbheartach Ua Brolchain; and he obtained a horse from every *taoiseach* (local ruler); a cow from every two *betagii*, a cow from every three *saerthach* (free-holders); a cow from every four *díomhaoin* (villeins); and twenty cows from the king (of the province); a gold ring of five ounces, his horse, and his battledress, from Muircheartach, son of Niall Ua Lochlainn, king of Ireland'.

The importance of cattle is evident here. The same annals, for the year 1161, give the value of an ox as three ounces of silver. However, silver was mainly used as a unit of calculation; actual wealth in the twelfth century still meant the ownership of cattle. The Annals of Loch Cé report the devastating effects of a murrain in 1133 and 1134 that reduced the herds of cattle throughout Ireland to an extent not experienced, according to this report, since the year 432. This would have affected all sections of society.

The Reform of the Irish Church

Despite many signs of secularisation in the Viking Age the Irish monasteries retained their reputation as centres of learning until the late eleventh century. This is shown by the career of Sulien, bishop of St David's in Wales (1073–78) who had been trained at Glendalough around 1050. His sons Rhigyfarch, Daniel and Ieuan were among the leading representatives of the Welsh Church in the early twelfth century; they were eminent both in literature and in Church affairs. The achievements of this family show that Ireland was still valued as an intellectual centre by the Welsh.

Besides this there were indications from the eleventh century onwards of a new leaning towards Rome. The pilgrimage to Rome by Donnchadh Ua Briain in 1064 has been mentioned (p. 116). He was not the first man to make the journey at that time. King Sitric of Dublin had been in Rome in 1028. The attachment to Rome becomes even more obvious in a literary work, a Life of Pope Gregory the Great, written presumably in the eleventh century. Gregory the Great had been called the Church's most important teacher in Ireland in the seventh century (PL 87, 975); he also appears in the Martyrology of Oengus (c. 800). In the Middle Irish Life (*Betha Grighóra*) this pope is linked with Ireland in an attractive way. For, according to this work, Pope Gregory was of Irish descent and had been buried on Inismore (Aran Islands). It is also of interest to note that Gregory's position as bishop of Rome is described in a similar way to the position of the bishops of Armagh in Ireland: *Grirorius pápa i. Grigóir náom comarba Petair* ('Pope Gregory, i.e. Saint Gregory, heir of Peter).[18]

The attachment of the Irish Church to Rome in the eleventh century, even before the Synod of Sutri of 1046 and the 'Gregorian Reform', has to be emphasised in order to counter the widespread idea that the reform of the Irish Church had been brought to Ireland from England. This is true only to a limited extent. It is, after all, possible to attribute the origins of the establishment of territorial bishoprics, one of the most important results of the Irish

Church reform, to King Sitric of Dublin. It is significant that the first bishops after the Roman model, that is bishops ruling territorial dioceses, appeared in the Scandinavian kingdoms on the Irish coast, in Dublin from 1074 at the latest, and some time later in Waterford and Limerick.

Four successive bishops of Dublin were consecrated in England by archbishops of Canterbury (Patrick, 1074; Donatus, 1085; Samuel, 1096; Gregory, 1121); Malchus, bishop of Waterford, was also consecrated by the archbishop of Canterbury, in 1096. All these bishops had been educated in England. We know less about the consecration of Gilbert, the first bishop of Limerick known by name. Neither the place nor the time of his consecration can be established; what is certain is that the archbishop of Canterbury, Anselm, did not consecrate him. Thus the first territorial bishoprics arose in the Scandinavian kingdoms, but not exclusively under English influence. It has been supposed that Gilbert was consecrated at Rouen. The influence of Canterbury on the reform of the Irish Church should not be underestimated, although it lasted only a few decades.

Moves towards reform, particularly in Munster, coincided with Canterbury's involvement in the ecclesiastical affairs of Ireland. King Tairrdelbach O'Brien corresponded with Pope Gregory VII who advised him to reform the Church, and in particular to change the Irish marriage laws which were unacceptable to Rome. This point had also been made by Archbishop Lanfranc in an exchange of letters with the same ruler. Yet just at the time of Canterbury's greatest influence on the Irish Church the king of Munster took the initiative. In 1101, Muirchertach, Tairrdelbach's son, handed over Cashel to the Church and presided over a reform synod there; unfortunately, the decisions of that gathering have not been preserved. However, it can be assumed that the need for a territorial structuring of the Irish Church had been of central concern along with the reform of the Irish marriage laws.

The Munster-based reform of the Church under the leadership of the O'Briens had wider repercussions; it was carried out without regard to the ambitions of Canterbury, without, indeed, any reference to England. In 1111 a further reform synod was assembled at Ráith Bressail; it was attended by 50 bishops, 300 priests and 3,000 clerics (AU). It was presided over by Gilbert of Limerick; in his capacity as papal legate, he showed the first signs of close links with Rome and an independent attitude towards Canterbury. The most important decision of this synod was to organise the Irish Church on the basis of two provinces (perhaps following Gregory the Great's model for the English Church as reported by Bede), with archbishoprics in Cashel and Armagh. The 'Scandinavian' bishoprics, especially Dublin, were not included.

Less spectacular, although not less important, were other aspects of the reform. In 1106 Cellach became abbot of Armagh; he was also in episcopal orders and the first cleric to hold this position for two centuries. Similar developments can be seen in other monasteries. The religious orders show that Ireland was at that time closely connected with the most advanced developments on the Continent. The Cistercian Malachy of Armagh (1113–48) provides a good example of this connection. He was a close friend of St Bernard of Clairvaux who after his death wrote a *Vita Malachiae*. Malachy begged the pope to be released from his episcopal office, without success; he is known to have founded the first Cistercian monastery in Ireland, Mellifont (Co. Louth). A few years later daughter houses were added, seven by 1153, eight more by 1172. Malachy is also credited with the introduction of the Rule of Augustine which spread widely and rapidly; in 1170 this Rule was observed in 63 houses in Ireland.

With Malachy as the driving force, the focus of reform in the Irish Church shifted noticeably to the north. The centre of reform remained in the north even after his death, and also under strong Cistercian auspices. In 1152 a further synod met at Kells and Mellifont which was presided over for the first time by a papal legate sent from Rome. The legate Paparo brought four pallia from the Cistercian pope Eugenius III, for the archbishoprics of Armagh (also primate), Tuam, Dublin and Cashel. This synod completely restructured the Irish Church, including the 'Scandinavian' bishoprics. The order that was established then lasted into modern times.

Finally, it should be mentioned that the reform of the Irish Church showed visible results. The creation of territorial dioceses was followed by the construction of cathedral churches, built of stone; these only occasionally show any influence of contemporary Continental or English architecture of that time. Generally speaking they were larger and lasted longer than the monastic churches of previous centuries. Many of the church ruins still visible in Ireland

today were the cathedrals of the new dioceses of the twelfth
century. The reform of the Irish Church stimulated building
activity until the end of the century, and this was carried out
predominantly by the Irish.

In the twelfth century the Irish Church was more closely linked
to the Continental Church than ever before; the synod of 1152 did
not herald the end of the reforming activities. The reform continued
and was now to include the older monasteries. At a synod at Brí
Maic Thaidg in 1158 the monasteries of the congregation of Colum
Cille were joined and placed under the abbot of Derry as general
abbot. Reforming activity continued uninterrupted into the first
years of the English intervention in Ireland.

A reform rarely comes to a satisfactory conclusion, but in Ireland
the Church had been reformed and modernised considerably in the
century after Gregory VII and largely without English influence.
In the light of this, Pope Adrian IV was not justified in 1155 in
granting the English king Henry II permission to go to Ireland in
order to reform the Church, which he did in the Bull *Laudabiliter*.[19]
Henry II did not come to Ireland until 1171, and then under
completely different circumstances and with different aims. Only
later generations were to establish a link between the coming of the
English and the English pope's mistaken ideas about Ireland. We
will come back to that at a later stage (pp. 160–61). It is now time
to look at the background to the 'Norman conquest of Ireland'.

The English Intervention in Ireland

The year 1169 is regarded by most Irish people as the nation's year
of destiny 'when the Normans came'. Before describing the political
events to which this phrase refers it is necessary to consider what
the inhabitants of the neighbouring island in the later twelfth
century should be called. Were they Normans, Anglo-Normans or
English?

The Norman Conquest of England had taken place a century
earlier, in 1066. The small groups of influential people who had
come with William the Conqueror to England and settled there
had adapted to native life in many ways in the course of a century.
From 1154 to 1399 the Plantagenets, who were of French descent,
ruled England. In accordance with the customs of the time this

dynasty was rooted in the European nobility that transcended national boundaries. But the aristocracy in England was less internationally-minded. From the late eleventh century onwards the nobility were gradually restricted limited to England partly because Normandy and England did not constitute a natural political unit. Nevertheless, for more than a century the English aristocracy cultivated the French language as the language of their social class; yet this should not be taken as an indication of their 'nationality'. Though the contrary has usually been assumed, it is now becoming clear that by the second half of the twelfth century the mother tongue in English aristocratic circles was predominantly English, not French. A confirmation of this is provided in the preamble to the Statutes of Kilkenny of 1366 (a document written in French!) where it is said unmistakably: 'At the time of the conquest of the land of Ireland and long thereafter the English of this country used the English language and English dress'. In his *Expugnatio Hibernica* Giraldus Cambrensis, one of the contemporary chroniclers of the English intervention in Ireland, referred to the conquerors nearly always as *Angli* 'English', and his usage is by no means unique.[20] This term is worth adopting even at the risk of disregarding long traditions in historiography: those who intervened in Ireland from the 1160s onwards will be called English or Anglo-Welsh, not Normans, Anglo-Normans or Cambro-Normans.

It has been shown already in the case of Dublin that Ireland had close contacts with England and France from the eleventh century on. The reform of the Irish Church shows links with these same countries. There is evidence of political connections which extended beyond Ireland, although on a smaller scale. For example, in 1102 Muirchertach Ua Briain married the daughter of Arnulf of Montgomery, one of the leading nobles of the Anglo-Norman kingdom. Munster maintained connections with the Continent. A tradition from Cashel claims that the king of Munster was to be elected according to the model of the German emperor. Cormac's Chapel on the Rock of Cashel was completed in 1135 under Cormac Mac Carthaigh, king of Munster, after the Regensburg model. There were further connections with Germany, such as the Irish monasteries (*Schottenklöster*) the first of which was established in the eleventh century. Even in these examples one can see a development of the Irish perspective on the world; perhaps one day a complete reassessment of this will be possible. As so often before, the south of Ireland was particularly open to innovations; yet the north also looked out beyond the sea. The Annals of Ulster record in the year 1174 the death of Flann Ua Gormáin 'arch-lector (*ardferleighinn*) of Armagh and of all of Ireland, a learned man, having been 21 years learning among the Franks and the Saxons and 20 years directing the schools of Ireland'. Contacts such as these between Ireland and the rest of Europe detract from the supposedly all-important Anglo-Irish link in the period after 1169. The circumstances surrounding the creation of this link were to develop in Leinster.

After the O'Briens the leadership of Ireland in the twelfth century was taken over by the O'Connors of Connacht. In 1120 Turloch O'Connor (1118–56) celebrated once again the Feast of Tara, thereby underlining his claim to the kingship of Ireland. He commissioned a magnificent reliquary cross, the Cross of Cong, c. 1123, the artistry of which shows Scandinavian influence, and this gives an impression of the way in which he wanted to be seen. His son Rory O'Connor (1166–86, † 1196) followed his father's example. His rule was celebrated by traditional encomia: 'A good mast this year as well as wealth and abundance of all things good has been given by God in this year of the reign of Rory O'Connor'. This is reported by the Continuator of Tigernach for the year 1168. By this time Dermot Mac Murrough of Leinster had already asked for support from England for his own plans.

Dermot Mac Murrough was king of Leinster from about 1134. In 1152 he abducted Devorgilla, wife of Tiernán O'Rourke, king of Bréifne. Devorgilla had allegedly agreed to her own abduction, but she returned to her husband in the following year. This, however, did not end the animosity between Mac Murrough and O'Rourke. In 1156 Murtough Mac Loughlin of the Uí Néill became high-king 'with opposition'. This opposition came especially from Rory O'Connor of Connacht who was also supported by O'Rourke. Mac Murrough was for the time being on the winning side. But his circumstances changed decisively when Rory O'Connor became high-king in 1166. Mac Murrough was driven from his kingdom; he went to England to seek support for its reconquest.

Henry II, king of England and ruler of a considerable part of France (1154–89), one of the most powerful monarchs of his time, was then on the Continent. Mac Murrough followed him there, became his vassal and requested permission to ask English nobles to help him in Ireland. Henry II agreed; in 1167 Mac Murrough managed to persuade some nobles from the Welsh Marches to help him, including the powerful earl Richard FitzGilbert de Clare, called Strongbow, Lord of Strigoil, to whom he offered his daughter Aoife (Eva) in marriage and the succession in the kingdom of Leinster. On his journey to Ireland he gained the support of further nobles from south Wales, the FitzHenries, Carews, FitzGeralds and Barrys, as well as some Flemish families, Prendergast, Fleming, Roche, Synnott, etc. whose ancestors had been settled in Pembrokeshire since the early twelfth century. The men who came with Mac Murrough were mostly the younger members of noble families whose prospects of success at home were poor.

When Mac Murrough did return to Ireland in the autumn of 1167, only a few of these new allies were with him. He managed, however, to regain Ferns, the monastery of which was closely connected with his family, but then had to submit to the united force of O'Connor and O'Rourke. In this situation he approached his allies in Wales for help. In May 1169 the first knights landed near Wexford, supported by Welsh cross-bowmen under the leadership of Robert FitzStephen, Robert de Barry and Maurice de Prendergast. With their help Dermot managed to take the town of Wexford. O'Connor and O'Rourke then decided to recognise Mac Murrough as king of Leinster once again but did so on the condition that he send back his foreign helpers. Mac Murrough, however, called for more help. In August 1170 Strongbow arrived with more knights. Waterford was taken, and in September 1170 Dublin fell into the hands of the Anglo-Welsh troops. Dermot gave his daughter to Strongbow in marriage, and when he died at Ferns in the spring of 1171, Strongbow, as agreed, became his successor as king of Leinster. He encountered some degree of opposition in his new kingdom, but his achievements, particularly the successful defence of Dublin in the spring of 1171 against massive attacks by Irish and Norse, had created a new situation.

The Irish, although numerically far superior, could not stop the Anglo-Welsh troops. It now became evident that it had not been entirely to the advantage of the Irish to have lived for centuries rather undisturbed by military attacks from outside. The Irish had not adopted recent innovations in armament, and the mail-coated Anglo-Welsh knight could not easily be harmed. Giraldus Cambrensis was right in this respect when he drew attention to the antiquated way in which the Irish fought with primitive arms and riding their horses without saddles.

The Anglo-Welsh nobles, on the other hand, were equipped in a far more modern fashion; they fought on horseback and were supported by the effective Welsh cross-bowmen. They fought with superior arms; in addition, they were well trained through their fights against the Welsh. As they had done in Wales, they built castles of the motte and bailey type, i.e. fortified houses with pallisade fencing, set up on hill tops which were sometimes man-made. These were their first strongholds from which they could determine to some extent the course of events.

Without wishing to detract from the achievements of the Anglo-Welsh, it should be pointed out that their success against a numerically superior enemy was not only due to their superior equipment and fighting techniques. Particularly during the first two years their successes were often threatened and they seem to have fought for many months in what would have appeared a hopeless situation. They had taken a dangerous gamble and they fought with determination born of desperation. Where possible, they fought in places where they had a strategic advantage; they fought in areas which until then had hardly been involved in the wars among Irish rulers. These qualifications must be made because they highlight the difficulties the English were to face when they tried to conquer the whole island.

The situation in the east of Ireland developed a stage further in October 1171 with the arrival of King Henry II. He came for a number of reasons: on the one hand he was concerned that his vassals in Ireland should not become too strong and wanted to show them that he was still their king. On the other hand, after the murder of Archbishop Thomas Becket of Canterbury in December 1170, a crime for which he was widely blamed, it seemed appropriate for Henry to withdraw for a while from the main stage of events. What is more, he could be seen to act meritoriously by fighting for Christianity in a remote country. Now he could apply the spirit of the Bull *Laudabiliter* to his own advantage without having to submit implicitly to the pope as feudal overlord as the Bull had implied.

All these considerations played a part in the events of the year that Henry II spent in Ireland. Strongbow submitted to the king, and received Leinster as a fief. The king took Dublin under his protection and in 1172 issued the first charter for 'his' city.[21] The Irish kings in the southeast of the country submitted. Waterford and Wexford received royal garrisons. The entire clergy under the leadership of Christian, bishop of Lismore and papal legate, recognised him in Cashel as their highest lord. Henry granted Meath to Hugh de Lacy. Even though Connacht and Ulster still remained outside the reach of the English king, his success in Ireland was remarkable. When Henry II left Ireland, he appointed Hugh de Lacy as justiciar (king's representative) and administrator of Dublin. In 1173 Pope Alexander III congratulated him on his successes in Ireland which he thereby implicitly recognised. In 1175 Henry went a step further: in the Treaty of Windsor, Rory O'Connor of Connacht submitted to the king in return for the overlordship over those areas which had not yet been conquered. These are the first indications of a division of Ireland into an English and an Irish area. Two years later, in 1177, Henry appointed his youngest son John, who up until then had not been provided for, as Lord of Ireland (*Dominus Hiberniae*).

From these events it can be seen that Ireland did not experience an English 'Conquest' in the manner of the Norman Conquest of England a century earlier. This type of conquest was impossible simply because Ireland had no effective central government which the English king could take over. Thus their relatively archaic political system proved to be of advantage to the Irish. A better comparison than England would be the Norman conquests in southern Italy in the eleventh century. More generally, the English intervention in Ireland may be seen as yet another example of the widespread expansion of the greater European states in the twelfth and thirteenth centuries.

Dublin in the Late Twelfth Century

In 1172 Henry II granted in a charter 'to my people from Bristol my city of Dublin to inhabit', and thus conferred on Dublin the liberties and customs of Bristol (which in turn were based on the customs of Breteuil in Normandy).[22] Dublin was the first town in Ireland to be directly subject to the Crown; others were to follow.

From the late twelfth century there exists a list of Dublin burghers,[23] which in some cases gives information about their places of origin. The list contains around 1600 names. In about 400 names we can recognise toponyms that can be taken as more or less reliable (e.g. *Willielmus de Licifelt* 'William of Lichfield'); where no toponym is given, it might be assumed that the person concerned was a Dubliner by origin. According to this list, many people in Dublin originated from various places in England, Scotland and Wales, as well as in Ireland (cf. Map 3); few, on the other hand, had come from the Continent, only thirteen from St Omer and seven from France generally (*Francigena*).

It is noticeable that London is well represented, with 30 names, but it does not take first place. The first position is held by Cardiff in Wales with 33 names. Five out of the seven English towns (London apart) that are represented by ten or more names are situated in the southwest and in the vicinity of the Welsh Marches. They are (with the numbers of the names in brackets) Gloucester (28), Worcester (28), Bristol (14), Exeter (13), Northampton (11), Hereford (10), Bedford (10). Especially interesting, in view of the charter of 1172, is the relatively small number of names from Bristol.

Of the 400 people whose place of origin is mentioned, the area of south Wales is particularly well represented with 108 names; it is that area from which many nobles originated who came to Ireland in 1167 and later. Significantly, it is an area that was only loosely connected with the English Crown. In addition to Cardiff the following places appear (with the number of names in brackets): Haverford(west) (11), Strigoil (the place Strongbow came from) (10), Tenby (5), Kidwelli (5), Pembroke (4), Brecon (3), Carmarthen (3), Swansea (2), Newport (1), Fishguard (1), Gwent (1), Ewias (1), Gower (1), Beaumaris (1). There are a further five non-localised *Walenses*. The frequent reference to *Flandrensis* (13 cases) probably refers to the Flemings who were settled in Pembroke in 1108 by Henry I and who are known to have kept their separate identity for more than a century.[24]

Lastly, it must be mentioned that Irish people who were not born in Dublin also lived in Dublin under English rule, few (39), however, compared to Welsh people. They originated from Cork (10), Castledermot (Tristeldermot) (4), Kildare (3), Kilmainham (2), Lismore (2), Waterford (2), Leighlin (2), Naas (2), Clonard (2), and one representative each from Bray, Carlow, Drogheda,

Map 3: Ireland and western Britain c. 1200

Kilkenny, Limerick, Oxmantown, Trim, Wexford, Ulster and one unlocalised *Hibernensis*.

The figures given here apply only to a quarter of the burghers of Dublin, but even as an approximate guide these figures have their significance as they reflect to some extent the political situation in Ireland in the second half of the twelfth century. The Anglo-Welsh nobility had brought a number of dependents with them; relatives and acquaintances were to follow later. In this respect, the composition of Dublin's population seems to have accurately reflected the range of influence of its new lords. People from the southwest of England, south Wales and the south of Ireland were much more numerous within the walls of Dublin than people from other parts of England and the neighbouring countries.

Intellectual Life

In the intellectual life of twelfth-century Ireland, native traditions mingled with new influences to an even greater extent than at any previous time. There emerged a more comprehensive presentation of Irish history, both in compilations and in original compositions. As far as is known, the most important developments in this field took place in the west of Ireland.

A 'history' of the reign of Brian Boru was written in Munster in the early twelfth century: *Cogadh Gaedheal re Gallaibh* 'The war of the Irish against the foreigners'; it was probably commissioned by Muirchertach Ua Briain. According to this work, the king of Munster's main motivation in the political struggles had been to expel the Vikings from Ireland. Brian is said to have pacified the country to such an extent that (using a topos quite widely employed) 'a woman could walk from Tory in the north of Ireland to Cliedhna in the south, and she was not molested even though she wore a gold circle'. By glorifying the Battle of Clontarf the author hoped to keep alive the historical claim of the O'Briens to the national kingship of Tara in the twelfth century.

Representative of the way native tradition was used is a manuscript from Clonmacnois, the so-called Book of the Dun Cow (*Leabhar na hUidhre*). According to the colophon the bulk of the manuscript was written by Maol Mhuire who died in 1106. Maol Mhuire came from a family of scholars and nobles; his genealogy can be traced back as far as the early ninth century and to an abbot of Armagh. *Leabhar na hUidhre* contains the earliest transmitted literary texts of some length in the Irish language, the *Táin*, the elegy on Colum Cille, as well as many other texts of secular and Christian subjects.

The Book of Rights, *Lebor na Cert*, dates from around 1100: in it, the hierarchical structure of Irish society is described and the rights and duties of the various kings are listed. This work continued a tradition which had been started in the Psalter of Cashel, *Saltair Caissil* (now lost) in the early tenth century. A further compilation of Irish texts in one volume, a typical Irish *bibliotheca*, was written around 1120, probably at Clonmacnois, and is now in the Bodleian Library in Oxford (MS Rawlinson B 502). This volume also contains Christian and secular texts, an indication that both kinds of literature were cultivated by clerics. The Book of Leinster, *Leabhar Laighneach*, with a lament on the exile of King Dermot Mac Murrough, can be dated to the 1160s. It was compiled by Aed Mac Crimthainn, abbot of Terryglass.

Apart from these works concerned with Irish history and mythology, Ireland was exposed to a new wave of European literature. At the close of the twelfth century works like the Aeneid, the Pharsalia and the Thebais were translated into Irish. These are tangible results of the increasing internationalisation of Irish society, although it is impossible to determine how exactly these works came into Irish hands. It could have happened through the religious orders, through nobles from England and Wales or through Irish people who had been abroad.

Furthermore, the emergence of the *filid* as the Bardic Order in the course of the late eleventh and the twelfth centuries should be mentioned. There had been poets, *filid*, in Ireland from prehistoric times, but in the course of the twelfth century new forms of poetry were developed, forms that were to persist for the next five centuries. The new methods of composition were so strict and were observed so closely that experts find it nearly impossible to determine on the basis of language when or where a particular poem was written. Bardic poetry is characterised by lines with seven syllables and stanzas of four lines, with a break after the second line. The number of stanzas is not prescribed. From the twelfth century onwards, the *filid* used this verse form to herald the qualities of their patrons, to record history and to comment on political events. These will be dealt with later (p, 103ff.). They are mentioned here because the development of the Bardic Order at this time shows that Irish intellectual life in the twelfth century displayed considerable dynamism and vitality. This is yet another indication that Irish society was not as archaic and immobile as Giraldus Cambrensis had maintained.

The increased openness of Ireland to the outside world can even be seen in the annals which until then had recorded mostly national events. In the course of the twelfth century the Annals of Ulster report more events from outside Ireland, particularly from England (the 'land of the Saxons'), even before 1169, but also from Scotland and Italy. An entry from 1098 should be mentioned because it combines the unusual with the general: 'Domnall Ua Enna, eminent bishop of the West of Europe and fount of the generosity of the world, doctor of either Law, namely of the Romans and of the Gaidil . . . died'. Until then Ireland had usually been the field of reference; now this field was to be western Europe. The explicit statement that Roman Law and Irish secular law had been mastered by one scholar is something quite new.

10.   Ireland from the Reign of John to the Statutes of Kilkenny

The history of Ireland in the thirteenth, fourteenth and fifteenth centuries is not easy to write without evoking anachronistic parallels to modern times. The very high degree of continuity in the history of Ireland in the first part of the Middle Ages is also a feature of the second part of the Middle Ages, albeit under somewhat different conditions. Central issues of the second part of the Middle Ages somehow seem to lead straight into the 'Irish question' of the present time. This view is often taken by Irish historians and is widespread among the general public. Those English historians who deal with Ireland – mostly in terms of how far Ireland exerted a negative influence on English politics – tend to complain that it has been impossible to settle the Irish question because the Irish keep changing it.

It is in some respects easier for the outsider to take a position which is beyond either Irish self-pity or English self-righteousness even at the risk of being accused by both sides of lack of understanding. The outsider can avoid the temptation to write 'them' while meaning 'us'. There is a historical reality to the view that there were two nations in later medieval Ireland, an idea developed in Ireland and quite widely held. In this case the existence of two nations meant that there were social groups which in other European countries appeared homogenous but which were treated differently in Ireland in that not all members of these groups had equal rights and duties as a matter of principle.

This applies throughout the second part of the Middle Ages. Ireland was under English rule. After the English conquest of Wales many of the privileges of the native aristocracy had at first been respected by the English conquerors and then gradually weakened. It was the intention of the English king that the Irish were to be ruled from the beginning according to the English model. To this end English institutions were transferred to Ireland and an administration was set up which was almost identical with that of England, only a few sizes smaller. It is hardly surprising that this English system failed in the long term; what is more surprising is that it was able to function at all.

The English system could not simply be transferred to Ireland for a number of reasons, all of which are interrelated

The most important reason seems to have been that there was no English ruler resident in Ireland who could assert his authority on a regular basis. Beginning with John, every English king was also Lord of Ireland (*Dominus Hiberniae*). It remains an open question whether it would have been more successful to continue to appoint a separate lord from among the royal family, as Henry II had done by naming John. In any case, the medieval English system of government was unthinkable without regular periods when the ruler was in his country, for it had been developed specifically to function on this assumption. Whenever the king was absent from the country for any extended time, the system soon showed considerable strains. When that system was transferred to Ireland and lacked even the occasional presence of a ruler, its effectiveness was reduced dramatically.

Relevant to this problem is the fact that the English conquest of Ireland remained incomplete. English law was only given to those who submitted to English rule. Those who did not were regarded as 'rebels' and could expect draconian punishment if they were caught. Such punishment was intended as a deterrent but because of this English law in Ireland often appeared harsher and more unfair than in England. Naturally, since the English conquest remained incomplete there were 'rebels' in Ireland throughout the second part of the Middle Ages, people who had no claim to Common Law. Common Law, as it developed under Henry II in England, gave equal treatment to all freemen whether of Saxon or Norman descent, and, a century after the Norman Conquest of England, the greatest differences between conquerors and conquered had disappeared. Those Irish who did not live under Common Law did not feel obliged to respect the royal peace, that most eminent symbol of rulership. This fact is indicative of the difference between royal rule in Ireland and England; in England internal wars were the exception and had no great prospect of success.

In the absence of the king local lordships emerged which were difficult to control. While the 'rebels' continued to use their own institutions and confirmed themselves by this as a separate 'nation' with their own language, culture and laws, the situation of the Anglo-Irish, the descendants of the Anglo-Welsh conquerors who settled in Ireland, was much more complex. In theory they were subject to the established English government in Ireland, but generally speaking they were not allowed to participate in this government, a fact that made them very different from their social equals in England. Westminster expected that the Anglo-Irish would submit to the authority of the government officials. It may have appeared appropriate to fill higher administrative posts in Ireland, where possible, with people who held no property in the country and who were thus less tempted to serve their own interests above those of the distant king. The situation was more difficult in practice because the Crown felt it could ill afford to send experienced first-rate people to Ireland when they were needed at home. This resulted in a dilemma: people from outside had to get used to the specific problems of Ireland; the longer they worked in Ireland, the more likely they became to make important decisions according to the actual situation on the spot, which could easily be misunderstood in England or interpreted as self-interest. It was often the case that English higher administrative officials in Ireland came to advocate Anglo-Irish interests eventually.

Finally it has to be remembered that from the English point of view Ireland in the later medieval centuries was only one of several areas which demanded the attention of the English Crown. More important, and geographically closer, for the English Crown in the thirteenth century was Wales, and in the later thirteenth and fourteenth centuries Scotland; and even more important in the fourteenth and fifteenth centuries, because war there promised greater rewards, was France. What may appear to Irish historians as a lack of interest in Ireland on the part of English rulers assumes a different dimension when one considers that the English kings treated Ireland within a wider framework, as only one of several countries which lay in England's sphere of influence.

The New Lords

The Anglo-Welsh nobles had come to Ireland with their followers because they had been given promises of land. Like the Normans in the first couple of generations after the conquest of England they had family, and often property, on both sides of the sea and remained, at least partially, integrated in the political system of their country of origin. This went beyond a theoretical subjection to their feudal lord the English king. Thus Strongbow and de Lacy, two years after their arrival in Ireland, were commanded by the English king to do military service in France. In the course of the thirteenth century, personal military service was largely abolished and replaced by a money payment (scutage), which the Anglo-Irish nobles had to pay just like their English counterparts.

In the course of the thirteenth century certain changes became evident. Families of English descent who no longer owned property in England gradually established themselves in Ireland. The proper term for these families is Anglo-Irish once all ties with England had been severed. Although of English descent and language they lived in Ireland without, as yet, integrating themselves into Irish society. In a letter to the papal curia in 1317 these people were referred to as a *media natio* but signs of this phenomenon can already be detected from the very beginning of the English intervention. Maurice FitzGerald, an uncle of Giraldus Cambrensis, is credited with the saying: 'To the English we are Irish, to the Irish we are English'.[25] Naturally, this phenomenon was less apparent in the uppermost layer of society. The families of de Clare, de Lacy or Marshall continued to have property and interests in England, Wales and Ireland. However, over the years they also were confronted with the question which of their properties, the Irish or the English, they should administer in person. When income from the Irish properties declined, or when the defence of these properties became more difficult, the landlords' interest in them soon declined, and they concentrated their attention on the more profitable of their estates. What applies in general to the king's policy regarding the Lordship of Ireland was reflected in the attitude of each individual landlord to his property.

It is necessary to return once more to the first generation of English in Ireland. The prospects of land and wealth had brought the English to Ireland. They had to fight for that land. Once they had occupied an area, the first step was to build a fortification, usually of the motte type. The mere existence of these castles is an important indication of the legal position of the English nobles in Ireland vis-à-vis the Crown. In England the building of castles was a royal prerogative, jealously guarded by Henry II after the civil wars under King Stephen (1135–54). In Ireland, on the other hand, the English nobles built their castles with the approval of the king. Those parts of Ireland which were under English control showed, through the very existence of the castles, the essential characteristics of Marcher land: that the aristocracy could, and indeed had to, act largely according to their own decisions.

Within the protective range of these castles, manors of the English type were established. In the first part of the Middle Ages the Irish economy had not been as exclusively cattle rearing as Giraldus Cambrensis among others had claimed, but nevertheless the English lords with new methods and more capital reaped far better harvests than their Irish predecessors had done. This intensification of agriculture from the late twelfth century onwards should not, however, be equated with the internal colonisation that was taking place elsewhere in Europe at that time. The English lords rarely opened up new farmland. Instead, they tended to settle in areas which were already being used for agriculture. A particularly good example of this is Meath which the de Lacys exploited more intensively than had been done previously. Most towns in Meath developed around English castles; the same can be said for the whole of Ireland with the exception of the coastal towns of Scandinavian origin.

The English lands were generally worked with the help of immigrants from England or Wales; these would normally receive a piece of land (a burgage plot) from the lord of the castle which they would work themselves, often free of obligations or dues for a certain period. Not all of these settlements developed into towns, many remained 'rural boroughs' in effect, mere villages. In addition, there was the lord's demesne which he usually worked himself. The manors sometimes developed into villages, a form of settlement hitherto unknown in Ireland. There are some indications that Irish of unfree status were taken over by the English without a change in their legal position. These people are called *betagii* in the Latin sources, a loan from the Irish *betagh* (derived from the verb *bíathaid*, 'feeds').

The Irish and English coexisted on all levels of society. The marriage of Strongbow and Aoife was not an exceptional case; Hugh de Lacy married a daughter of Rory O'Connor and others were to follow these examples. Initially there was no major confrontation between English and Irish. Just as in the Viking Age, there was no expression of the feeling that national freedom was threatened. The political circumstances which might have led to such a feeling did not exist and no such consciousness had developed. Personal interests were paramount, and alliances were formed according to individual and short-term gain. One should not read too much into the fact that the Irish annals describe the English, as they had once described the Vikings, as the foreigners. They continued to be called 'foreigners' when they had developed characteristics which were highly regarded by the Irish.

At first sight it does not appear that English rule meant fundamental change in Ireland. Like the Vikings three centuries earlier the English were an additional element on the political scene, nothing more. There were new names, but little change in the manner of rule. However, on closer inspection, there are some important differences between Scandinavian settlements in Ireland and those of the English. The Norsemen in Ireland had from very early on detached themselves completely from their home country and had long remained isolated from the Irish. Culturally, the Irish could feel superior to the Vikings as long as the latter remained pagan. Integration came in the end largely through the assimilation of the Scandinavians.

A similar development also occurred in the case of the English although over a longer period of time. Initially, they brought new methods of government to Ireland, methods that had been tested and proven in England. There are indications that some Irish rulers had followed the English example even before 1169. Dermot Mac Murrough issued charters according to the English model, and he was not the only one to do so. According to their charters, other Irish rulers, especially in Connacht, employed chancellors and notaries. However, there are very few cases of such imitation of English (or Continental) modes of government, and they did not extend beyond the thirteenth century. Nevertheless, the English had a level of culture similar to that of the Irish, even though it manifested itself in very different ways.

When Strongbow died in 1176, his daughter Isabella de Clare was a minor. At that time most of Leinster was in English hands, so English customs were applied. Until Isabella came of age, her land was administered by Crown officials. In 1189 Isabella married William Marshall, one of the most eminent nobles in England. The last Irish king in Leinster for some time was Murtagh Mac Murrough, Dermot's son, who died in 1192.

In 1177 John de Courcy came to Ireland from England, probably sent by the king. Subsequently he became active in Ulster, which had remained relatively unaffected until then. He was able to conquer the area east of the River Bann and established a number of castles which were later to develop into towns: Carrickfergus, Downpatrick, Dromore, Coleraine, Newry, Carlingford. John de Courcy went his own way in some respects. He did not hesitate to cooperate with the Irish and he was the first English noble to take an interest in Irish tradition. In 1185 he asked Jocelin de Furness to write a Life of St Patrick; after all, he ruled a part of the country which was believed to have been Patrick's main area of activity.

'John Lackland, son of the king of the Saxons, came to Ireland' (in 1185) (*hEoan Sinter /idon sineterra/ mag rígh Saxan, do techt i n-Eirinn*, AU, 1185). He arrived in Munster from south Wales, coming via a route which was to be the one most widely used for another two centuries. Among his companions was Giraldus Cambrensis who already had relatives in Ireland (he was a de Barry) and who now used the opportunity to collect material for his books about Ireland. According to the report of Giraldus, the young English prince and Lord of Ireland behaved in an impossible manner; he pulled the beards of the Irish kings who had come to honour him, and was amused by their infuriated reaction. But John's visit was not the disaster Giraldus claimed it had been.

John was accompanied by new people to whom he granted land. A part of Limerick he gave to Theobald Walter († 1205), from the family of the hereditary butlers of England (Botiller, later Butler), a nephew of the future English justiciar and archbishop of Canterbury, Hubert Walter. Philip of Worcester and Hubert de Burgh received extensive lands in Tipperary; some of those lands were still in Irish hands and had yet to be conquered. From Munster, John went to Dublin via Kildare. He appointed John de Courcy justiciar, the highest secular office and the king's representative in his absence. De Courcy remained in this office until 1192. Philip of Worcester was made temporary administrator of Meath.

Hugh de Lacy, the last important representative of the first generation of the English in Ireland, died in 1186. In the following years, John de Courcy advanced from Ulster into Connacht. Difficulties arose with the English Crown after the accession of King John in 1199 when John de Courcy apparently refused to do homage for Ulster. What is more, he openly allied himself with the Irish, particularly with the O'Connors of Connacht. The Crown

therefore gave a free hand to Hugh de Lacy the Younger in Ulster
and in 1205 he was made earl of Ulster.

In 1207 William Marshall came to Ireland to look after his
possessions in Leinster. He remained in the country for almost six
years and became an important support for the Crown when John
ran into difficulties with the Church and his barons in England. In
1210 King John came once again to Ireland, mainly in order to
restrain some defiant nobles. In contrast to his visit 25 years
earlier, he now came as king of England and with much greater
authority. He drove Hugh de Lacy out of Ulster, which was not
restored to him until 1227. But his particular wrath was aimed at
the de Braose family. William de Braose, a Welsh Marcher Lord,
had quarrelled with him in 1210 and afterwards spread the rumour
that John had personally strangled his nephew Arthur of Brittany.
John allowed William's wife to starve in prison. He repossessed the
de Braose lands in Limerick and subsequently treated them as
Crown property. Almost all Irish kings payed homage to John
during this visit. He ordered prelates and magnates to implement
English law. John's visit conveys some idea of what English rule
could have achieved had a king been resident in Ireland, but after
his departure at the end of the year no English king was to come to
Ireland for almost two centuries. This was to have important
consequences.

This outline of the first 50 years of the English presence in
Ireland shows that the overall situation in the country remained
rather complex. Although the English king regarded himself as the
highest feudal lord in Ireland, both of the English and the Irish, his
power reached only as far as that of his officials and of his direct
feudal vassals. Those Irish kings who still remained had submitted
only because John was in the country. Since each new English king
after John was also Lord of Ireland, it should have been required of
Irish kings to do homage to their new lord; this, however, none of
them did.

The area of English rule was not uniformly under royal control.
Almost all of the towns were directly subject to the Crown and
were endowed with special privileges. The Crown land was
subdivided into counties and administered by royal officials under
the supervision of sheriffs. The establishment of these counties
shows the growth of English control: Dublin (1199), Cork,
Waterford (1207), Munster, Tipperary, Limerick (1211), Louth,

Kerry (1233), Connacht (1247), Roscommon (1292), Carlow (1306). In those areas where there were no counties, the Irish territorial units remained more or less intact, even though under new rulers. The so-called Liberties were comparable with English palatine earldoms: the most important were Leinster, Ulster and Meath. These Liberties were not yet granted through titles. They were also to be subject to English law which was not to be administered by Crown officials but independently by the administration of the franchisal lord.

It was generally intended that Ireland would be administered from Dublin and on the English model. It received English administrative personnel except that it usually took some years or even decades for English institutions to be established in Ireland. Justiciars are attested from 1172, the Exchequer from 1200, the Treasury from 1217, Itinerant Justices from 1218, the Chancellor from 1232. Of special importance was the office of the Escheator which was charged with the administration of royal fiefs that, for whatever reasons, had temporarily fallen to the Crown. It is significant, particularly in view of the Lord of Ireland's absence from the country, that no offices were created which were specifically designed for the Irish situation.

The Church had caused the least difficulty in the early years. As early as 1172 the bishops of the country had submitted to the English king at Cashel; in the following year, Pope Alexander III wrote to Ireland, approving of what the English king had done there. The most important representative of the Irish clergy in these decisive years was Lorcán Ua Tuathail, popularly known as Laurence O'Toole, archbishop of Dublin from 1162. He had attempted from the beginning to mediate between the English and the Irish; he is villified for this by Irish historians to the present. It does not improve his reputation that he later ran into difficulties with Henry II and died an exile in Normandy in 1180. Instead, historians point to his 'collaboration' during the siege of Dublin in 1170 as well as to his intervention in the negotiation of the Treaty of Windsor in 1175. Yet all the Irish clergy regarded themselves as forming part of the supranational Church, and it was therefore their Christian duty to promote peace by all possible means. The fact that the clergy came to terms with the Crown is hardly surprising since most Irish rulers had done precisely the same in a similar situation.

Lorcán Ua Tuathail was the last archbishop of Dublin of Irish descent for several centuries, he was canonised in 1225. Yet the initiative for that did not come from Ireland, but from Eu in Normandy where he died. In 1181 John Comyn became archbishop of Dublin, and in 1192 he laid the foundation for the second of Dublin's cathedrals, St Patrick's. His successor, Henry of London, is famous as the builder of Dublin Castle which was started in 1212. At the time of the Fourth Lateran Council in 1215, only a quarter of the 36 Irish bishoprics were held by Englishmen; the election of English candidates was due largely to the Anglo-Irish, not to the Crown. Under Henry of London, the first tensions surfaced in the Irish Church, but these were due mainly to him personally, not to the Irish. For he claimed the primacy for the see of Dublin and thereby came into conflict with the successor of St Patrick at Armagh.

In 1213, King John had submitted to Pope Innocent III as his feudal vassal and received England and Ireland as a papal fief. The arrangement that had been suggested by Pope Adrian IV in the Bull *Laudabiliter* in 1155 and which had been rejected at that time by the Crown now became law under completely different circumstances. As the highest feudal authority, the pope now had more scope for intervention in the affairs of Ireland than in other countries.

Giraldus Cambrensis was still alive at that time. The last two chapters of his *Expugnatio Hibernica*, a work completed in its first version around 1189 and later revised several times, describe how Ireland should be conquered and subsequently ruled. It is important to remember that Giraldus advocated the initial creation of local centres of power through the building of castles which were then to be extended; this had more or less happened. Most interestingly of all, he regarded it as particularly important to adapt to the existing circumstances in Ireland. In his opinion, heavily armed knights on horseback could not achieve much in the woodlands and bogs of Ireland. Instead, the English should be prepared to fight on foot in order not to let the Irish enemy escape. That did not mean, however, that Irish weapons should be adopted. On the contrary, Giraldus emphasised the great advantage which the English had in the effective Welsh long-bow. He generally recommended that the English rely on the experiences of the first generation who had fought in Ireland; their success had largely been due to their experience of guerilla warfare in the Welsh Marches. In addition to this technical advice, he also emphasised the importance of taking the psychology of the enemy into account. Giraldus thus recommended that those Irish who were prepared to cooperate be treated well; in the case of temporary defections, harsh punishment was justified, but the English should also be prepared to forgive.

These considerations deserve attention because they deal with the essential nature of England's problems in Ireland. Ideas such as these surfaced from time to time during the following centuries. They also help to explain why Ireland was never completely conquered and anglicised in the Middle Ages.

The Limits of Expansion

In the course of the thirteenth century the English conquered more than three-quarters of Ireland, or so we are told in most of the textbooks. The question is often raised why the whole of Ireland was not conquered, and it is answered in various ways.

When one charts the success of English activities in Ireland, considerable variations emerge. It had started promisingly in 1169 and received its greatest boost through John's visit in 1210. The next 50 years of English rule, on the other hand, show a remarkable levelling-off, and at the close of the thirteenth century the downward trend begins to show. This is revealed by small symptoms at first, but by the early fourteenth century it had become more noticeable. There are a number of reasons for this course of events; none of these is decisive in itself but they combine to support each other.

One part of the answer is that the English-ruled areas of Ireland reflected to a remarkable degree the course of English history. The turbulent and crisis-ridden reign of Henry III (1216–72) did not allow the Crown to take an active part in Irish affairs. From the year 1234 we have the first request from Ireland that the king should come or at least send his brother.[26] Requests of this kind were made with increasing frequency and urgency over the next two centuries; they were never adequately answered.

Due to the complex structure of the areas of Ireland under English control internal English politics could only have a limited influence on what happened in Ireland. It was only in the counties, which were directly administered by Crown officials, that the effects of English internal politics were felt immediately. These areas were, however, only part of the English sphere of influence. The impression is given that the king did little to expand these areas for the political structures that had arisen unsystematically in the first half-century were to a large degree maintained.

Outside the areas organised into counties, there were other areas like the Liberties which had their own lords; these were on the whole fully occupied with looking after their lands and keeping the peace. These lords did not have any official mandate to enlarge the area of English rule and were only intermittently prepared to attempt it. Adventurers like those of the first generation were no longer attracted in such numbers, especially once the richest prizes in land had been distributed. Besides, once the English king had become the Lord of the whole of Ireland, in title at least, the scope for such people had become much more limited. The political situation made it, for the time being, unnecessary to push for the conquest of the whole island. It was more important for the Crown to have English rule recognised in all parts of Ireland and particularly by the Irish kings; this also cost less. It was to take the Crown quite some time to realise that there was a wide gap between its theoretical position and the actual state of affairs; when they finally became aware of this, nothing was done to narrow that gap.

There are, however, other considerations. The English and Welsh lords of the first two generations had been successful mainly because they could attract large numbers of immigrants from England and Wales who could provide a relatively stable basis for the new lordships. However, these immigrants were not in unlimited supply. It soon emerged that many of these people preferred to live in the towns rather than in the country. If English rule could expand at all under these circumstances, this was due only to a few dynamic men who were able to exploit the disagreements among the Irish to their own advantage. Nevertheless, throughout the thirteenth century there remained in the whole of Ireland enclaves in which Irish people lived quite unaffected by English rule. It should be emphasised that there were enclaves of this kind all over the island, including Leinster, the province where English rule was strongest.

This can be explained by taking into consideration both geographical factors and the different fighting methods used by the

Irish and English. The Irish may well have been inferior to the English in open battle, but they avoided open battle as far as possible. On the wooded hills, however, as well as in the lowland bogs, English arms and methods of fighting were not very successful. The knight on horseback was well protected but also rather slow. It is significant that, in the course of the following century, the Anglo-Irish increasingly went over to the Irish way of fighting, even to the extent of giving up the use of saddles. The Irish, on the other hand, felt no need to adapt to English methods of fighting. This was to work to their advantage in the long term.

The expansion of English rule in the thirteenth century is due mainly to one family, the de Burgo or de Burgh (later Burke). As early as 1192 this family had been offered Connacht; the offer was renewed in 1222 to Richard de Burgh. In 1232 he fell from favour because his brother Hubert de Burgh had run into political difficulties in England. It was only after a reconciliation with the king that Richard could begin the advance into Connacht in 1235. He was quite successful in this and with King Felim O'Connor he was able to arrange a partition of their respective spheres of influence. This arrangement did not last long, but it showed de Burgh's readiness to come to some kind of accommodation with the Irish. This was almost inevitable since there were hardly any English settlers available for the economic exploitation of Connacht. De Burgh had to rely largely on the cooperation of the Irish. On the other hand, English influences can be detected at O'Connor's court. From the thirteenth century on, the family employed an official, *marasgál*, whose title had obviously been borrowed from the English.

These are undeniable signs of the expansion of English influence, but a number of setbacks occurred as early as the thirteenth century, due primarily to the nature of the English system. In the years 1243 and 1245 the heads of important families, those of de Lacy and Marshall, died without leaving male heirs. Had they left male heirs, inheritance would have been according to primogeniture; had they died without any legitimate heirs, their lands would have reverted to the Crown to be disposed of at the king's pleasure. As it happened, the lords were survived by sisters and daughters, and the lands were divided between these. Because of this, Anglo-Irish rule weakened considerably in these Liberties, which effectively balanced out the gains in Connacht. This also drew attention to the catastrophic consequences of the fact that the highest feudal lord did not reside in the country and, in the case of minority inheritance, could not effectively protect the land of the heirs as was his duty.

In 1263, Walter de Burgh became Earl of Ulster. This marks the real beginning of the granting of Irish titles by the Crown, a practice that was to become more common in the following century. Walter's son Richard, known as the Red Earl, became the most important man in Ireland during his long period of rule, 1286 to 1320. He extended the sphere of English influence westwards beyond Derry into Donegal. In 1302 he gave his daughter Elizabeth in marriage to Robert Bruce, the future Scottish king. Richard de Burgh was quite successful since, like his uncle in Connacht, he did not hesitate to cooperate with the Irish.

Alongside the English lordships Irish rule also survived, although to a limited extent. The Irish lords owed some of their power to the system to which they belonged, and in the course of the fourteenth century they managed to regain a dominant position. It is true that internal disputes about the kingship regularly arose among the O'Connors of Connacht; yet despite these disputes there was some kind of continuous kingship in Connacht between 1233 and 1274 with the reigns of Aedh and Felim O'Connor. The O'Neills survived in a similar manner in Ulster. In 1258, the Irish were even able to agree on a king of Ireland, Brian O'Neill, who did not last long, however. In 1263 some Irish kings invited the king of Norway, Haakon, to lead them in the fight against the English. The fact that many of the Irish had come to terms with the English did not mean that the descendants of the old dynasties, particularly the provincial kingdoms, had renounced their claims to rule. The archaic Irish marriage laws, which still pertained, ensured that there was no shortage of candidates for the kingdoms. On the other hand, the English law of succession, in the form of primogeniture, brought many advantages to the feudal lord, although it had fatal consequences for the vassal when the heir was a minor.

The Annals of Ulster demonstrate this quite clearly for the thirteenth century. Rather repetitive entries relating to the deaths of royal heirs (rígdomnae) indicate that there were numerous potential successors. It was unusual for Irish kings to die a natural death, e.g. Domnal Mór Ua Domnaill, king of Tir Conail, Fir Manach, Cairpri and Airghialla (AU 1241) but it is never recorded that an Irish king died without an heir entitled to succeed.

It is worth comparing these impressions of the Irish ruling class with the picture that emerges from the annals of St Mary's, Dublin, that is from within the area dominated by the English. In 1284 and 1290 respectively these annals start to mention once again Irish *reguli* and *reges* in Offaly and Meath. By now even Dublin had realised that Irish kingship was once again a reality.

Since the Irish on their own were not able to weaken the English to any appreciable extent, they sought help from outside. From the second half of the thirteenth century there are reports of mercenary troops in Ireland, the *gallóglach* (literally 'foreign troops', anglicised 'gallowglass') who had come from the southwest of Scotland and from the Hebrides; due to their success in Tir Connell and Tyrone, they settled there in the course of the fourteenth century and ultimately founded their own dynasties.

There were never any clear frontiers in Ireland between the English and the Irish, even in the thirteenth century, the time of greatest success for the English. English rule could not even be imposed in the Wicklow Mountains, south of Dublin. Around 1280 the peasants of Saggart (near Dublin) complained in a letter to London that in the past seven years the Irish had stolen from them 30,000 sheep, 200 head of cattle and 200 pigs.[27] However, these figures also show that the settlers in the lordship were not badly off, although everyday life was dangerous. On the other hand, the increasing violence in the close vicinity of Dublin gave some cause for concern.

Around 1270 came the first complaints from Dublin that Crown officials had had to advance money in order to carry out their duties, and that the London Treasury had been slow in paying them back.[28] These are the first signs of the impending financial crisis which was to affect the lordship of Ireland. During the previous two generations the Irish administration had regularly produced a financial surplus, particularly through the export of wool and cereals; this money had been welcomed by the English Crown and spent elsewhere.

It is clear that the political situation in Ireland in the thirteenth century cannot be described in simple terms. In many areas, however, it was still possible to lead a relatively uncomplicated existence. The complaint from Cork in 1278 that the Irish were hostile to the Crown, that the political scene resembled that of a

Marcher land,[29] was at that time unusual. It still looked as if the Irish and English would eventually be persuaded to live side by side peacefully. In the case of the Church, however, it appears that the integration of Irish and English had not occurred, and the Church in the Middle Ages meant much more than religion; the term covered a wide social spectrum.

The Church

The Church in thirteenth-century Ireland conveys rather contradictory impressions. In comparison with England and with other countries, there is very little documentation; this is surprising for a society with a highly developed learned élite and for a country that had been decisive in the Christianisation of central Europe.

The diocesan structure that had originally been created in the twelfth century lasted, with few changes (e.g. the joining of the diocese of Glendalough to Dublin) into modern times. In the thirteenth century, the bishoprics were subdivided into parishes; this process was particularly intensive in the anglicised areas and these subdivisions were to remain into the nineteenth century. In the course of the thirteenth century the monastic chapters of cathedrals were changed into canonical chapters. The reform of the Church also continued; the organisation appeared to become more and more 'European'. The arrival and success of the mendicant orders indicate a similar trend. The Dominicans first came to Ireland in 1224 and had established 25 houses by the end of the century; the Franciscans came in 1231 and were equally successful. However, taken in isolation, these facts do not say much.

It is difficult to determine the extent to which the decisions of the Fourth Lateran Council were implemented in Ireland. The most persistent abuse seems to have been that of hereditary succession in high ecclesiastical offices. The bishopric of Derry was firmly in the hands of the O'Cerbhalláin family between 1185 and 1293; this was, however, a particularly notorious example. In the closing years of the thirteenth century there were indications that this situation would be improved considerably; but by the fourteenth century, popes became more generous in giving dispensations in return for appropriate payment, and the old abuse could continue.

The bishops of Ireland were divided by their different

nationalities. Attempts in the early thirteenth century to exclude the Irish from the bishop's office met with united and determined resistance from the papal curia. Because of this, the provinces of Armagh and Tuam had almost exclusively Irish bishops, Dublin was completely anglicised while Cashel, under strong English influence, had bishops from both sides. However, the classification of bishops according to nationality was not the only dividing element, nor the most important one. It was more important that the primacy of Armagh, which had been recognised for centuries and had been confirmed in 1152, was not accepted unquestioningly within the Church. Dublin attempted to withhold recognition of that primacy – and was later to be successful in this – but Cashel also created difficulties.

Life in the monasteries is generally poorly documented. Due to the unusual structure of the Cistercian Order whose abbots held an annual general chapter in order to examine the observance of the Rule, there is better information on this Order in Ireland. It gives a rather gloomy impression. The Cistercians had about 35 houses in Ireland the majority of which had been founded by Irish people. The well-documented visitation by Stephen Lexington in 1228, in itself a sign that the Irish Cistercians were in a bad state, contains detailed information. Lexington, who was to become abbot of Clairvaux in 1243, would appear to have acted in accordance with the expectations of his Order. He stated that discrimination according to nationality was practised in some monasteries; the Irish refused entry to the English, and vice versa. As a consequence of the visitation, the Irish abbot of Mellifont, the mother house of many Irish monasteries, resigned. Stephen dissolved the filiation of Mellifont altogether and subjected fifteen monasteries to other houses, all of them outside Ireland. In view of Mellifont's high reputation due to its foundation by the revered Malachy, this was a considerable blow. Even if Stephen's motivations had not been explicitly anti-Irish but had instead been intended to maintain or restore the high international standards of Cîteaux in Ireland, the Irish monks felt badly treated. After all, as a result of the reorganisation they had mostly English superiors. This arrangement lasted almost half a century; in 1274, the filiation of Mellifont was reconstituted. However, by this time the Cistercian Order as a whole had experienced a gradual decline and its central organisation was noticeably weakened.

This is really all that can be said in any survey of the Irish Church in the thirteenth century. The influence of the Church in daily life and its position in society are both largely unknown. There are, however, some exceptions. Marriage law had been a favourite subject of the reformers from the eleventh century onwards and had also played a prominent part at the Fourth Lateran Council; in this case, the official policy of the Church was not accepted in practice. Although the evidence of this is found mainly in the higher echelons of society, there is no reason to assume that the situation was different and better in other sectors. Except among the English, the Irish secular marriage laws continued to be observed throughout; according to these laws, marriages could be dissolved rather freely and no distinction was made between illegitimate and legitimate children regarding inheritance.

This was an issue which concerned not only the English bishops in Ireland; Irish bishops also regarded themselves as belonging to the universal Church and were interested in changing the existing situation. This at least is the interpretation given by some historians to the effort to have English law extended to all the inhabitants of Ireland. Up until then, English law was applied only to those who lived in anglicised areas and who obeyed the orders of the English administration. It is known that some Irish people managed to buy themselves English legal status, but in general there were huge differences between the Irish social structure and that of the English, and these differences manifested themselves most clearly in the different legal systems.

The attempt to extend English law to the whole Irish population was lead by Mac Carwill, the Irish archbishop of Cashel (1253–1289). Several attempts at this are recorded between 1276 and 1280, and the sources name a sum of 7,000 marks which were to be payed to the Crown in order to obtain the desired privilege. These offers were refused, and two legal systems continued to exist; the Crown even accepted explicitly that Irish families as a whole were accountable for the misdeeds of their individual members. Irish historians often regard this negative attitude on the part of the Crown as a missed opportunity to reconcile the two nationalities. Reconciliation of this kind, namely equality before the Law, equal treatment of Irish and English, did not seem possible, since the political and military situation remained unclear. Furthermore, there is nothing to show that the archbishop of Cashel acted on behalf of the Irish upper class; on the contrary, there are enough indications that the Irish legal system was firmly established and could not be abolished within a short time.

The First Crisis: Edward Bruce in Ireland (1315–18)

Ireland experienced its greatest crisis for 150 years in the early fourteenth century when Edward Bruce invaded the country from Scotland. The assumption that this crisis mainly concerned the English lordship of Ireland demands some modification.

While it is true that Dublin was once in danger of being taken by Bruce, it is by no means certain that the conquest of Dublin would have guaranteed Bruce's victory in Ireland; nor was Dublin identical with English rule in Ireland. The invasion created a serious crisis since Bruce terrorised the whole country for three years. The invasion coincided with a succession of three disastrous harvests that resulted in severe famine both in Ireland and in Europe generally. The Scottish strategy of 'scorched earth' affected everyone in Ireland.

This invasion relates back to the various unsuccessful attempts by Edward I of England (1272–1307) to conquer Scotland. He had already been successful in conquering the Principality of Wales in 1282–84, although at great financial cost. He later attempted to do the same in Scotland, only more cheaply: in 1292, he imposed a compliant vassal king. However, his creature, John de Balliol proved uncompliant, and he had to resort to war. Once again, England's finances were exhausted and Ireland was also obliged to contribute. Edward's campaigns brought the English far into the north of Scotland, but his means proved insufficient and the country too large. Towards the end of his life, Edward I acquired in Robert Bruce an opponent just as able and unscrupulous as he himself. Shortly afterwards, Edward II came to power in England. His turbulent reign lasted twenty years; he was finally deposed, with the approval of parliament, and murdered in prison. But it was to take many years of misrule before the English barons rebelled against their king. Part of the problem lay with Edward II's system of favouritism, since by this he excluded most of the nobility from government. The first major crisis arose because of his favouritism of Peter Gaviston in 1311. This was followed by

Edward's catastrophic defeat at Bannockburn in 1314 by Robert Bruce and the Scots: although the outcome was for a long time in the balance, it was all the more catastrophic since the Scots had never before been equal opponents.

Robert Bruce now went on the offensive: in the following year, he sent his brother Edward to Ireland in order to establish a kingdom for himself. This move would appear to have been directed primarily against the English. The new Irish front eased the pressure on the Scottish king, since Ireland had been called upon in the preceding years to help finance the Scottish wars. This was now no longer possible, and, what is more, English troops were needed in Ireland.

Edward Bruce was the brother of the son-in-law of the Earl of Ulster. However, his invasion was directed against his kinsman. Edward had gained the support of Donal O'Neill, who had invited him to Ireland to become king. Donal had extended this invitation in the name of all the Irish, mindful, it seems, of the historic claims of the O'Neills to the national kingship. However, he acted without a mandate from other Irish leaders. He was interested in his own personal gain and must have hoped that in the case of Edward's success he would somehow benefit, too. He may have been hoping that Bruce would later marry into the Irish aristocracy. In any case, it must be made clear that O'Neill's invitation to Bruce was in no sense a 'Celtic alliance'. Bruce was of Norman descent; his ancestors had come to England in the late eleventh century and had subsequently gone to Scotland. It was only by the thirteenth century that they had succeeded in rising to prominence.

Edward Bruce landed in Ulster in the spring of 1315. His first opponent was the Earl of Ulster whom he defeated after some of the Earl's followers had refused him support. The Dublin administration thought this highly improbable and suspected instead a conspiracy between de Burgh and Bruce. Bruce then advanced from Ulster into Connacht against another de Burgh who had allied himself with Felim O'Connor. Bruce later defeated Roger Mortimer, Lord of Trim, continued his march into Leinster and finally returned to Ulster. In May 1316, he was crowned king of Ireland at Faughart.

Edward Bruce had initially been quite successful. However, it should be taken into account that the Liberty of Kildare was without effective lordship after the death of the Earl of Gloucester at Bannockburn. In addition, it was reported to London that the Treasury of Dublin was empty. This message was presumably intended to underline the request for more help from England. Early in 1317, Roger Mortimer took over as leader of the English army.

That year was to bring some new developments. Robert Bruce came over from Scotland for several weeks, to support his brother; the Earl of Ulster was taken into custody in Dublin; Roger Mortimer succeeded in securing the sea passage to England. The Scottish troops advanced as far as the walls of Dublin; four suburbs were burned down by the Dublin administration. However, the Scots avoided an open confrontation. Instead, they turned to the southwest and devastated Tipperary and Limerick. They then went back to Ulster and Robert Bruce returned to Scotland.

In this context, a letter from Donal O'Neill to Pope John XXII in 1317 deserves close attention. In this letter, known as the Irish Remonstrance, he asked the pope to support the new king of Ireland. This document is a political pamphlet of considerable length.[30] O'Neill began by arguing that the Irish had been a free people, decent and God-fearing, until an English pope (Adrian IV) had, under false pretences, given permission to the English king to conquer Ireland and reform the Church. O'Neill here referred to the Bull *Laudabiliter* from which he quoted verbatim. He further claimed that even had the Bull not been issued wrongly, the behaviour of the English since their arrival in Ireland showed that they had not fulfilled the task which they had been given in that Bull. Instead of treating the Irish as fellow Christians, the English had driven them from their rightful possessions and lands into the bogs and wasteland, and treated them in inhuman ways. He wrote that some English clerics even boasted that it was no sin to kill an Irishman. In these circumstances, the Irish had invited a man from Scotland to be their king because the English had forfeited their right to rule Ireland, which had been questionable from the very beginning. The pope was asked to approve of this action and to ensure that the English would leave Ireland. However, O'Neill made no reference to the fact that the pope was feudal lord of the king of England.

The Irish Remonstrance did not have much practical effect. By the time the pope reacted to it and asked the English king to put a stop to mismanagement in Ireland and treat the deserving Irish as fellow Christians, the kingship of Edward Bruce had already been decided on the battlefield. Nevertheless, the way O'Neill used past events in his argument deserves attention. The Remonstrance shows that it was then argued that English rule in Ireland was based on the grant by Pope Adrian IV to Henry II. As we have seen, this argument lacks any historical basis although it is impossible to say whether or not O'Neill was aware of this at the time. The view is expressed here for the first time, a view never completely abandoned in Ireland, that *Laudabiliter* represents an 'English plot' against the Irish. The fact that the central issue in this Bull was the state of Christianity in Ireland gave added poignancy to this fixation right up to modern times, especially after the Reformation.

It is certain that O'Neill did not act in the name of all the Irish in sending this pamphlet to the pope. When Edward Bruce was killed at Faughart in 1318, the Irish Annals have the following entry: 'Edward Bruce, the destroyer of Ireland in general, both foreigners and Gaidhil, was killed by the foreigners of Ireland. . . . And there was not done from the beginning of the world a deed that was better for the men of Ireland than that deed. For there came dearth and loss of people during his time in all Ireland in general for the space of three years and a half and undoubtedly people used to eat each other throughout Ireland' (AU 1318).

Despite its short duration, the Scottish invasion of Ireland had considerable consequences for the whole country. It had become apparent that the might of the English had its limits; Roscommon was lost by the English after only 60 years; the attacks from the Wicklow Mountains became more frequent and more intense. However, these facts should not be interpreted as a deterioration in Anglo-Irish relations. It seems equally important that the Annals of Ulster should, at that time, make positive mention of the 'foreigners', giving the impression that the term 'foreigner' had lost many of its negative connotations. De Cogan is called 'the noblest baron that was in Ireland' (AU 1316); ten years earlier it was written about Sir William Prendergast: 'a young knight of the best repute and liberality and disposition that was in Ireland' (AU 1306). Edward Bruce's war in Ireland had accelerated a process that had begun earlier, namely that the Anglo-Irish nobles made very positive impressions on the Irish annalists. It can be argued that the Irish and Anglo-Irish, in the face of a common threat, had come much closer to each other.

In addition to this general improvement in atmosphere, the war brought considerable changes with regard to lordship. In 1316, the FitzGeralds of Kildare were given the title 'Earl'; this family were to be Earls of Kildare for the next two centuries. John de Bermingham, who had defeated Bruce, was made Earl of Louth (1319–29) but did not found a dynasty. In the following decade, the earldoms of Ormond and Desmond were created for the Butlers and for another branch of the FitzGeralds respectively; these lines were to survive into the sixteenth century. This policy signals a new type of lordship in Ireland.

During these years life in Dublin was quite comfortable despite dwindling income from the lordship. The Annals of St Mary's report in 1308 that John le Decer, Mayor of Dublin, ordered the repair of the acqueduct for the supply of drinking water and had a marble cistern built. A new bridge across the Liffey was also built during his rule; a further bridge was built in 1322. John le Decer died in 1332, apparently a very popular man.[31] Immediately after the Scottish wars, Alexander Bicknor, Archbishop of Dublin, founded a university which, however, did not survive. Of the four masters who started teaching there in 1320, one came from Wales, Edmundus de Kermerdyn (Carmarthen).[32] These examples would seem to indicate that the financial hardship of Dublin was limited.

Ireland in the Reign of Edward III

After the victory over Edward Bruce, the importance of Ireland to the English Crown once again diminished and Ireland became a secondary issue. Internal crises, particularly those around Thomas of Lancaster and the Despenser family, dominated the political scene in England during the following decade. The intrigues of Isabella and Mortimer against Edward II, his deposition and subsequent murder, Mortimer's three years' regency in England and his execution in 1330, these were the decisive events in England and they also receive much attention in the Irish annals. The accession of Edward III seemed to mark a new departure in Anglo-Irish politics. The king made preparations to go to Ireland personally in 1332, but changed his mind at the last minute:

France took priority. This is not to say that Edward III neglected Ireland but his policy could not succeed in halting the decline of the English Lordship. By the time his son Lionel of Clarence went to Ireland, the situation had changed quite fundamentally.

Several factors contributed to this change. In the area controlled by the English only a few leading families had succeeded in establishing themselves for any length of time. Family matters play a part in this decline as can be seen in the example of Ulster. The Red Earl had made a vigorous start when he took control personally in 1286 and was able to extend his sphere of influence considerably. For a long time it did not seem to matter that he cooperated with the Irish local lords. However, when the Scottish invasion occurred, doubts were expressed about the earl's loyalty, which were probably unfounded. He died in 1326, leaving a young heir. In the following year, taking advantage of the chaos in England, Robert Bruce invaded Ireland once again and threatened Ulster. Although he did not do much damage, neither did he encounter any serious resistance. The young Earl of Ulster was murdered in 1333; as his sole heir he left a small child, Elizabeth, who later was to marry Lionel of Clarence, Edward III's son. The new lord of Ulster was, however, busy with the wars in France; he was not to come to Ireland until 1361, and when he came it was not to administer his earldom but to participate for a very short time in the Dublin administration. The earldom of Ulster therefore remained for 60 years without an effective lord in the country. English rule west of the River Bann disintegrated soon after 1333 and further to the east could only be maintained with difficulty.

Ulster's case was not unique. Families who still held property in Ireland and England generally did not reside in Ireland, but had their lands administered for them. From 1327 onwards, the Mortimers were the only English family of consequence to take any real interest in their Irish possessions. In 1360 it was established that 80 per cent of the English landowners did not look after their land in Ireland themselves. The family bonds between England and Ireland which could have contributed to cooperation in peacetime as well as in times of crisis had now largely been broken.

This accounts for the increasing importance of the Anglo-Irish, the descendants of the conquerors who lived in Ireland and whose links with England and Wales had almost disappeared. Their main concern was the defence of their lands which they were prepared to do by all available means.

They were quite ready to ally themselves with the Irish if necessary, but, like the Earl of Ulster, their loyalty became suspect because of that. Were they still loyal subjects of the Crown, particularly in view of the fact that they frequently allied with the Crown's Irish enemies? They also acted increasingly like their Irish counterparts: they took hostages to guarantee good behaviour and gave presents to the Irish leaders in order to win their favour.

The Dublin government had also been using these methods since the mid-fourteenth century. Although the administration's finances had deteriorated drastically (compared to the thirteenth century by around 50 per cent), administrative documents report between 1295 and 1361 no fewer than 50 official campaigns against the Irish. Despite these campaigns, they were unable to maintain control of all their land. Apparently, the means available were insufficient for effective measures. It nevertheless happened in the course of these campaigns that even representatives of the Lordship would deal with Irish leaders, receive hostages and tribute and give presents to those Irish who cooperated with them. It has been argued that in doing so the Dublin administration was not acting very differently from the high-kings of earlier centuries.[33] While there is much to justify this view, it must be pointed out that the long-term effects were certain to be different. Alliances which were based on personal agreements lost their validity if one of the partners of the alliance, a representative of the central government, left office. It was characteristic of the English administration of Ireland in the fourteenth century that leading officials were replaced frequently. It was unusual for a justiciar to hold office for more than a year or two. New administrators came with ideas that were often impracticable; they had to get used to their new posts and had to gain the confidence of others; having done so, they were often suddenly recalled. In the fourteenth century it became official Crown policy to give the most important administrative positions to English people, not to the Anglo-Irish. These would only be appointed when no English alternative could be found.

In view of these considerations it is not surprising that the area under English control, particularly the counties, shrank rapidly. From 1327 at the latest, Connacht is assumed to have been outside English influence, and there were further losses in Tipperary and elsewhere. The stretch of land connecting Dublin with Cork was lost in 1325, and soon after with the connection with Waterford and Wexford. In 1339, the Dublin Annals state succinctly: *Guerra generalis per totam Hiberniam* ('General war throughout all Ireland').[34] These serious developments were to force Edward III into action. Perhaps it was due to bad advice, or perhaps he wanted to show that he was in overall control, when in 1341 he declared void all grants that had been made in Ireland after the accession of his father (1307) and reserved the right to renew them as he wished. By doing so he called into question the lordship of all major Anglo-Irish families, particularly the Earls of Kildare, Ormond and Desmond. These resisted strongly the plans of the king and pointed to their loyal services in past crises. This was the greatest confrontation so far *inter Anglicos in Anglia oriundos et Anglicos in terra Hiberniae oriundos* ('between the English from England and the English from Ireland').[35] The king was ultimately forced to concede, but the conflict did not end there. In 1343 he appointed a very able justiciar, Ralph Ufford, who was related by marriage to the royal family and who represented the interests of the Crown with determination. The conflict now became more acute: Desmond and Kildare rebelled openly, and there was considerable relief when Ufford died in 1346.

Two years later, the plague first arrived in Ireland. It appears that both the Anglo-Irish and the townspeople were affected more severely than the Irish living in the country, but ultimately the plague affected everyone. The following entry was written in the margin of an Irish manuscript: 'It is 1350 years tonight that Jesus Christ was born, and in the second year after the coming of the plague to Ireland was this written, and I am 21 years old. And let every reader in pity recite a *pater* for my soul. It is Christmas Eve tonight, and under the protection of the King of Heaven and Earth am I on this eve tonight. May the end of my life be holy and may this great plague pass by me and my friends and restore us once more to joy and gladness. Amen. *Pater noster*. Hugh, son of Connor Mac Egan, wrote this on his father's book, in the year of the great plague. It is just a year tonight since I wrote the lines on the margin below; and, if it be God's will, may I reach the anniversary of this great evening once more. Amen. *Pater noster*'.[36]

Edward III was never really able to make decisive changes. In 1361 he sent his son Lionel of Clarence to Ireland in the new position of royal lieutenant (*tenens locum*). The situation remained as before; the new man realised the changes which had to be made and issued laws accordingly, but he did not remain long enough to ensure their implementation.

A number of reasons explain Edward's decision to send someone of Clarence's importance. Through the Peace of Bretigny in 1360, the war with France had ceased to be a priority, and the situation in Ireland had meanwhile deteriorated rapidly. In Leinster, the heart of the Lordship, great unrest had surfaced. In addition to sending Clarence, the king instructed the English landowners of Ireland to look after the security of their lands personally or risk having it confiscated.

Clarence came from Liverpool directly to Dublin. He seems to have considered transferring the capital to Carlow; the Exchequer and the Common Bench were transferred to that town and remained there until the end of the century.

Clarence came to Ireland a second time in 1364 and stayed for two years. On his initiative the Statutes of Kilkenny were issued.[37] These laws, approved by the parliament of Kilkenny in 1366 for the King's subjects, can be taken as an accurate reflection of the situation which they were intended to improve. The most important provisions were:

- no relationship with the Irish in marriage, concubinage or adoption;
- no trade with the Irish;
- exclusive use of the English language, even by the loyal Irish; only English names for children;
- above a certain level of income the saddle was to be used in riding;
- prohibition of Marcher Law and Irish Law (Brehon Law); exclusive use of Common Law;
- no mutual diffamation between English and Anglo-Irish (the insult 'Irish dog' is mentioned);
- hurling forbidden; instead, continuous training in arms (bow, lance);
- no unofficial wars against the Irish; no peace with them on the basis of gifts; when peace was made, the Irish were to give hostages;

- no ecclesiastical benefices of any kind to be granted to Irish people;
- no contact with Irish musicians, poets and singers in view of the danger of espionage;
- offers to be made to English people to take over farmland in Ireland;
- farm labourers forbidden to leave Ireland;
- wars between the English forbidden.

The extent to which these instructions were observed was to be assessed twice annually.

The earliest regulations of this kind had been issued in the late thirteenth century. In 1347, it was ordered that marriages between English and Irish needed the explicit permission of the government. In 1351, the justiciar Thomas de Rokeby had instructed the English to use only English, not Irish law and to avoid any contact with the Irish. All these regulations remained without much effect; some of them were not even observed by the administration itself. The fact that they went into such detail shows the extent to which the Anglo-Irish had already adapted themselves to the Irish. The appointment of Clarence at least made the financial situation clear: because of his visit, London became aware that the English Lordship in Ireland could not maintain itself by its own means. From this time onwards, financial help began to come from England, though never regularly and never sufficiently.

In the year after the passing of the Statutes of Kilkenny the administrative documents from Dublin mention for the first time the following significant terms: *Irrois, enemys nostre seignur roi, ou Englois rebeaux et enemys reputez et aiugges en Irlande* ('Irish, enemies of our lord the king, or English rebels who are reputed and judged [our] enemies in Ireland').[38] The Anglo-Irish who did not submit to the regulations of Kilkenny were increasingly described as enemies of the Crown, just as the Irish had been.

Irish Society: Old and New Structures

The adoption of Irish culture by the Anglo-Irish in the fourteenth century is one of the basic themes of modern Irish historiography. This phenomenon is not surprising when one considers that many of these families had been resident in Ireland for more than a century, in an environment that was dominated by the Irish, who were in the majority. Something similar had, after all, happened to the Normans in England.

However, as with most historical comparisons, this is only valid to a limited extent. While it can be argued that in England a social and cultural symbiosis had come about between the Normans and the English in the twelfth century, the same cannot be said about Ireland in the fourteenth century. It is now necessary to take a closer look at the politics of Irish society at that time.

Discussions among Irish historians about when the so-called Gaelic revival began are often intense and opinion tends to vary considerably. However, it is rarely pointed out that the political structures which evolved in the fourteenth century in Irish society were quite different from those predominant in the twelfth century. This is not immediately apparent for two simple reasons: the dynasties now surfacing again were originally descended from old Irish dynasties, and a number of old institutional terms were revived even though their meanings had changed. It should be remembered that the learned élite in Ireland was extremely conservative and used very conservative language. Professions such as lawyers, poets, historians, healers and musicians were the preserve of certain families, and these claimed to be able to trace their ancestors back into early historical times. As has been mentioned earlier, the classical Irish law tracts are preserved only in late medieval manuscripts and these handed on the classical terminology.

There is, fortunately, a legal text in which such archaic terms do not occur; this can be dated to around 1300. Its author is Giolla na Naomh Mac Aodhgáin.[39] This text helps to confirm that the terms for important social institutions had changed, something which occasionally surfaces also in the annals. It can be assumed from this that the institutions themselves had changed and that the stratification of Irish society had become more pronounced. On the basis of this legal text, the *túath* and the *rí* seem to have virtually disappeared even though the terms continued to be used, particularly in literary texts. The *rí* had largely been replaced by the less-respected *taoiseach* (Latinised as *dux*) or *tigerna* (Latinised as *dominus*); the *túath* had been replaced by the *oirecht* (lit. 'gathering, assembly'). The term denotes the cooperation between political

leadership and *populus*; there was greater emphasis on the mutual
obligations between the two than there had been between the n
and the *túath*. Although the institution of *tánaise* still existed, his
nomination was no longer the sole right of the assembly, but
neighbouring leaders also had a say in this.

The term *ardrí* 'High-King' reappears in the annals in the
fourteenth century; however, it merely referred to kings who ruled
over a province, not over the whole island.

The richer supply of sources shows more clearly than in earlier
times that political units did not exist completely independent of
each other. Those parts of the old system which had survived into
the twelfth century collapsed due to the English conquests. When
the English were pushed back, the Irish lordships which appeared
again were based entirely on military power. As a consequence,
political leadership built on new concepts. This also meant that
new families could rise to the highest positions as long as they were
successful in war; they began to rival the descendants of the old
dynasties.

This can be seen particularly clearly in Ulster. The O'Neills did
not succeed in regaining the provincial kingship of Ulster. Instead,
they became a dynasty like many others: the O'Donnells of
Tirconnel, the Maguires of Fermanagh, the O'Dohertys of Derry,
the Mac Quillans who originated from Scotland, the Mac Sweenys
and Mac Donnells who were descendants of the *gallóglach*
(mercenaries), as well as the descendants of the English, the
Savages. With the collapse of English rule lordships of very small
size began to appear once again. From the political viewpoint, the
most important group within these lordships was the clan. This
was the term used for them by the English administration in 1310
when a law was passed ordering that the leaders of each clan would
be held responsible for the actions of their dependents. It should be
pointed out that the clans only made up the upper class in these
lordships. This kind of lordship was also adopted by the Anglo-
Irish families from the early fourteenth century at the latest, by the
Dillons, Daltons, Delamares, Tyrrels, etc.

With this we have outlined the political dimension of the Gaelic
revival; the controversial nature of this term has now become more
obvious. There was also the fact that the Anglo-Irish had adopted
a wide range of Irish customs. This was evident even in their
external appearance: they wore their hair long, grew moustaches

and no longer rode with saddles. Similar developments also occurred in the social sphere. In the fourteenth century the Earl of Ormond had in his service an Irish legal expert, a *brehon*, who administered justice in his earldom. John de Bermingham, Earl of Louth, counted among his followers the most famous Irish musician of the time, Mulroony Mac Carroll, as well as twenty of his pupils. Yet Bermingham had originally been appointed earl because he had fought for the survival of English Lordship in Ireland and had defeated Edward Bruce; it is therefore interesting to note the extent to which Irish customs had spread among the 'loyal' Anglo-Irish. Intermarriage took place at all levels of society. The Anglo-Irish, apart from the greatest lords, also treated their illegitimate children in the same way as their legitimate children, with full right to inherit, although these offspring had no claim to English law. Finally, the Anglo-Irish had also adopted the Irish language. It is not clear when this process began, but the preamble to the Statutes of Kilkenny of 1366 states explicitly that the Irish language was being spoken by the Anglo-Irish. FitzGerald Earl of Desmond (1363–98), is regarded as the first great lyrical love-poet in the Irish language. This would certainly have required great familiarity with Irish language and culture.

In the areas in which English rule had collapsed, the manors and villages which they had established soon disappeared. The last main vestiges of English rule were the towns, by now almost without hinterland, strongly fortified and dependent on trade for survival. For this, however, they had to retain contact with the surrounding areas. Both English economic patterns and the money-economy soon disappeared outside the towns. Barter, services and the duty of hospitality once again became predominant. It should be added, however, that these changes were taking place at a time when the whole of Europe was going through a deep economic recession.

In 1310, Felim O'Connor was inaugurated as king of Connacht in a style that was meant to evoke times long past; it was an anachronism, even at the time. Felim subsequently fought with the de Burghs of Connacht against Edward Bruce and died in 1316. The Annals of Ulster gave only brief mention of his accession; on the occasion of his death he received less praise than the annalist had given Sir William Prendergast on his death in 1306. Felim was succeeded by his son Turlough O'Connor, but the traditional type of provincial kingship which had been suggested by the form of the inauguration was never to come about. It was not enough merely to revive old ceremonies. What has been said about Ulster and Connacht also applies to Leinster. In 1350, John O'Byrne was elected leader of the O'Byrnes, in the presence of the justiciar Thomas de Rokeby. He was given money in order to keep his area of influence peaceful for two years. In 1354, Muirchertach Mac Murrough became king of Leinster, at the same time accepting money from the Dublin treasury in return for good behaviour. These were old names which awakened old memories, but they were, in fact, new and smaller lordships.

11. The End of the Middle Ages

The political map of Ireland in the fifteenth century, like those of Germany and northern Italy at the time, resembles a patchwork, consisting of many elements of varying size. The titles of the rulers may well have changed, but their influence did not stretch beyond the areas where they themselves were active. These lordships were of the size of one or more of the earlier *túatha*. Some lordships, particularly the former Liberties, were comparable in size to the provincial kingdoms of earlier centuries. It is significant that the centre of the Lordship of Ireland, Dublin and its surrounding area, was no longer the greatest or most important of the individual lordships. However, this is the only area for which it is possible to trace the political development.

The End of the Lordship

The political turmoil in England from the later fourteenth century onwards had devastating consequences for English rule in Ireland: the country was to feel the repercussions of the crises under Richard II, the takeover of the House of Lancaster in 1399, the rivalries with the House of York and finally the accession of the Tudors in 1485.

The cost of administering the lordship had risen steeply since the late fourteenth century, at a time when income was falling. In 1369, William of Windsor came to Ireland as *locum tenens*. He demanded high taxes from the Anglo-Irish in order to be able to impose his authority on Leinster. It is reported that it cost £6,720 to hire 120 soldiers and 200 archers for one year; however, little could be achieved with such a small troop.

Limerick was burned, Munster was in rebellion. The Anglo-Irish complained to London, and Windsor was recalled. The sharp criticism of the government of the senile Edward III, which reached its climax in the Good Parliament of 1376, had its repercussions even in Ireland. Almost all the Crown officials were replaced. In 1378, James Butler, the second Earl of Ormond (there were five Earls of Ormond of that name in succession) was appointed

Map 4: Ireland c. 1500

justiciar; he received £50 per annum in expenses. He was replaced in the following year by Edmund Mortimer, the Earl of March. Mortimer had made a precondition of his service that he receive the sum of £13,000 over three years. He had with him 200 knights and 700 archers. As Lord of Meath he could have had a considerable income in Ireland; his wife, daughter of Elizabeth de Burgh and Lionel of Clarence, was heiress to Ulster and Connacht. There was, however, little to be got from there. What had begun in a promising way ended by achieving nothing. After the departure of the Earl of March, both Ormond and Desmond refused to accept the justiciarship. It was a position that cost the holder money instead of earning him an income, and he could not expect thanks. In 1393, Galway fell to the Irish.

King Richard II came to Ireland in the following year; this was to be the last major attempt to halt the rapid decline. Richard brought an army 10,000 strong, the biggest which had ever been brought to Ireland although the English government had often raised armies of that size for the French wars. It was therefore hardly surprising that Richard II made an impression. Most Irish clan-leaders submitted to him and swore loyal cooperation in the future, with the exception of the O'Donnells in the northwest. However, few of the 'rebel English' appeared in order to make peace with the Lord of Ireland, since they feared the confiscation of their possessions. The king stayed in the country for barely six months. He transferred the treasury from Carlow back to Dublin. Five years later, Richard II once again came to Ireland, and Henry of Lancaster used this opportunity to chase him from the throne.

By the fifteenth century, the lordship had become even smaller and now included only Dublin, Kildare, Meath and Louth, an area of about 20 × 30 miles; in addition, some towns were still held, Trim, Athlone, Wicklow, Greencastle and Carrickfergus. In 1494 orders were given to fortify the area around Dublin, now named the 'Pale', with a wall and a ditch.

Richard of York acted as *locum tenens* for an unusually long period, from 1447 to 1460. Though he was only briefly in Ireland during this time, he made such a favourable impression generally that some Anglo-Irish remained loyal to the House of York even after the Tudor victory in England of 1485. Pretenders to the English throne twice gained considerable support in Ireland; Lambert Simnel in 1487, claiming to be Edward V, and Perkin

Warbeck in 1491, claiming to be Richard of York – the two princes who had disappeared under Richard III. Lambert Simnel was crowned king in Dublin. In order to prevent similar events in future, the Irish parliament, which had hitherto been in large measure independent, was directly subjected to the English Crown Council by Sir Henry Poynings in 1494.

The English government was more dependent than ever on cooperation with the Anglo-Irish, since they could at least achieve something. When the families of Desmond and Ormond were no longer able or willing to cooperate – particularly after the execution of Thomas FitzJames, Earl of Desmond, in 1468 – the House of Kildare assumed the leading position. Three earls in succession became Chief Governor of Ireland, though not without interruptions. They were Garrett Mor FitzGerald, the 'Great Earl', about 1478 and again 1496–1513, his son Garrett Ōg 1513–19, and his grandson, Silken Thomas, who ended his life as a rebel on the scaffold. Two years after his execution, in 1536, the Irish parliament recognised Henry VIII as the head of the Irish Church, and in 1541 as king of Ireland.

This marked the beginning of a new chapter in the history of Ireland, a period dominated by religious wars, the appointment of Irish clan leaders to the position of earls, and, when that did not succeed, the military conquest of the country by the Tudors and Stuarts and the plantations by numerous settlers from England and Scotland. It was only then that Ireland became a colony.

Ireland outside the Lordship

While the area of the English lordship decreased considerably after the middle of the fourteenth century, to become in the end almost totally insignificant, affairs in other parts of Ireland gained in importance. At present, the history of these parts of Ireland remains seriously under-researched. This may appear surprising, but a closer look reveals the reasons for this imbalance in the state of research. It becomes apparent that the history of research and modern political history are interrelated.

Let us begin by considering the sources. Administrative documents from the area of the English Lordship are preserved in relative abundance in the English Public Record Office and elsewhere. In England the continuity of central government guaranteed their preservation. In Ireland, the sources which were contained in the Public Record Office were almost completely destroyed in the Civil War of 1922. In the Gaelic parts of Ireland, the areas outside English control before the sixteenth century, there was no such continuity. The political disturbances of the following centuries, when the aim of the English government was the increasing anglicisation of Ireland, also contributed to the destruction of source material. For example, we know only from indirect references that some Gaelic rulers in the last medieval centuries issued laws which have not been preserved.

This, however, is not the complete story. It is assumed that the rulers of the Gaelic parts of Ireland issued fewer written documents than did the English administration in the Lordship. After all, the Lordship had in Westminster a place to which it could turn with written requests or complaints. Documents of this type contribute largely to the assessment of the English situation in Ireland. Lordship of the Gaelic and 'gaelicized' lords was more immediate; it was based on the power of the sword.

This is not to say that there are no written sources whatever from Gaelic Ireland, but what has been preserved deals only to a small extent with political matters. In the first place there are the very detailed annals. More important are the sources of a less overtly political nature. In the last medieval centuries, a very rich literature in the Irish language was created, so rich indeed that its editing and interpretation is still in the early stages. The intensive study of Irish literature really only began with Romanticism, just as the scientific approach to history in general derived much of its impetus from Romanticism. However, the Celtic scholars experienced more difficulties than others: the Irish language is so complex that an intensive study of it has always been a minority choice, and for a long time Irish culture was insufficiently appreciated in England. English scholars and the general public show a lack of appropriate interest in the history of her Celtic neighbours. More generally, it must be said that scholars tend to research the early period of Irish language and literature more closely than the later developments because it is here that they expect to find greater originality. The literature of the later Middle Ages offers little that is spectacular: new literary genres were rarely tried; the older forms were used which by the later Middle Ages frequently display epigonous features. Finally, a large proportion of late medieval literature in Irish consists of translations of Continental material, another area which scholars have tended to neglect.

Irish historians proudly contrast the Gaelic revival with the decline of the English Lordship in Ireland. As already indicated in the previous chapter, this view has certain limitations. It is not enough to declare that many Anglo-Irish adopted the Irish language, customs and culture; it is true that they did this and this is certainly an indication of the vitality of Irish society. On the other hand, it must be emphasised that contacts with England and the Continent also left their marks on Irish society. The idea of a homogenous Irish culture outside the English Lordship in the last two medieval centuries is simply incorrect. There are in fact numerous indications of mutual influences, and ultimately Irish and non-Irish traditions mixed. One might therefore consider whether it would be preferable to speak of an 'Irish Renaissance' which, like the Italian Renaissance, combined old and new elements and was in the end different from the sum of its components.

The openness of Ireland to the outside world which had existed since early historical times, started to increase from the eleventh century onwards. It is important to realise that the English intervention in Ireland in the late twelfth century therefore merely accelerated a process which had started long before. Through the Continental religious orders which had settled in the country, as well as through its nobility, merchants and scholars, Ireland was a part of Europe more than ever before. This is difficult to show in every respect, but some examples may serve to illustrate the general idea.

Ireland as a Land of Travel

Nobility and clergy contributed in many ways to increase the contact between Ireland and the Continent in the second part of the Middle Ages. There was also an early form of tourism, the pilgrimage, for which Ireland was one of the well-known destinations.

St Patrick's Purgatory, situated in Lough Derg, Co. Donegal, was, from the thirteenth century at the latest, one of the most celebrated places of pilgrimage in the whole of Europe. Apparently, the pilgrims were given the opportunity to glimpse the Next World. The Purgatory first appears in the sources in the twelfth century. An English knight named Owen visited there around 1153; what he experienced on that occasion made him enter a monastery. His stories about the Purgatory soon became very popular and began to be included in entertaining and edifying literature. Giraldus Cambrensis certainly did not get as far as Donegal during his stay in Ireland in 1185, but nevertheless referred to the Purgatory as a matter of course (*Topographia* II, v).

Visits to the Purgatory are mentioned quite frequently from the thirteenth century onwards. The visitors are not thought to have come in very large numbers; however those who came visited not only Lough Derg but also used the opportunity to visit other Christian places and to admire the by then renowned *mirabilia* (marvels) of Ireland. Giraldus himself may well have contributed to this popularity since a third of the space in his widely-read *Topographia Hibernica* was given to the *miracula et mirabilia* of Ireland. It is certainly remarkable how easily this 'tourism' could continue and this at a time when most modern historians would have us believe that there was nothing but continuous fighting between the English, Anglo-Irish and Irish.

Let us examine the report of one particular pilgrim. In 1411, the Hungarian knight Laurent Rathold de Pasztho came to Ireland. He had started his journey from the court of King Sigismund three years earlier with a small group of companions; he intended to visit St Patrick's Purgatory and the holy places of Santiago de Compostella. He travelled to Lough Derg via Dublin and Armagh. In the Purgatory, he got the desired glance into the Next World, which he reported to the ecclesiastical authorities as well as to others. A Dublin notary, Jacobus Yonge, wrote an authenticated account of it.

This account forms part of another work which an anonymous cleric wrote a few years later for the edification of monks. From this work we learn that the Purgatory in Lough Derg at that time attracted many curious people but that only few had Pasztho's courage to actually enter the Purgatory after performing the required severe penitential exercises. We also learn something else: that God had instituted the Purgatory for St Patrick 'on account of the blindness of incredulity of the Irish' (*propter Hibernicorum incredulitatis caecitatem*). Is it possible to take this remark as a comment on the insufficient commitment to Christianity on the part of the Irish in the later Middle Ages?

In any case, the reputation of the Purgatory and of Ireland as a land of miracles was widespread in Europe. The Hungarian Pasztho had come, as he himself said, *ad videndum mirabilia et sanctorum miracula Hibernie, quia multum audivi de ipsis mirabilibus et miraculis* ('in order to see the marvels and miracles of the saints of Ireland because I have heard much about these marvels and miracles'). Two priests from Lyons, Franciscus Proly and Johannes Garhi, who came to Ireland in 1485, gave an almost identical reason for their journey. Apparently Ireland was accessible without great difficulty even in the late fifteenth century, and was a popular destination. These accounts help to modify the impression conveyed in the annals that Ireland was a country where there was no peace.

Education

The first viable university in Ireland was founded by Elizabeth I in 1591; it is the present Dublin University (Trinity College). There had been earlier attempts to found universities, in Dublin in 1320, in Drogheda and Youghal in 1464. Since these earlier foundations had not been successful, students from Ireland had to go abroad. Most of them went to England, preferably to Oxford. They experienced pressure there, particularly in times of crisis, but the English king never gave in to demands to expel them from the country.

Most of these Irish students have remained unknown. However, there are some who rose to the highest positions and must be counted among the intellectual élite of Europe. One of these was the scientist Michael Scottus, who worked at the court of Emperor Frederick II and who was chosen by the pope to become archbishop of Cashel in 1223; he refused to accept the appointment because he did not understand the language of his flock. Another important Irish scholar was Peter of Ireland, one of the teachers of St Thomas Aquinas.[40]

Reference should also be made to Richard FitzRalph, the contentious archbishop of Armagh (1346–60) who made important contributions to the dispute about Franciscan poverty.[41] All three scholars seem to have been of Anglo-Irish descent. Michael Scottus and Peter of Ireland had left their country of origin permanently, but FitzRalph had come back to Ireland after completing his studies. The many Irish bishops from the mendicant Orders, most of whom seem to have been native Irish judging by their names, had also studied outside Ireland. Thus, through the Church leaders the whole of Ireland participated in European intellectual life.

Similar claims can be made about the medical profession. It is known that Ireland had had an indigenous medical tradition from prehistoric times, which was continued into the later medieval centuries; there are also indications, from the fourteenth century onwards, that Irish people studied medicine abroad, especially at Montpellier. This is shown by the existence of medical school books which have been preserved in Irish adaptations and translations from Latin.[42] The general educational requirements of the Church brought about the foundation of simple schools (*studia particularia*), in which most Irish clerics were educated. This education was often the first step to studies at Oxford, Cambridge, St Andrews in Scotland (from 1410 onwards) or on the Continent. In 1453, a synod at Limerick forbade the admission of nobles or other lay people to these *studia particularia*, with the exception of those who intended to embark on a clerical career. Apparently these schools had previously also trained lay people.

The Augustinian Order in Connacht in the Fifteenth Century

As stated earlier, the Rule of Augustine was brought to Ireland in the twelfth century by Malachy of Armagh and had been widely adopted, apparently because of its flexibility. In 1256, the Order was reformed by Pope Alexander IV, and from 1280 onwards these reformed Augustinians were also active in Ireland, mainly in the areas of the English lordships. One exception was the community of St Mary's at Ballinrobe, Co. Mayo, founded in the first half of the fourteenth century. In 1387, a reformed congregation of Augustinians established itself at Leccete near Siena. These so-called Augustinian Observants were to become quite important in Ireland, especially in Connacht. In 1423, the first house of this Observant movement was established in Banada, Co. Sligo, perhaps through the mediation of the canons of Ballinrobe. An Irish landowner, Donough O'Hara, had granted land to the community, and in 1430 he joined the Order himself. The community of Banada remained poor for many years, that was, however, in accordance with the spirit of the Augustinian reform, the most important aim of which was to put Christian teaching into practice by serving one's neighbour.

In 1456, on the initiative of the canon Hugh O'Malley of Banada, another house was set up in Murrisk, Co. Mayo. The reason given for setting up an Augustinian community there was: 'The people of that area have not been taught in the faith until now'. This is an indication of the poor state of Christianity in the west of Ireland at that time; but clearly the decline of Christian teaching in the last decades before the Reformation was not irreversible.

It is significant that this reform movement from Connacht was to affect other areas of Ireland also. In 1461, Sir Edmund Butler founded the Augustinian house of Callan, Co. Kilkenny and eleven years later this community joined the Observant movement. In 1479, Callan was made the head of the Irish congregation, which was now able to act independently of the Augustinians under English control. In 1500, a community of Augustinian Observants settled in Galway.

Observant movements also had been established in the mendicant Orders, and these soon reached Ireland. The Dominican Observants established themselves in Portumna, Co. Galway, in 1425, the Franciscans in Quin, Co. Clare, in 1433. It is perhaps only due to the abundance of sources or the state of research that the Augustinians appear as particularly active in the fifteenth century. In any case, there was certainly plenty of scope for activity by such committed Christians in the west of Ireland.

It should be added that these communities were not affected by the dissolution of the monasteries under Henry VIII. This is one of the reasons why the old religion could survive the Reformation in the west of Ireland and could gain new influence during the Counter-Reformation with the help of Spain.

Society

In the society generally one also observes the merging of Irish and English customs. The Irish social system had one inherent advantage over the English feudal system, in that the Irish nobility never lacked potential leaders; if anything, there were rather too many. However, the annals report that this also worked to the advantage of the Irish. Consider the situation of a minor inheriting land in the English lordships. If he were fortunate, the land would be administered on his behalf by Crown officials until he could take it over personally. In the course of these critical years, the property could often sustain considerable damage.

The situation among the Irish was different. It becomes clear from the continuous reports in the annals of the deaths of *rígdomnae* that there was no shortage of potential heirs. This was due to the Irish secular marriage laws which were still observed widely. Philip Maguire, lord of Fermanagh († 1395), is said to have left 20 sons and at least 50 grandsons by 8 women; Turlough O'Donnell of Tirconnell († 1423) had 18 sons and 59 grandsons by 10 women. Since all were eligible to succeed, it did not matter greatly if many of them died in battle before they could inherit. The large pool of potential heirs also ensured that weaklings did not come to the top. From this point of view it seemed relatively unimportant that few Irish kings or clan leaders died peacefully; the annals report only rarely that someone had died 'on the pillow' (cf. AU 1241). Human life was cheap, even in the highest circles.

From the fourteenth century onwards, it can be seen that the Anglo-Irish adopted the same marriage customs as their Irish neighbours. It would seem to have been necessary for long-term survival in this society. It was unusual for Irish families to practise inheritance by primogeniture, but this was the case, for example, with the Mac Carthy Mór for six generations between 1359 and 1508.

In the fifteenth century, the rules governing the social order were changed once again. By now the family names of important people could be given to children even where no blood relationship existed. This was also sometimes done later in life, but was generally accepted as a valid legal bond. In this way the group of potential heirs increased even further.

It was mentioned previously that the social innovations in Ireland in the second part of the Middle Ages put an end to some traditional ways of achieving social cohesion. The leaders who needed troops could no longer rely on the obligations of protection and military service. This was the case both with the feudal system and the Irish system which in any case shared a number of important features. It is not certain whether the raising of private armies, which is attested since the fourteenth century, was started by the Anglo-Irish or by the Irish. The sources mention these first among the Anglo-Irish where the lords offered equipment and food to those who were willing to serve ('coyne and livery'). Something similar is attested among the Irish from the later fourteenth century onwards under the term *buannadha*. This apparent time difference in the introduction of private armies may only be due to the nature of the source material, as mentioned earlier.

The building of stone castles had been introduced into Ireland by the English. Since the English had penetrated almost the whole of Ireland at various times, castles had been built all over the country. In the fourteenth, and more particularly in the fifteenth century, it is known that Irish kings also had castles. The ruins of these 'castles' show them to have actually been quite modest fortified dwellings or 'tower houses'; however, it at least shows that the Irish upper class had adopted the English custom of building stone houses.

On the other hand, the Anglo-Irish used their money economy less and less and returned instead to the barter system. Cattle once more became a unit of account.

From the few examples it can be seen that the two social systems had to some degree merged. Whatever had proved viable was retained. In the final analysis, the Irish lords had become more European than their ancestors, and the Anglo-Irish had in turn adopted Irish customs: the two groups could no longer be distinguished from each other in terms of language and social behaviour.

The Learned Tradition

The learned tradition, that great pride of the Irish, shows hardly any sign of compromise and in this field the Anglo-Irish adapted themselves completely. The highly-developed Irish intellectual tradition was maintained without interruption and with only minor modifications from the earliest times into the seventeenth century.

The bardic schools in which the *filid* were trained are the best known: the most detailed description of these schools comes from

Thomas O'Sullevane in the year 1722. According to his account, the schools existed under the patronage of a secular lord and the students were provided for by the people of the neighbourhood. A master (*ollam*) taught at the school, and it was his task to record the deeds of his patron and important events such as marriages, births and deaths in high-quality verse. The *fili* had to be familiar with the history and genealogy of his patron and had to observe political events in order to transform them into literature.

The mastery of the Irish language came first in importance, for the rules of versification were very strict. The students were taught during the winter months, from Michaelmas to 25 March (the use of Christian dates is significant). The master gave the students a theme; they retired to their rooms and lay in the dark for 24 hours, working on their composition. Afterwards, they wrote their poems down and submitted them to the master for criticism and correction. The inherited conventions were to be strictly observed and there was no room for improvisation.

The poet's profession was highly respected and he was guaranteed high rewards; poets were exempted from military service and they enjoyed protection throughout Ireland. It is reported in the fifteenth century that the killing of a poet had to be compensated for with 120 head of cattle. The first attempts to study the Irish language systematically were made within the bardic schools. This is evident since the sixteenth century in the works of grammatical analysis. However, it is possible to tell from poetry that has been preserved that these language studies were being carried out as early as the twelfth century. In the important genre of praise poetry the last medieval centuries display unbroken continuity. This is evidence of the inherent vitality of the system, but does not show its flexibility which can be seen elsewhere.

The importance of the learned tradition in Irish society is shown by the example of a passage in the Annals of Clonmacnois from the year 1351:

William O Donogh Moyneagh O Kelly (lord of the Uí Mhaine, 1340–75) invited all the Irish poets, brehons, bards, harpers, gamesters . . . jesters and others of their kind of Ireland to his house upon Christmas this year, where every one of them was well used during Christmas and gave contentment to each of them at the time of their departure, so that every one was well pleased and extolled William for his bounty, one of which assembly composed certain Irish verses in commemoration of William and his house which began thus: *filidh Ereann go haointeach* 'the poets of Ireland in one house'.

The author of this poem was Gofraidh Fionn O Dálaigh.

In the year 1387 it was recorded that Niall O'Neill had established a place for the scholars from all of Ireland in Emhain Mhacha. This was obviously an attempt to recall the glory of the heroic age; it was almost a thousand years since Emhain Mhacha had had any real political significance. It was the scholars who had seen to it that the memory of this place had remained alive.

What is well documented in the case of the *filid* seems also to have applied to other branches of the learned élite, namely that tradition was cultivated and kept alive in schools. The professions of the lawyers, musicians and healers were kept within certain families and passed on from one generation to another. There were the famous families of lawyers such as the Mac Egans, Mac Clancys and the O'Dalys, and traditional families of poets like the O'Malcronys, O'Clerys, O'Duignans, etc. Occasionally, the term of the profession became the family name, as is the case with the family of healers called O' Hickey (*ícide* 'healer') or Mac Inlea (*liaigh* 'healer', cf. English 'leech'). Some families claimed to be able to trace their professional ancestors back over many centuries, but it is difficult to be sure whether such pedigrees were historically reliable or were manipulated simply in order to satisfy society's expectations.

The high regard in which these professions were held is shown in the case of the poet Niall O'Higgins who was said to have killed the English *locum tenens* Sir John Stanley in 1414 by means of a malediction. In this case tradition appears to have been combined with historical facts in order to impress people with the power of the poet.

Occasionally it is reported that some scholars were masters in more than one of these professions, e.g. 'Maurice Ó Gibillán, greatest master of Ireland in new and in old jurisprudence, in the canon and in the civil law, one eminent in wisdom and knowledge, master of poetry and Ogmic and many other arts', whose death was recorded in the Annals of Ulster in 1326. It is difficult to decide whether this was a more general development or simply an exception. The O'Daly family in Meath and the O'Donnellans in Connacht were considered masters of music and history from the twelfth century onwards, the Magraths and the O'Quils in Munster as poets and historians; Seán O' Dubhgain († 1372) was master of poetry and history with the Uí Mhaine.

The Anglo-Irish families also adopted this tradition. Although it is generally maintained that they had begun by employing musicians, as attested for the Earl of Louth as early as 1329, of equal if not greater importance for them were legal scholars as is indicated clearly in the Statutes of Kilkenny. Around 1432, the Earl of Ormond appointed Donnell Mac Clancy and his descendants to be his legal scholars. It was only by establishing its own dynasty of scholars that a family could become completely integrated into Irish tradition.

It would nevertheless be wrong to convey the impression that Irish culture was adopted by the Anglo-Irish without any opposition or modification. One opponent of this was Richard Ledrede, the quarrelsome bishop of Ossory (1318–60) who tried to ban all secular songs and to popularise hymns instead; he apparently wanted to continue using the secular melodies which appear to have been very popular. Influences were, however, more effective in other ways. The history of the wars in Clare in the late thirteenth century was written in Irish following the model of Lucan's *Pharsalia* on the Roman wars. This work was called *Caithréim Toirdelbaig*; its author, Seán Mac Ruaidhri Meic Craith, was influenced by the classical Latin model. As mentioned in the last chapter, a genuine innovation in the literary field, love lyrics in the Irish language, was introduced by an Anglo-Irish man, FitzGerald Earl of Desmond.

Generally speaking, the Anglo-Irish went over to the Irish learned tradition. How much this was valued may again be shown by one example. The Butlers of Ormond were generous patrons of Irish scholars. Two important manuscripts, British Library, London, Add. 30 512 and Bodleian Library, Oxford, Laud Misc. 610 (containing extracts from the now lost Psalter of Cashel) were written around the middle of the fifteenth century. In 1462, these manuscripts were offered and accepted as pledges for good behaviour following a war between the houses of Ormond and

Desmond. These books with their accounts of Irish history seem to have had the same value as hostages.

Finally, some of the more important late medieval manuscripts should be mentioned briefly in order to show what was then regarded as being worth preserving. A typical manuscript of this period is the Book of the Uí Mhaine. It contains historical and pseudo-historical material, genealogies of Irish saints, secular and spiritual poetry, placename legends (*dinsenchas*, i.e. popular explanation of placenames and fieldnames by allegedly historical events), biblical stories, excerpts from the Book of Rights as well as treatises on metrics, grammar and lexicography. Other wide-ranging volumes, almost small libraries in their own right, are the Yellow Book of Leccan and the Great Book of Leccan (named after the Mac Fírbhisig family of Lacken, Co. Sligo) from the later fourteenth century; the Great Book of Duniry (*Leabhar Breac*) containing mainly theological material, around 1411; the Book of Ballymote and others. In the Book of the Dean of Lismore, preserved in Scotland, are the love lyrics and poems of courtly love ascribed to FitzGerald, Earl of Desmond (*Gearóid Iarla*).

It is only due to this learned and scholarly tradition that so much historical material about Ireland has been preserved. Because of the political developments under the Tudors and Stuarts, the history of Ireland became a topic of serious investigation at quite an early stage. Traditional Irish society came to an end with the flight of the last Irish earls in 1607. During the Reformation many clerics were forced to leave the country and found refuge on the Continent. The Irish Franciscans bought a house in Louvain in 1617 and it has been in their possession ever since. The lay brother Mícél Ó Cléirigh, descendant of an old Irish scholarly family, joined this community. He was sent to Ireland in 1626 in order to collect hagiographical material. Over the next six years, he copied many important Irish texts in Donegal, including the Martyrologies of Donegal and of Oengus, *Leabhar Gabhála*, and others. In 1632, he set himself the task of collecting annalistic material about Irish history. This work was completed in 1636 by Mícél Ó Cléirigh together with Cúcoigríche Ó Cléirigh, Fearfeasa Ó Maolchoncaire and Cúcoigríche Ó Duibhghennáin: the Annals of the Four Masters.

These annals represent both the end of an era and the beginning of another; they marked the end of a learned tradition with a thousand years' history, carried on by the descendants of old learned families whose livelihood in Ireland had now been destroyed; they marked a new departure in that the first steps had been taken to make Irish history available to modern scholarship. A tradition had come to an end; the task was now to study and assess it.

12. The Enduring Tradition

In this book an outline has been given of a thousand years of Irish history. Instead of a summary the author would like to conclude by dealing with a few questions which occurred to him in the course of working on this book. Are there any constant features in the history of Ireland in the Middle Ages? What is to be gained by writing this history apart from adding a few facts to the knowledge of the interested reader? Does the history of Ireland in the Middle Ages concern us?

The last of these questions would seem to be the easiest to answer. It is a fact that Ireland in the first part of the Middle Ages stimulated developments on the Continent in several ways. This has been clearly demonstrated in the work of Ludwig Bieler. The achievements of the Irish missionaries are the first to come to mind; however, one should also consider the achievements of the missionaries from England who had been strongly influenced by Irish spirituality. Besides the contributions to the conversion of central Europe, one must also remember their contributions in the field of learning. Those who consider the political and intellectual world of the Carolingian Empire to have been formative for the future development of Europe, must be made aware that the intellectual achievements of that empire, which in turn influenced political decisions, are unthinkable without the insular contribution, without people like Willibrord, Winfrid/St Boniface, Virgil of Salzburg, Sedulius Scottus, Eriugena and others. But to label Ireland the island of saints and scholars can be misleading unless it is taken into account that sanctity and scholarship were rarely combined in the same individual. Moreover, Irish contributions in the field of learning are various and should therefore be treated in various ways.

Denis Bethell, an English medieval historian, taught for many years in Ireland and came to perceive the history of Ireland both from without and within. In the last lecture he gave before his death he put forward the concept of the dualism of the Christian Church in western Europe in the first part of the Middle Ages. The dualism he had in mind was one of the 'Southern Church' and the 'Northern Church'; he contrasted the diocesan Church which had risen on the territory of the former Roman Empire with the monastic Church which predominated in Europe north of the Alps and of the Loire. According to Bethell, the repercussions of this dualism were of decisive importance for the first part of the European Middle Ages and could still be felt until the Fourth Lateran Council (1215). The 'Northern Church' originated in non-Romanised areas, and the Irish made decisive contributions to its formation. This concept can be accepted in outline, although it is necessary to elaborate on details and thus to modify it. This is the beginning of a more comprehensive appreciation of Ireland's contribution to the formation of medieval Europe.

Those who consider this topic will soon realise how important it is to take a closer look at the history of Ireland itself. Once the Irish impact on Europe has been established, the question arises how Ireland could have become so important. A more detailed study of the history of Ireland in the Middle Ages is required to answer this question.

In dealing with the specific development of their people, Irish historians invariably point to the island's geographical position as a key factor in the development of its history. While this may well be relevant, it has to be put into perspective. What may appear to the modern observer to be a peripheral geographical position has not always been peripheral in history and politics. In the first part of the Middle Ages in particular Ireland lay at the crossing of busy trade routes which stretched from Spain to Scandinavia. The political and intellectual consequences of this have been mentioned several times in the preceding chapters; they have contributed to the fate of Ireland. It is therefore necessary to call into question the contention of many Irish historians that Ireland had had only one powerful and overwhelming neighbour – England.

The development of any one society has to be considered in comparison with the development of other societies, because only by comparison do specific strengths and weaknesses become apparent. Compared to other countries, Ireland was much less threatened from abroad than most others. We have seen that the impact of the Viking and English invasions did not destroy the core of Irish society even though they affected it. Viewed from the end of the Middle Ages, the impact of the Vikings seems to have been as formative as that of the English. This perspective is all too easily distorted by what happened in post-medieval times.

It has often been suggested that Ireland's political fragmentation
provided the strongest protection against a complete takeover of
the country by the Vikings or the English. This view is shared by
the author. Yet even the term 'political fragmentation' has strongly
negative connotations. It is tempting for the modern observer to
give absolute priority to national unity or even the nation state as
the desirable end product of political development. It is worth
considering the opposite point of view. There has been considerable
debate as to whether Ireland was moving in the direction of a
national kingdom in the twelfth century, a process interrupted
shortly before its completion by the intervention of the English. An
attractive challenge for the student of history is to take account of
the actual course of events whatever his own personal point of
view. Participants in that debate may be reminded that the
evolution of societies is rarely linear. Thus it is by no means certain
that national unity would have been achieved had it not been for
the intervention of the English, or, if it had been achieved, whether
it would have lasted. On the contrary, there are important
indications to the contrary.

The term 'political fragmentation' demands closer examination.
It may be significant that in the popular view of their own history
the Irish are reluctant to assign any great political importance to
individual figures, with the exception perhaps of Brian Boru and
Dermot Mac Murrough. There is no serious modern biography of
an Irish medieval king; this is an astonishing lacuna. There was
always a multiplicity of kings who had to struggle for survival in a
political situation that appears to have been quite well balanced.
Surely this shows the strength of the system as a whole even though
it makes it for many both difficult and frustrating to come to terms
with the political history of Ireland.

The political map of Ireland around 1500 can be drawn with
some degree of confidence. When compared with the picture of
Ireland around 500, the contours of which are much less precise, it
can be argued that the two pictures resemble each other to a
surprising degree. Around 500 just as around 1500 there were a
great number of small lordships and there were also some lordships
that were of greater influence without, however, dominating the
country. If this description is correct, then it seems, as argued
previously, that English influence had been neutralised and that

the strength of the Irish system had prevailed. This is quite a remarkable phenomenon.

The history of Ireland in the Middle Ages is all too rarely studied as a whole. From such a perspective, the strength of Irish society in the first part of the Middle Ages is fully appreciated only when it becomes apparent that this society was able to absorb the impact of the Vikings and that of the English. In this respect the last two medieval centuries clearly demonstrate the essential stability of the Irish system. In the case of Ireland, political history must be seen as only a part of the whole. If indeed political fragmentation is one of the main features of Irish medieval history, then the outstanding richness and vitality of Irish culture is a further characteristic, closely linked to that fragmentation. It has been argued that Irish society was able to encounter Latin civilisation on equal terms and therefore successfully to withstand it. This was the case throughout the Middle Ages. This is one of the fundamental conclusions to be drawn from an examination of Ireland in the second part of the Middle Ages.

A second feature that marked Ireland very strongly was the openness of society to intellectual and cultural influences from outside. As far as the first medieval centuries are concerned, the effects of such influences can in general be perceived only indirectly and vaguely. Later they can be associated more easily with particular individuals. These range from Palladius and Patrick to Giraldus Cambrensis and Laurent Rathold de Pasztho. These men spent stimulating weeks, months or years in Ireland. Due to the fact that Ireland's history was relatively undisturbed from outside, such foreign influences could be assimilated in the most beneficial ways by Irish society.

In the course of this book several 'firsts' were claimed for Ireland in early medieval Europe. The most important of these 'firsts' seems to me to have been the wide-ranging use of the vernacular. Irish was developed as a written language and applied in many different ways before any other non-Latin language of western Europe. Unlike the Germanic languages which were developed as written languages on the basis of religious texts, the Irish language was first used for secular material and only at a later stage for religious texts. One of the preconditions for that was the existence of a non-Latin intellectual tradition in Ireland from prehistoric times. In the face of an incoming Latin civilisation, as it was then current in the Church, this tradition continued unbroken. One could go further and suggest that the native civilisation was even strengthened by competition with Latin culture. It is possible, though it cannot be proved, that non-Latin intellectual developments, non-Latin literature, were introduced by the Irish into other European countries. It was in Ireland, however, that the effect of the widespread use of the vernacular was strongest. It apparently became possible to receive new ideas without having to abandon one's own cultural identity. On the contrary, this identity emerged more strongly than ever. All this was made possible by the existence of a socially respected and privileged intellectual élite which had developed from an archaic stage of culture in prehistoric times. The survival of this élite in Christian times is partly due to the fact that classical Roman civilisation could not, as elsewhere, eclipse and largely destroy things non-Roman and pre-Roman. Because of this, the archaic features of Irish society could become or remain dynamic in the Middle Ages. This is a view which attempts to order the facts so that they make sense even if certain details have yet to be worked out.

Should all this be so, then the history of Ireland in the Middle Ages shows that there was a viable alternative development to that of the rest of Europe, dominated by Christian Latin culture. Those who claim not to understand the political problems of Ireland today, problems often labelled 'medieval', are well advised to look more closely at Ireland in the Middle Ages. It seems clear that Ireland developed quite differently in many essential respects from Continental Europe. It is impossible to reach a full understanding of Ireland's past without recognising and appreciating this fact.

Abbreviations and Sigla

AI   Annals of Inisfallen
AU   Annals of Ulster
Conf.   Patrick's Confessio (quoted by chapters)
Ep.C.   (Epistolae =) Letters of Columbanus (quoted from Walker's edition)
Ep.P.   (Epistola =) Letter of Patrick to the soldiers of Coroticus (quoted by chapters)
HE   Bede, *Historia Ecclesiastica Gentis Anglorum* (quoted by book and chapter)
Hib.   Collectio Canonum Hibernensis
JRSAI   Journal of the Royal Society of Antiquaries of Ireland
MGH   Monumenta Germaniae Historia (and the common subsections)
PBA   Proceedings of the British Academy
PL   J. P. Migne, *Patrologia Latina*
PRIA   Proceedings of the Royal Irish Academy
S.   (Sermo =) Sermons of Columbanus (quoted from Walker's edition)
Tig.   Annals of Tigernach
VC   Adomnán's *Vita Columbae* (quoted after the edition of the Andersons)

Bibliography and References

GENERAL STUDIES

T. W. Moody, F. X. Martin (eds), *The Course of Irish History* (Cork, 1965) (reprinted frequently). Liam de Paor (ed.), *Milestones in Irish History* (Cork and Dublin, 1986). *Gill History of Ireland*, eds James Lydon and Margaret MacCurtain (Dublin, 1972), with good maps. Gearóid Mac Niocaill, *Ireland before the Vikings*; Donncha Ó Corráin, *Ireland before the Normans*; James Lydon, *Ireland in the later Middle Ages*; Kenneth Nicholls, *Gaelic and Gaelicized Ireland* (Dublin, 1972). *Helicon History of Ireland*, eds Art Cosgrove and Elma Collins (Dublin, 1981), Charles Doherty, *Early Medieval Ireland*, forthcoming; Robin Frame, *Colonial Ireland, 1169–1369* (Dublin, 1981); Art Cosgrove, *Late medieval Ireland, 1370–1541* (Dublin, 1981). Frank Mitchell, *The Irish Landscape* (London, 1976). William Nolan (ed.), *The Shaping of Ireland. The geographical perspective* (Cork and Dublin, 1986). *Irish Historic Towns Atlas*, No. 1 Kildare, eds J. H. Andrews and Anngret Simms (Dublin, 1986). P. J. Corish (ed.), *A History of Irish Catholicism*, 6 vols (incomplete), (Dublin, 1967ff.). Fergal McGrath, *Education in Ancient and Medieval Ireland* (Dublin, 1976).

GENERAL SURVEYS
F. J. Byrne, in: *Handbuch der europäischen Geschichte*, Vol. 1, ed. Theodor Schieffer (Stuttgart, 1976); M. Richter, Vol. 2, ed. Ferdinand Seibt (Stuttgart, 1987). *A New History of Ireland*, eds T. W. Moody, F. X. Martin, F. J. Byrne; Vol. 2, *Medieval Ireland (1169–1534)* (Oxford, 1987); Vol. 8, *A chronology of Irish History to 1976* (Oxford, 1982); Vol. 9 *Maps, genealogies, lists* (Oxford, 1984).

LITERATURE
Kenneth Jackson, *A Celtic Miscellany* (Penguin Classic, Harmondsworth, 1971); Robin Flower, *The Irish Tradition* (Oxford, 1947).

LATEST BIBLIOGRAPHICAL GUIDES
In *Lexikon des Mittelalters* (1977ff.).

PARTS I AND II

J. F. Kenney, *The sources for the early History of Ireland. I. Ecclesiastical. An Introduction and Guide* (first published in 1929; revised edition Dublin, 1961). Michael Lapidge and Richard Sharpe, *A Bibliography of Celtic-Latin literature, 400–1200* (Dublin, 1985). Kathleen Hughes, *Early Christian Ireland: Introduction to the Sources* (London, 1972). Ludwig Bieler, *Ireland. Harbinger of the Middle Ages* (Oxford, 1963). Myles Dillon and Nora Chadwick, *The Celtic Realms* (London, 1967). Máire and Liam de Paor, *Early Christian Ireland* (London, 1958). E. R. Norman and J. K. S. St Joseph, *The early Development of Irish Society: the evidence of aerial photography* (London, 1969). F. J. Byrne, *Irish Kings and High Kings* (London, 1973). Eoin Mac Neill, *Phases of Irish*

History (London, 1919). T. F. O'Rahilly, *Early Irish History and Mythology* (Dublin, 1946). James Carney, *Studies in Irish Literature and History* (Dublin, 1955). Kathleen Hughes, *The Church in early Irish Society* (London, 1966). A. P. Smyth, *Warlords and Holy Men. Scotland 80–1000* (The New History of Scotland I), (London, 1984). Emile Benveniste, *Indo-European Language and Society* (London, 1973). M. W. Barley and R. P. C. Hanson (eds), *Christianity in Britain, 300–700* (Leicester, 1968). Dorothy Whitelock *et alii* (eds), *Ireland in early mediaeval Europe*, (Studies in Memory of Kathleen Hughes), (Cambridge, 1982). Heinz Löwe (ed.), *Die Iren und Europa im früheren Mittelalter*, 2 vols (Stuttgart, 1982). P. Ní Chatháin and M. Richter (eds), *Ireland and Europe. The early Church* (Stuttgart, 1984).

1. THE CELTS

J. Raftery, *The Celts* (Cork, 1964). Jan Filip, *Celtic Civilization and its Heritage*, (Prague, 1977). Ann Ross, *Pagan Celtic Britain* (London, 1967). Proinsias Mac Cana, *Celtic Mythology* (London, 1970). L. Fleuriot, 'Le rôle des Celtes dans l'Europe du haut moyen-âge', *Revue de l'Université de Bruxelles*, 1977, pp.146–58.

2. IRELAND IN PREHISTORIC TIMES (BEFORE C. A.D. 500)

Táin Bó Cúalnge from the Book of Leinster, ed. and transl. Cecile O'Rahilly (Dublin, 1967). *The Táin*, transl. Thomas Kinsella (Oxford, 1948). Rudolf Thurneysen, *Die irische Helden – und Königsage* (Halle, 1921). Eoin MacNeill, *Celtic Ireland* (Dublin, 1921, reprinted 1981). R. Thurneysen, *A Grammar of Old Irish* (revised and enlarged edition, Dublin, 1946). Whitley Stokes and John Strachan (eds), *Thesaurus Palaeohibernicus*, 2 vols (Cambridge, 1901–03). D. A. Binchy, *Celtic and Anglo-Saxon Kingship* (Oxford, 1970). *Críath Gablach*, ed. D. A. Binchy (Dublin, 1941). John V. Kelleher, 'The Táin and the Annals', *Ériu* 22, 1971, pp.107–27. Myles Dillon, 'The Archaism of Irish Tradition', *PBA* 33, 1947, pp.320–40. D. A. Binchy, 'Some Celtic legal terms', *Celtica* 3, 1956, pp.221–31. T. M. Charles-Edwards, 'The Heir-Apparent in Irish and Welsh Law', *Celtica* 9, 1971, pp.180–90. P. Mac Cana, '*Regnum* and *Sacerdotium*: notes on Irish tradition', *PBA* 65, 1979, pp.443–79.

1. K. H. Jackson, *The Oldest Irish Tradition: a Window on the Iron Age* (Cambridge, 1946). It should be emphasised that Jackson shows parallels between the *Táin* and the Homeric epics which suggest direct influence.
2. Eoin MacNeill, 'The Law of dynastic Succession', in *Celtic Ireland*, pp.114–43.

3. POLITICAL DEVELOPMENT IN EARLY IRISH TIMES

Peter Sawyer, *From Roman Britain to Norman England* (London, 1978). James Campbell (ed.), *The Anglo-Saxons* (Oxford, 1982). Kenneth Jackson, *Language and History in Early Britain* (Edinburgh, 1953). D. A. Binchy, 'The Fair of Tailtiu and the Feast of Tara', *Ériu* 18, 1958, pp.113–38. Wendy Davies, *Wales in the early Middle Ages* (Leicester, 1982).

3. Bede, *Vita S. Cuthberti*, 'Two *lives of Cuthbert* Ch. 24, ed, Bertram Colgrave (Cambridge, 1939, reprint New York, 1969), p.230ff. Dungallen, Vita Wilfridi, Ch 28 (MGH SS. rer. Merov. 6), p.221.

4. THE BEGINNINGS OF CHRISTIANITY IN IRELAND

D. A. Binchy, 'Patrick and his Biographers, Ancient and Modern', *Studia Hibernica* 2, 1962, pp.7–173 (review article of fundamental importance). R. P. C. Hanson, *Saint Patrick. His Origins and Career* (Oxford, 1968). James Carney, *The Problem of Saint Patrick* (Dublin, 1973). A. B. E. Hood (ed. and transl.) *St. Patrick. His Writings and Muirchu's Life* (Arthurian Period Sources 9, Old Woking, Surrey, 1978). Peter Dronke, 'St. Patrick's Reading', *Cambridge Medieval Celtic Studies* 1, 1981, pp.21–38. P. A. Wilson, 'St. Patrick and Irish Christian Origins', *Studia Celtica* 14–15, 1979–1980, pp.344–79. C. E. Stancliffe, 'Kings and conversion: some comparisons between the Roman mission to England and Patrick's to Ireland', *Frühmittelalterliche Studien* 14, 1980, pp.59–94. *Landévennec et le monachisme breton dans le Haut-Moyen-Age*. Actes du colloque du 15ème centenaire de l'abbaye de Landévennec, 25–27 avril 1985 (Landévennec, Plomodiern, 1985). The quotation from *Bethu Phátraic* is taken from Ludwig Bieler, 'The Mission of Palladius', *Traditio* 6, 1948, pp.1–32. Interchange between Irish and British, David Greene, 'Some linguistic evidence relating to the British Church', in Barley and Hanson, *Christianity in Britain*, pp.75–86. For new suggestions see Damian MacManus, 'The so-called *Cothrige* and *Pátraic* strata of Latin loan words in early Irish', in *Ireland and Europe*, pp.79–96.

4. R. Weijenburg, 'Deux sources grecques de la "Confession de Patrice"', *Revue d'Histoire Ecclésiastique* 62, 1967, pp.361–78.
5. See E. A. Thompson, 'St Patrick and Coroticus', *Journal of Theological Studies*, NS 31, 1980, pp.12–27. I find E. A. Thompson's *Who was Saint Patrick?* (Woodbridge, Suffolk, 1985), far from convincing.
6. Walahfrid Strabo, *De exordiis et incrementis rerum ecclesiasticarum* 7 (MGH Capit. II), p.481.

5. THE FORMATION OF THE EARLY IRISH CHURCH

Map of Monastic Ireland (Ordnance Survey, Dublin, 1964). John Ryan, *Irish Monasticism. Origins and early Development* (London, 1931). A. O. Anderson and M. O. Anderson (eds), *Adomnan's Life of Columba* (Edinburgh, 1961). 'Columba', article by Próinséas Ní Chatháin *Theologische Realenzyklopädie*, Vol. 8, pp. 156–59, D. A. Bullough, 'Adomnan and the Achievement of Iona', *Scottish Historical Review* 43, 1964, pp.111–30, 44, 1965, pp.17–33. G. S. M. Walker (ed.), *Sancti Columbani Opera* (Scriptores Latini Hiberniae 2, Dublin, 1957). H. B. Clarke and M. Brennan (eds), *Columbanus and Merovingian Monasticism* (British Archaeological Reports, International Series 113, 1981). F. J. Byrne, 'The Ireland of St Columba', *Historical Studies* 5, 1970, pp.37–58. M. Richter, *Der irische Hintergrund der angelsächsischen Mission*, in Löwe, *Iren*, pp.120–37.

7. Wendy Davies, *The Llandaff Charters* (Aberystwyth, 1979). Wendy Davies, 'The Latin Charter Tradition in western Britain, Brittany and Ireland in the early medieval period', in *Ireland in mediaeval Europe*, pp.258–80.

8. Denis Bethell, 'The Originality of the early Irish Church', JRSAI 111, 1981, pp.36–49.

6. CHRISTIAN IRELAND IN THE SEVENTH AND EIGHTH CENTURIES

INSULAR LATIN

Louis Holtz, *Donat et la tradition de l'enseignement grammatical* (Paris, 1981). Michael Herren, 'Sprachliche Eigentümlichkeiten in den hibernolateinischen Texten des 7. und 8. Jahrhunderts', in Löwe, *Iren*, pp.425–33. Michael Herren, 'Hisperic Latin; "Luxurious Culture-Fungus of Decay"', *Traditio* 30, 1974, pp.411–19. For a different view see J.-M. Picard, 'Une préfiguration du latin carolingien: la syntaxe de la *Vita Columbae* d'Adomnán, auteur irlandais du VIIᵉ siècle', *Romanobarbarica* 6, 1981–82, pp.235–83.

IRELAND AND SPAIN

J. N. Hillgarth, 'Ireland and Spain in the seventh century', *Peritia* 3, 1984, pp.1–16.

THE BIBLE

Próinséas Ní Chatháin and Michael Richter (eds), *Ireland and Christendom. The Bible and the Missions* (Stuttgart, 1987). Bernhard Bischoff, 'Turning-points in the history of Latin exegesis in the early Middle Ages', in Martin McNamara (ed.), *Biblical Studies. The Medieval Irish Contribution* (Proceedings of the Irish Biblical Association No. 1, Dublin, 1976), pp.74–160. P. Grosjean, 'Sur quelques exégètes irlandais du VIIᵉ siècle', *Sacris Erudiri* 7, 1955, pp.67–98. Patrick McGurk, 'The Irish Pocket Gospel Book', *Sacris Erudiri* 8, 1956, pp.249–69. M. McNamara, 'Psalter Text and Psalter Study in the early Irish Church (A.D. 600–1200)', *PRIA* 73 C, 1973, pp.201–72. R. E. McNally (ed.), *Scriptores Hiberniae Minores* (CCSL CVIII B, 1973).

PENITENTIALS

Ludwig Bieler (ed.), *The Irish Penitentials* (Scriptores Latini Hiberniae 5, Dublin 1963). Raymund Kottje, 'Überlieferung und Rezeption der irischen Bussbücher auf dem Kontinent', in Löwe, *Iren*, pp.511–23.

ANNALS

A. P. Smyth, 'The earliest Irish Annals: their first contemporary entries and the earliest centres of recording', *PRIA* 72 C, 1972, pp.1–48. Gearóid Mac Niocaill, *The Medieval Irish Annals* (Dublin Historical Association. Medieval Irish History Series 3, Dublin 1975). Seán Mac Airt and Gearóid Mac Niocaill (eds), *The Annals of Ulster* (to A.D. 1131) (Dublin, 1983). Dáibhi O Cróinín, 'Early Irish annals from Easter-tables: a case restated', *Peritia* 2, 1983, pp.74–86.

KINGSHIP

Audacht Morainn, ed. Fergus Kelly (Dublin, 1976). Hans Hubert Anton, 'De duodecim abusivis saeculi und sein Einfluss auf den Kontinent, insbesondere auf die karolingischen Fürstenspiegel', in Löwe, *Iren*, pp.568–617. Michael J. Enright, *Ioan, Tara and Soissons. The origin of the royal Anointing Ritual* (Arbeiten zur Frühmittelalterforschung, Vol. 17, Berlin, New York, 1985).

IRISH LAW

Rudolf Thurneysen *et alii* (eds), *Studies in early Irish Law* (Dublin, 1936). D. A.

BIBLIOGRAPHY AND REFERENCES

Binchy, 'Bretha Crólige', *Ériu* 12, 1938, pp.1-77, 1) A Binchy, 'Irish law-tracts reedited', *Ériu* 17, 1955, pp.52-85. D. A. Binchy, *The date and provenance of Uraicecht Becc*', *Ériu* 18, 1958, pp.44-54. T. M. Charles-Edwards, 'The Corpus Iuris Hibernici, Review Article', *Studia Hibernica* 20, 1980, pp.141-62. D. Ó Corráin, L. Breatnach and A. Breen, 'The laws of the Irish, *Peritia* 3, 1984, pp.382-438.

COLLECTIO CANONUM HIBERNENSIS
H. Wasserschleben (ed.), *Die irische Kanonensammlung* (second edition, Leipzig, 1885, reprint Aalen, 1966). M. P. Sheehy, 'The Collectio Canonum Hibernensis: a Celtic Phenomenon', in Löwe, *Iren*, pp.525-35.

ART
Françoise Henry, *Irish Art in the early Christian Period (to 800 A.D.)* (London, 1967). F. Henry, *Irish Art during the Viking Invasions, 800-1020 A.D.* (London, 1967). Françoise Henry, *Irish Art in the Romanesque period, 1020-1170* (London, 1970). *Great Books of Ireland*, Thomas Davies Lectures (Dublin, 1967). *Treasures of Irish Art, 1500 B.C.-1500 A.D.* (Metropolitan Museum of Art, New York, 1977).

9. John W. Waterer, 'Irish Book Satchels or Budgets', *Medieval Archaeology* 12, 1968, pp.70-82.
10. D. H. Wright, 'The Tablets from Springmount Bog: a key to early Irish palaeography', *American Journal of Archaeology* 67, 1963, p.219. Reproduction in E. A. Lowe, *Codices Latini Antiquiores*, Supplement (Oxford, 1971), No. 1684.
11. *Acta Sanctorum* (1 Feb., Antwerp, 1666) p.99ff. The translation given here is the one from the forthcoming critical edition of Cogitosus's work by Dr Seán Connolly and Dr J.-M. Picard whose generous permission to quote from their translation is gratefully acknowledged.
12. John Morris, 'The Chronicle of Eusebius: Irish Fragments', *Bulletin of the Institute of Classical Studies of the University of London* 19, 1972, pp.80-93. A bifolio containing fragments of the Latin 'Eusebius' written in an Irish hand in the early seventh century was sold by Sotheby (London) in June 1985.
13. See JRSAI 110, 1980, with the articles by Hilary Richardson, F. J. Byrne and Próinséas Ní Chatháin. Michael Ryan, 'The Derrynaflan and other early Irish eucharistic chalices: some speculations', in Ní Chatháin and Richter, *Ireland and Europe, the early Church*, pp.135-48. Michael Ryan, *The Derrynaflan Hoard I*. (A preliminary Report, Dublin, 1983).
14. Alcuin, Ep. 287, MGH Epp. 4.
15. Einhart, *Vita Karoli Magni*, Ch. 16 (MGH SS rer. Germ. Hannover, Leipzig, 1911).

7. SECULARISATION AND REFORM IN THE EIGHTH CENTURY

L. Bieler (ed.), *The Patrician Texts in the Book of Armagh* (Scriptores Latini Hiberniae 10, Dublin, 1979). Wendy Davies, 'Clerics as rulers: some implications of the terminology of ecclesiastical authority in early medieval Ireland', in N. Brooks (ed.), *Latin and the vernacular languages in early medieval Britain*, (Leicester, 1982), pp.81-97. Peter O'Dwyer, *Céli Dé. Spiritual Reform in Ireland 750-900* (second edition, Dublin, 1981). E. J. Gwynn and W. J. Purton, 'The Monastery of Tallaght', *PRIA* 29 C, 1912, pp.115-79. Heinz Dopsch, Roswitha Juffinger (eds), *Virgil von Salzburg. Missionar und Gelehrter* (Salzburg, 1985). John Hennig, 'A feast of all the saints of Europe', *Speculum* 21, 1946, pp. 49-66.

16. MGH SS. rer. Merov. II. 463 (B).
17. *Conversio Bagoariorum et Carantanorum*, ed. Herwig Wolfram (Wien, Graz, Köln, 1979), Chs 3 and 5, pp. 40 and 44.

8. THE AGE OF THE VIKINGS

Brian O'Cuiv (ed.), *The impact of the Scandinavian Invasions on the Celtic-speaking Peoples, 800–1000* (Dublin, 1975). Peter Sawyer, 'The Two Viking Ages in Britain, a discussion', *Mediaeval Scandinavia* 2, 1969, pp.63–207. A. P. Smyth, *Scandinavian Kings in the British Isles, 850–880* (Oxford, 1977). P. H. Sawyer, *Kings and Vikings. Scandinavia and Europe* A.D. *700–1100* (London, New York, 1982). Patrick F. Wallace, 'The English presence in Viking Dublin', in M. A. Blackburn (ed.), *Anglo-Saxon monetary History*, (Leicester, 1986), pp.201–21.

PART III

Bibliography: P. W. A. Asplin, *Medieval Ireland, c. 1170–1495* (Dublin, 1971). E. Curtis and R. B. McDowell (eds), *Irish Historical Documents, 1172–1922* (Dublin, 1943). H. G. Orpen, *Ireland under the Normans*, 4 vols (Oxford, 1911–20). A. J. Otway-Ruthven, *A History of Medieval Ireland* (London, 1968). H. G. Richardson and G. O. Sayles, *The Administration of Ireland, 1172–1377* (Dublin, 1963). J. A. Watt, *The Church and the Two Nations in Medieval Ireland* (Cambridge, 1970). M. P. Sheehy (ed.), *Pontificia Hibernica. Medieval papal chancery documents concerning Ireland, 600–1261*, 2 vols (Dublin, 1962–65). For the chronology of the most important English administrative officials and the bishops see E. B. Fryde, D. E. Greenway, S. Porter and I. Roy (eds), *Handbook of British Chronology* (third edition, London, 1986).

9. IRELAND UNDER FOREIGN INFLUENCE: THE TWELFTH CENTURY

Robert Bartlett, *Gerald of Wales, 1146–1223* (Oxford, 1982). English version of the *Topographia* by J. J. O'Meara (Penguin Classic, Harmondsworth, 1982). Michael Richter, 'The European dimension of Irish history in the eleventh and twelfth centuries', *Peritia* 4, 1985, pp.328–45.

DUBLIN

Patrick F. Wallace, two articles in H. B. Clarke and Anngret Simms (eds), *The comparative history of urban origins in Non-Roman Europe: Ireland, Wales, Denmark, Germany, Poland and Russia from the Ninth to the Thirteenth century* (British Archaeological Reports, International Series 255, 1985).

MAP

Dublin c. 840 – c. 1540: the medieval town in the modern city (Ordnance Survey, Dublin, 1978).

REFORM

M. Richter (ed.), *Canterbury Professions* (Torquay 1973), Introduction.

P. A. Breatnach, "The might of the Irish monastic tradition at Ratisbon (Regensburg), *Celtica* 13, 1980, pp.58–77.
John van Engen, 'The Christian Middle Ages as an historiographical problem', *American Historical Review* 91, 1986, pp.519–52.

WALES
William Rees, *An Historical Atlas of Wales* (third edition, London, 1967).

18. J. Vendryes, *Betha Grighora* (Revue Celtique 42, 1925), pp.119–53, quotation on p.128; see also John Hennig, 'Ireland's contribution to the martyrological tradition of the popes', *Archivum Historiae Pontificiae* 10, 1972, pp. 9–23, esp. pp.21–2.
19. M. Richter, 'The First Century of Anglo-Irish Relations', *History* 59, 1974, pp.195–210.
20. M. Richter, 'Giraldiana', *Irish Historical Studies* 21, 1979, p.425; for more detail see M. Richter, 'Towards a methodology of historical sociolinguistics'. *Folia Linguistica Historica, Acta Societatis Linguisticae Europae*, VI, 1, 1985, pp.41–61.
21. *Historic and Municipal Documents of Ireland, 1172–1320*, ed. J. T. Gilbert (RS 53, London, 1870), p. 1.
22. *Ibid.*, p.2.
23. *Ibid.*, pp.3–48.
24. M. Richter, *Giraldus Cambrensis. The Growth of the Welsh Nation* (second edition, Aberystwyth, 1976), pp.18–21.

10. IRELAND FROM THE REIGN OF JOHN TO THE STATUTES OF KILKENNY

G. W. S. Barrow, *The Anglo-Norman era in Scottish History* (Oxford, 1980). J. Lydon (ed.), *The English in Medieval Ireland* (Dublin, 1984), and on this see M. Richter, 'The interpretation of medieval Irish History', *Irish Historical Studies* 24, 1985, pp.289–98. Geoffrey J. Hand, *English Law in Ireland, 1290–1324* (Cambridge, 1967). Robin Frame, *English Lordship in Ireland, 1318–1361* (Oxford, 1982).

FELIM O'CONNOR
Myles Dillon, 'The Inauguration of O'Connor', in *Medieval Studies presented to Aubrey Gwynn*, (eds) J. A. Watt, J. B. Morrall, F. X. Martin (Dublin, 1961), pp.186–202.

25. Giraldus Cambrensis, *Expugnatio Hibernica*, (eds). A. B. Scott and F. X. Martin (Dublin, 1978), p.80.
26. G. O. Sayles (ed.), *Documents of the Affairs of Ireland before the King's Council* (Dublin, 1979) (abbr.: *Affairs*), No. 3.
27. *Affairs*, No. 41.
28. *Affairs*, No. 14.
29. *Affairs*, No. 35.
30. There is no modern critical edition of the Remonstrance. The best text is in Thomas Hearne (ed.), *Johannis de Fordun Scotichronicon* (Oxford, 1722), vol. 3, pp.908–926; English translation in Curtis, McDowell, *Irish Historical Documents*, pp.38–46. See also J. A. Watt, 'Negotiations between Edward II and John XXII concerning Ireland', *Irish Historical Studies* 10, 1956, pp.1–20, and M. Richter, *Irish Historical Studies* 24, 1985, p.295 and n.46.

31. *Annals of Ireland, 1162–1370, Chartularies of St. Mary's Abbey Dublin*, ed. by J. T. Gilbert (RS 80, London, 1884), p.377ff.

32. *Ibid.*, p.361. See also A. Gwynn, 'The Medieval University of St. Patrick's, Dublin', *Studies* 27, 1938, pp.199–212; 437–54.

33. Robin Frame, 'English Officials and Irish Chiefs in the fourteenth century', *English Historical Review* 90, 1975, p.771.

34. *Annals of Ireland* (as above n.31), p.381.

35. *Ibid.*, p.383.

36. C. Plummer, 'On the Colophons and Marginalia of Irish scribes', *PBA* 12, 1926, pp.41–2.

37. *Statutes and Ordinances and Acts of the Parliament of Ireland King John to Henry V*, ed. H. F. Berry (Dublin, 1907), pp.430–68.

38. *Affairs*, No. 238.

39. Gearóid Mac Niocaill, 'A propos du vocabulaire social irlandais du Bas Moyen-Age', *Études Celtiques* 12, 1970–71, pp.512–46.

11. THE END OF THE MIDDLE AGES

GENERAL

Kenneth Nicholls, *Gaelic and Gaelicized Ireland in the Middle Ages* (Dublin, 1972).

THE IRISH LANGUAGE

Osborn Bergin, 'The Native Irish Grammarian', *PBA* 24, 1938, pp.205–35. Osborn Bergin, *Irish Bardic Poetry*, (eds) D. Greene and F. Kelly (Dublin, 1970). J. E. Caerwyn Williams, 'The Court Poet in Medieval Ireland', *PBA* 57, 1971, pp.1–51.

ST PATRICK'S PURGATORY

J.-M. Picard and Yolande de Pontfarcy, *Saint Patrick's Purgatory* (Blackrock, Co. Dublin, 1985). H. Delehaye, 'Le Pèlerinage de Laurent de Pasztho au Purgatoire de S. Patrice', *Analecta Bollandiana* 27, 1908, pp.35–60.

AUGUSTINIAN REFORMS

F. X. Martin, 'The Augustinian Friaries in pre-Reformation Ireland', *Augustiniana* 6, 1956, pp.346–84. F. X. Martin, 'The Irish Augustinian Reform Movement in the Fifteenth Century', in *Medieval Studies presented to Aubrey Gwynn* (as above in Ch. 10), pp.230–64.

LEARNED TRADITION

Robin Flower, *The Irish tradition* (as above General Studies). R. A. Breathnach, 'The Book of Uí Mhaine'; Cathaldus Gibilin, 'The Annals of the Four Masters', both in *Great Books of Ireland* (as above bibliography to Ch. 6), pp.77–103.

40. M. B. Crowe, 'Peter of Ireland: Aquinas's teacher of the *artes liberales*', in *Arts Libéraux et Philosophie au Moyen-Age* (Montreal, Paris, 1969), pp.617–26.

41. Katherine Walsh, *A Fourteenth-century Scholar and Primate. Richard FitzRalph in Oxford, Avignon and Armagh* (Oxford, 1981).

42. Norman Moore, 'An Essay on the History of Medicine in Ireland', *St. Bartholomew's Hospital Reports* 11, 1875, pp.45–64. See also Whitley Stokes, 'On the *materia medica* of the medieval Irish', *Revue Celtique* 9, 1888, pp.222–44. Francis Shaw, 'Irish medical men and philosophers', in *Seven Centuries of Irish Learning*, (ed.) Brian Ó Cuîr (Dublin, 1961), pp.75–86.

List of Irish words

pl. – plural; gen. – genitive case
The stress falls normally on the first syllable in Irish words.

áes dána [ois da:na] – people of learning
aire ard [ar'e a:rd] – high noble
aire déso [ar'e de:so] – lowest of nobles
aire forgill [ar'e forgil'] – noble of superior testimony
aire túise [ar'e tu:ʃe] – noble of leadership
ard-rí [a:rd ri:] – high-king

báire [ba:r'el] – 'hurling'
bíathach [b'i:ataχ] – 'betagh'
bíathaid [bi:aθiδ'] – feeds, nourishes
biáit [b'ia:d'] – *beati* (opening word of Psalm 118)
bóaire [bo:'ar'e] – freeholder (who probably owes a cow a year in tribute)
bothach [boθaχ] – cottier, crofter
brithem [b'r'iθev], (brehon') pl. brithemin – maker of judgements, jurist
buada [bu:aδa] – special qualities, attributes
buannadha [bu:аnaδa] – quartering, billeting soldiers

cáin [ka:n'] – written law, tribute
caisel [kaʃel']– stone fort
caplait [kablit'] – Maundy Thursday
cathach [kahaχ] – reliquary (taken to battle), 'battle book'
céle [k'e:le], pl. céli – companion
céle giallnai [k'e:l'e g'i:aLni] – base client
cenn [k'eN] – head
cland [klaN] – child
cléirich ind deiscirt [kle:r'ix' in' d'εʃkir't'] – clerics of the south
cloicthech ['klog'θ'ex] – bell-house, tower
clúain [klu:in'] – meadow, pasture land
cóiced ['ko:k'eδ] – a fifth, province
comarba [kovarba] – heir
corcur [korkur] – purple

corgus [korɣus] – Lent
crann [kraɴ] – tree
cruimther [kriv'θ'er] – priest
cumal [kuval] – female slave, bond-woman
cuthe [kuθ'e] – pit

deorad dé [d'o:raδ d'e:] – exile of God
derbfine [d'erevin'e] – 'certain kin group', family
díomhaoin [d'i:voin'] – villein
dísert [d'i:ʃert'] – secluded retreat
druí [dri:] – druid
dún [du:n] – fortification

enech [en'eχ] – face

feis [feʃ] – feast
fénechas [fe:neχas] – body of custom of freemen
féni [fe:ni] – freemen of legal standing
ferann claidibh [feraɴ klaδ'iv] – sword land
fer fothlai [fer foθli] – man of secret removal
fer léighinn [fer le:ɣiɴ'] – man of (Latin) learning
fer midboth [fer miδvoθ] – man of temporary habitation on his
    father's land
fili [fil'i], pl. filid [fil'iδ] – poet, seer
fírchlérigh [fi:rχle:riɣ'] – real clerics
foaid [fo'iδ'] – spends the night, sleeps
for-cain [for'kan'] – teaches, predicts
fuidir [fiδ'ir] – tenant at will

gaisced [gaʃkeδ] – weapons (spear and shield)
gaiscedach [gaʃkeδaχ] – warrior, champion
gallóglach [gaʟ'o:glaχ] – gallowglass, heavily armed soldier
gessa [gesa] – taboos
grád féne [gra:δ'e:ne] – grade of nobles
grád flatha [gra:δ laθa] – grade of nobles

iarfine [i:arv'in'e] – extended family
íccide [i:kiδ'e] – healer
indfine [ind'in'e] – extended family

haigh [Ⅱ.aγ'] – physician, leech

mac bethad [mak beθaδ] – 'son of life'
muinter [mun't'er] – community of a monastery

nemed [neveδ] – sacral person/place
ní anse [ni:'anse] – it is not difficult

ócaire [o:g'ar'e] – low-grade noble
oenach [oinaχ] – assembly
oifrend [of'reɴ] – Mass
oirecht [or'reχt] – assembly
ollam [oʟav] – master
ortha [orθa] – prayer

peccath [pekaθ] – sin

ráth [ra:θ] – fort
rechtaire ['rextir'e] – stewart, bailiff
rí [ri:] – king
rígdomna [ri:γδovna] – material of a king
rigid [riγiδ] – stretches
rí ruirech [ri'rur'eχ] – king of overkings
ruiri [rur'i] – king of kings

saerthach [soirθaχ] – freeman
sechithir [ʃeχiθir] – follows
senchaid [ʃenχiδ'] – historian
sen-chléithe [ʃen'χl'e:θe] – hereditary serf
slige [ʃliγe] – road
sligid [ʃliγiδ] – fells, cuts down

tánaise [ta:niʃe] – second, heir apparent
taoiseach [toiʃeχ] – leader
tigerna [tiγerna] – lord, leader
túath [tuaθ], pl. túatha, gen. túaithe – people, territory

Index

(A note on the spelling and pronunciation of Irish words and names:

Placenames are given, as far as possible, in the modern form and in the anglicised version. Personal names have not been standardised throughout. In general, for the period prior to the twelfth century, the Old Irish or Middle Irish forms are given, thereafter mostly the anglicised forms. In quotations from sources the names are given as they occur in the sources; hence some inconsistencies. The simplified phonetic transcription of Irish terms and names is intended to help the reader who is not familiar with the Irish language and to whom the orthography may appear to be forbidding; it makes no claim to scholarly perfection. The stress falls normally on the first syllable in Irish words and has not, therefore, been marked in each case.

For further guidelines to the pronunciation of Irish terms and names see K. H. Jackson, *A Celtic Miscellany* (Harmondsworth 1971), E. G. Quin, *Old-Irish Workbook* (Dublin 1975) and F. J. Byrne, *Irish kings and high-kings* (London 1973), pp. 305–7. For indispensable advice in this matter I should like to record my profound gratitude to Professor Próinséas Ní Chatháin.)